SAGE was founded in 1965 by Sara Miller McCune to support the dissemination of usable knowledge by publishing innovative and high-quality research and teaching content. Today, we publish over 900 journals, including those of more than 400 learned societies, more than 800 new books per year, and a growing range of library products including archives, data, case studies, reports, and video. SAGE remains majority-owned by our founder, and after Sara's lifetime will become owned by a charitable trust that secures our continued independence.

Los Angeles | London | New Delhi | Singapore | Washington DC | Melbourne

Love,
Labour
and Law

Thank you for choosing a SAGE product!
If you have any comment, observation or feedback,
I would like to personally hear from you.
Please write to me at **contactceo@sagepub.in**

Vivek Mehra, Managing Director and CEO, SAGE India.

Bulk Sales

SAGE India offers special discounts
for purchase of books in bulk.
We also make available special imprints
and excerpts from our books on demand.

For orders and enquiries, write to us at

Marketing Department
SAGE Publications India Pvt Ltd
B1/I-1, Mohan Cooperative Industrial Area
Mathura Road, Post Bag 7
New Delhi 110044, India

E-mail us at **marketing@sagepub.in**

Subscribe to our mailing list
Write to **marketing@sagepub.in**

This book is also available as an e-book.

Love,
Labour
and Law

Early and Child Marriage in India

Edited by

SAMITA SEN
and
ANINDITA GHOSH

Los Angeles | London | New Delhi
Singapore | Washington DC | Melbourne

First published in 2021 by

SAGE Publications India Pvt Ltd
B1/I-1 Mohan Cooperative Industrial Area
Mathura Road, New Delhi 110 044, India
www.sagepub.in

STREE
16 Southern Avenue
Kolkata 700 026
www.stree-samyabooks.com

SAGE Publications Inc
2455 Teller Road
Thousand Oaks, California 91320, USA

SAGE Publications Ltd
1 Oliver's Yard, 55 City Road
London EC1Y 1SP, United Kingdom

SAGE Publications Asia-Pacific Pte Ltd
18 Cross Street #10-10/11/12
China Square Central
Singapore 048423

Published by Vivek Mehra for SAGE Publications India Pvt. Ltd. Typeset in 10.5/13 pt Book Antiqua by Fidus Design Pvt. Ltd, Chandigarh.

Library of Congress Cataloging-in-Publication Data

Names: Sen, Samita, editor. | Ghosh, Anindita, editor.
Title: Love, labour and law: early and child marriage in India / edited by Samita Sen and Anindita Ghosh.
Description: New Delhi, India; Thousand Oaks, California: SAGE, 2021. | Includes bibliographical references and index.
Identifiers: LCCN 2020044155 (print) | LCCN 2020044156 (ebook) |
   ISBN 9789381345580 (hardcover) | ISBN 9789381345627 | ISBN 9789381345597 (epub) |
   ISBN 9789381345603 (pdf)
Subjects: LCSH: Child marriage—India. | Child marriage—Law and legislation—India. |
   Teenage girls—India—Social conditions. | Women's rights—India.
Classification: LCC HQ784.C55 L68 2021 (print) | LCC HQ784.C55 (ebook) |
   DDC 305.235/20954—dc23
LC record available at https://lccn.loc.gov/2020044155
LC ebook record available at https://lccn.loc.gov/2020044156

ISBN: 978-93-81345-62-7 (PB)

SAGE Stree team: Aritra Paul, Amrita Dutta and Neena Ganjoo

Cover Design: Paramita Brahmachari

Contents

Preface and Acknowledgements

IN THE LAST decade or so, there has been a resurgence of interest in child marriage globally. My own interest in child marriage dates further back to the 1990s, when I began to research the question of marriage in colonial India. My aim was to investigate developments in the marriage system beyond the social reform paradigm. The purpose was two-fold. First, I wanted to explore marriage in non-elite contexts. Second, my lens was labour and I wanted to analyse the intersections between production/reproduction and marriage. My research had to reckon with (even start with) questions of child marriage, sometimes without the name, since the fact that participants in a marriage were 'children' was not considered either aberrant or noteworthy. In the nineteenth century, the colonial state grappled with the universalization of marriage as much as the normalization of child marriage. In the twenty-first century, we ask some of these questions in new ways and in different contexts. I was fascinated by the prospect of a research project on early marriage in contemporary West Bengal and its all-India implications and accepted the proposal with pleasure because it allowed me to draw a big arc from the early nineteenth to the early twenty-first century in my understanding of the marriage system in North India.

In 2016, we embarked on a two-year research project to investigate child marriage in West Bengal, which emerged as early marriage as the bride is no longer a child but a teenager below 18, in collaboration with and funded by the American Jewish World Service (AJWS). This book emerged from that project. In February 2018, there was a workshop to discuss the findings of the project in which many other researchers working in this field participated and presented papers. Three chapters (4, 5 and 6) are based on the contemporary research project. One historical chapter has been a contribution to the project by an external member. The other four chapters are from presentations in the workshop. Some of those who made presentations at the workshop in February 2018 were unable to give us papers for this volume; we hope to see some of their work in print elsewhere soon.

This project became possible because of the generosity of the American Jewish World Service. I would like to thank especially Dr. Manjima Bhattacharjya, Praneeta Kapur and Jyotika Jain for their enthusiasm and cooperation and for holding our hands when we needed help. The conclave organized by Partners for Law and Development and AJWS in February 2017 in Delhi was a huge help in taking the conversation forward.

I thank Dr. Bhaswati Chatterjee and Professor Deepita Chakravarty for participating in this project housed in Jadavpur University as external members.

This project brought together many researchers and field workers. I should thank the co-ordinator, Dr. Anindita Ghosh, who took a great deal of responsibility to enable the research and the running of the project. Over the two and half years of the running of the project, a number of assistants have worked on the project and I thank all of them: Avirup Jana, Biswajit Prasad Hazam, Ishita Chowdhury, Jay Bhattacharyya, Kaushik Mukherjee, Purbita Chowdhury, Rubina Khatun, Saheli Dutta, Soujanya Chakraborty and Utsarjana Mutsuddi. A special thanks is due to Seema Chatterjee, who helped us organize the field work and accompanied us on many occasions. Many NGOs have helped us with this work: Chandanpiri Ramkrishna Ashram (South 24-Parganas), DAISAI Welfare Society (Purba Medinipur), Forum of Communities United in Service (Park Circus, Kolkata), Gana Unnayan Parshad (Bagha Jatin, Kolkata), Jalpaiguri Centre for the Development of Human

Initiatives (Jalpaiguri). I thank all of them for their active cooperation. Some officers and state government agencies have shared their experience and expertise and helped us with the field; we thank, especially, the Office of the National Child Labour Project (Purulia), the SDO of Domkal Sub-Division (Murshidabad) and the BDO of Jalangi Block (Murshidabad).

The members of an administrative committee of the university helped us run the nitty-gritty. I thank particularly Dr. Iman Kalyan Lahiri, internal member, and Professor Ratnabali Chatterjee, external member, for their contribution to various discussions. We thank Jadavpur University for housing and facilitating the project. Our accounts were ably handled by Debaprasad Guha (as always). Debamitra Chakrabarty, Librarian, was wonderfully resourceful. We got some unexpected energy and enthusiasm from Professor Mary John who also began to work on child marriage and this enabled long conversations, which helped to clarify ideas and shape questions.

We hope this book will help to encourage more research on early and child marriage. There is an urgent need for a social history of marriage and an understanding of its changing dynamics in the present. We do not have much of this kind of research. It is perhaps not surprising that the most-married region in the world, where the universality of marriage is both a commitment and a curiosity, has woefully little by way of critical scholarship on the marriage system. This book will be a contribution, I hope, towards a field much thinner than it ought to be.

May 2020

Samita Sen
Vere Harmsworth Professor
of Imperial and Naval History
University of Cambridge

Introduction

Samita Sen

A T PRESENT, SCHOLARSHIP on child marriage or early marriage, as the case seems to be, in India is very uneven. This has become more evident in the context of the global push against child marriage in the past decade or so. Despite the importance given to child marriage as a social 'problem' since the early nineteenth century, and an efflorescence of didactic and creative writing in the nineteenth and early twentieth centuries, the issue appears to have quietly moved from a controversial social issue into a consensus development agenda. The country's legislative activity in the 1970s and 1980s reflected this shift. The discussion on child marriage became a matter of policy design rather than public debate. This shift is related, we suggest, to the changing nature of child marriage.

The chief 'problem' of child marriage is its persistence. We ask about causes of child marriage, even 'root causes', as though there are also other kinds of causes. The clear assumption in asking that question is a particular trope of modernization, which assumes that child marriage is an aberration, harmful, an 'evil', that is slated for obsolescence. If 'development' does not succeed in working its magic, however, it has to be 'eradicated' by the efforts of the state. Despite reform, awareness, policy and law, it persists, however, on a scale that continues to invite search for new or 'root' causes or at least their repeated reiteration. This framing of the problem obscures the other equally remarkable 'fact' that, while child marriage persists, the pattern has changed. First, infant marriage—of those below the age of 12 years—is no longer common. The numerically largest component of legally defined child marriage is teenage marriages in the age range of 15–17 years. Many observers have opted for the term 'early' rather than 'child' marriage to describe this phenomenon.

The shift from child marriage to early marriage means in effect that child marriage has declined. Indeed, the average age of marriage for women has increased from something like 10–12 to nearly 18 in the course of the twentieth century. We have assumed that it is the 'normal' trajectory of modernization that child marriage should give way to adult marriage. It may be helpful, however, to turn the question around and to pay some attention to the process of decline, which has so far been rendered null by the force of an assumed teleology of modernity. In this regard, two related sets of issues need attention.

First, we have to treat child marriage not as an isolated problem, but as a part of a marriage system. Thus, child marriage is not the only 'problem' in marriage and 'eradicating' child marriage will not solve many of the problems associated with it. The 'child' in a marriage is not the only or even the most important negative element of our marriage system. Indeed, 'child' is not a relevant marker of the Indian marriage system; adulthood is also not of concern in marriage; that is to say, age has not much to do with marriage. One major justification of the emphasis on adulthood relates to consent. However, in older understandings—in both Hindu and Christian legal systems—marriage was a sacrament, reflecting an unalterable divine will, rather than a social contract to be underwritten by the state. In the Hindu system, moreover, marriage was 'arranged' ostensibly by parents/guardians as part of a wider set of social alliances and networks. If there is no consent, then the question of child/adult is not legally relevant. Rather, marriage was (and, largely, is) a life cycle ritual, which marks the transfer of a women (with her productive and repro-ductive labour) from one family to another; it does not link directly with age, either physically (puberty) or legally (age of majority). Thus, there was no word for 'child marriage'. The word *balyavivaha* is a nineteenth-century translation of child marriage, which came into circulation in the tide of social reform, reflecting the responses of the British, one of the very few population groups in that period to practise late (and adult) marriage for men and women.

Marriage is defined as a union between a man and a woman; children born out this union are legitimate and recognized by society. It represents socially recognized institutional cohabitation of a man and a woman that allows them to engage in sexual activities and imposes on them certain responsibilities. One cannot deny, however, the cultural construction of marriage and its social and economic ramifications. Marriage is not only a legal union between two 'heterosexual' persons but also establishes cultural, social and economic alliances between families and kin-networks. It is a characteristic of the Indian marriage system that older/elder kin members take decisions on behalf of younger members of the family. In addition, marriage involves economic and cultural transactions, which the proximate community endorses. The most ambiguous part of this community-sanctioned institution is that it allows cross-cousin and uncle-niece marriage, polyandry and polygyny, sororate and levirate marriages, but does not allow love marriages and inter-caste or inter-religion marriages.[1] The range of prohibited marriages causes great familial anxiety about possible transgressions by the young; marriage becomes a political issue; parents are always afraid of a fragile family 'honour' threatened by sexual violation of daughters, which is cited as one of the main causes of early marriage.

The second set of issues is to do with the construction of 'childhood' in modern India. Following the trail-blazing work of Philippe Ariès (1960), there have been some attempts to unpack this process in nineteenth-century India. However, this too remains a much thinner field than one would imagine. The 'women's question' in the nineteenth century was essentially about the girl child (as wives and widows), as Mary John points out in Chapter 1 of this book. Indeed, there has been inadequate research into the construction of childhood in colonial India and within this limited literature, the girl child has got even less attention. However, attention is now turning to these issues and we have two major monographs on rather different themes. Ruby Lal (2013) has sought to recover the limited agency of girls within patriarchal constraints of segregation and domesticity. Ashwini Tambe (2019) has explored the definition of girls in relation to sexual choices. Both these works address the question of agency in different ways. On a different track, Ishita Pande (2020) in a very recent book explores how the digital age came to constitute a juridical childhood and its relationship with the age of consent and child marriage. In colonial India, the child was produced within the convergence of education, labour and marriage. Despite the new work on a variety of themes, there is insufficient attention paid to this triangular relationship, which can help us understand the convergence of the problem of the 'child' and the problem of 'marriage' into a single social issue. In Chapters 5 and 6, Deepita Chakravarty, Samita Sen and Anindita Ghosh have attempted to chart some aspects of these relationships in the contemporary period in West Bengal.

There was an engaged public debate on child marriage in the colonial period. We find its expression in novels and short stories in almost every Indian language. In Bengali, there were also essays, pamphlets, satires and writings in every imaginable genre. As a result, historians have given considerable attention to these questions. For instance, we have path-breaking interventions by Tanika Sarkar (2001) on the age of consent controversy and Mrinalini Sinha (2006) on the Sarda Act, and Ishita Pande (2020) discusses both these in a single frame. Why is there so little comparable scholarship on child marriage in postcolonial India? In the colonial period, child marriage was a 'problem' of the new elite, the *bhadralok*. It was linked to questions of class formation, and in that period, the marriage system came to be perceived as a hindrance to education, professionalization and the making of the colonial service elite. The education of boys (grooms) necessitated that of girls (brides). The crux of B. B. Malabari's appeal in 1884 was that men should finish their education before marriage. If they did so, however, they became ineligible grooms for uneducated child brides. Thus, the 'companionate marriage', which underpinned the new elite, was the basis for the construction of both the *bhadralok* and the *bhadramahila*. This was not an easy process because the force of colonial capitalism and modernity tore at everyday practices of the family. Hence, many bottles of ink were spilt on both sides of a heated debate. In 1929–30, at the time of the Sarda Act (Child Marriage Restraint Act or CMRA) (see Chapter 2), these issues were still very much on the boil. By the 1970s, however, when the age of marriage was raised to legal majority, aligning consent and contract in marriage, there was no controversy.

By then, child marriage was no longer a problem of the elite. Among the urban middle class, most girls went to school for a few years before they married. The problem had already been upgraded to early rather than child marriage. This was a secular change and progressed with great rapidity. In one generation, increasing numbers of women moved to higher education and professions, and adult marriage (at 18+ years) became the norm. The problem of child marriage was no longer a problem of the 'self' of the writing classes but of the 'other', that is, the working classes (and/or the rural poor). This allowed the shift from social controversy to policy consensus. In the case of the poor, debate was not necessary; once the change was accepted among the educated middle classes, it was to be extended to the rest of the population, for their own good. The 'problem' of child marriage became associated with the poor and, eventually, its 'root cause' became poverty (rather than culture/tradition as it had been in the earlier period); and its reform became associated with fertility rates, population growth and public policy. These are the domain of the state rather than society. The question of child marriage no longer involves discussions of scriptures and traditions, self-reflection or analysis of family dynamics, inter-generational relationships, wider social and economic change.[2] It registers on a two-dimensional matrix of state policy: population and development. Even the huge output in gender studies and cultural studies is virtually blank on child marriage in the contemporary period.

THE HISTORICAL PERSPECTIVE

The issue of child marriage was first flagged at the beginning of the nineteenth century, in relation to the practice of sati (the immolation of the widow on the funeral pyre of her dead husband). The issue was whether a child widow could commit sati and if so, whether this could be seen as 'voluntary'. Could a child, already married, consent to suicide? These debates were somewhat summarily closed with the Act in 1829 which prohibited sati (Mani 1998). The child widow, however, reappeared as a more controversial figure in the remarriage debates. There was discomfort about the role and the place of young widows in a society which put enormous importance to disciplining the sexuality of women within marriage. The emphasis on ascetic widowhood was not entirely an effective alternative. By the turn of the nineteenth century, when the decennial Census began counting, it was found that nearly a quarter of women in Bengal were widows! Historians have shown that Vidyasagar's concern was primarily with child widows and, especially, virgin widows, the rather clumsily-named *akshatayoni* (virgina intacta). Some of Vidyasagar's most passionate writings addressed the need to harness the sexuality of child widows within marriage and to recover their reproductive capacity. It is said that he witnessed the pain and difficulty of child widows in his own family (Sarkar 2007). One aim of legislating on widow remarriage was to bring the child (or the young) within the discipline of marriage. Thus, the child wife and the child widow are complementary images; the child wife becomes the child widow and, at times, again a child wife (Chakravarti 1989).

After the widow remarriage debates in the 1850s, B.B. Malabari's Notes on Infant Marriage and Enforced Widowhood (1884) once again raised these issues and for the first time made a direct link between child marriage and education. Soon after, there was the Rukhmabai case (1885–88), which has been richly documented by many historians. However, the legal precedent on child marriage was set by another case, more than ten years earlier. The history of social reform in India has not given the Huchi case the importance it deserved. Gauri Viswanathan briefly recounted the story in her book (1998) and it has been discussed in more detail in two papers (Sen 2009; 2012). The case was about child marriage but in the context of religious conversion. The case went on appeal to the Governor General and thus became a precedent for both child marriage and conversion marriage disputes.

From the 1830s, issues of consent had troubled Christian proselytizers. For instance, the conversion of minors led to parental challenge in the courts. Before 1857, the Company's courts often upheld such conversions and allowed missionaries to retain custody. From the 1860s, courts leant in favour of parental rights. The reinforcement of patriarchal authority within the family also found reflection in rulings against women in cases of marital disputes following conversion. Given that status and rights in marriage were linked to personal laws based on religious profession, conversions became the cause of disputes between parties claiming rights, each from their own personal law, within the same marriage. New legislation had to be adopted but it posed a formidable challenge; and the first Act—Act XXI of 1866 (The Native Converts Marriage Dissolution Act)—took nearly thirty years to pass. This Act, moreover, failed to solve the myriad marital issues raised by conversion.

From the 1870s, British Indian courts had to deal with a crop of disputes regarding the marriage of converts. In all these cases, the judicial as well as the policy verdict of the state was against any contravention of status quo and in favour of orthodox interpretation of Indian personal laws. The first of these was the Huchi case (1873, Madras). The impact of the Huchi case was felt on a number of other cases like those of Ganga (1880, Bombay), Radha Bhujaji (1881, Bombay), Lachmini (1889, Bengal), Ram Kumari (1891, Bengal), and a few others. Ram Kumari's case was cited even in the 1980s in the Sarla Mudgal Case in Bombay, not for child marriage but conversion marriage. These cases are not part of the social reform story; nevertheless, they had a quiet but telling effect on the laws on marriage in India.

Helen Gertrude Huchi, a daughter of Hindu parents, became a pupil in the Bangalore Central Female School of the London Missionary Society in 1865, when she was about seven or eight years old. In 1870, she asked for baptism, but it was not followed through because she was a minor. In 1871, she was married to her cousin (father's sister's son) Appaiah, against her will, and in spite of her professions of belief in Christianity. A few months later, Huchi escaped from her marital home, went to the Mission Chapel, and was there baptised. In July 1873, when she was about to marry a Christian convert, Appaiah objected, and the prospective groom withdrew. In August 1873, Miss Louise Hannah Anstey, in charge of the Mission School, instituted a case on behalf of Huchi in the civil court challenging the binding nature of the marriage between Huchi and Appaiah. The major issue before the court was the validity of the marriage conducted when Huchi was a minor, an unwilling party and desirous of conversion. The suit was dismissed; Appaiah was granted costs in the first court. On two subsequent appeals, higher courts found against Huchi on all counts. Since the case was instituted in Mysore, there was no possibility of appeal to the Privy Council. Huchi raised an appeal to the Governor General supported by the Madras Missionary Conference but this too was turned down.[3]

Huchi's memorial (dated 6 December 1873) supported by the opinion of some English lawyers, asked for legal remedy against the enforcement of an infant marriage on Huchi, since

Appaiah was unwilling to honour the spirit of it after her conversion.[4] The Madras Missionary Conference, forwarding her papers, asked that Hindu marriages among infants or minors should become void if one party ceased to be a Hindu, if the marriage was not consummated.[5] The question of infant marriage had been before the British in India ever since it 'possessed true legislative power', that is, since the passing of Act IV of 1833.[6] Huchi argued not only against infant marriages, but also against its enforcement in British Indian courts, an issue of some importance in light of the sanctions behind 'offences against marriage' in the Indian Penal Code (1866). The government, however, rejected their views, which, they argued, betrayed a profound misunderstanding of the nature of Hindu marriage. In such a marriage, the question of consent, and therefore of majority, of the woman played no role at all. It would, they argued, be 'a violation of Hindu religious liberties' to downgrade infant marriage to a betrothal. In Hindu custom, 'the father contracts a marriage for his infant daughter' and it could not be considered a betrothal subject to the adult daughter's discretion. Sir E. C. Bayley argued that it would be a violation of Hindu religious liberties to reduce a full-fledged marriage to a mere promise.[7] Government of India was not prepared to embark on any such legislation; marriage, even if conducted in infancy, was a sacrament and the British accepted that in Hindu law marriage was indissoluble.

In the debates over Act XXI of 1866 (The Native Converts Marriage Dissolution Act), W. Muir had already made this suggestion, and it had been rejected. He argued that Hindu doctrine be set aside in favour of asserting the basic principles of a free contract: 'The essence of marriage [is] that it is a contract entered freely into by the parties themselves after reaching years of discretion.'[8] He stressed the significance of the Penal Code, nearly contemporaneous, which had opened new and punitive avenues of enforcing marriages. According to him, 'no enlightened ruler' could enforce by penal provisions infant marriages not followed by cohabitation. He suggested a compromise that infant marriages be regarded as a 'simple betrothal'.[9] Sir Henry S. Maine, regarded as the chief architect of British Indian law, asserted that the preliminary marriage ceremonies did constitute a valid contract. Moreover, since divorce did not constitute dissolution of marriage in Hindu law, such a provision would render conversion a means of exercising marital choices. In the Indian context, he argued, marriages between children could not be downgraded and marital discipline relaxed. The government could not allow young men to abrogate their marital obligations without opening the door to grave abuses and causing 'great scandal'.[10] In this discourse of discipline, neither the notions of individual 'consent' and 'rights' nor the old arguments about 'protection' of women against the 'immoral and barbarous' customs of Hinduism cut any ice.[11] British law officers considered the father's right to give a minor daughter in marriage fundamental to the Hindu family. They were unwilling to allow the discourse of legal subjectivity (including questions of discretion and majority) to encroach upon familial authority over women (especially in matters of marriage). Tanika Sarkar has shown, quoting from H.H. Risley and Charles Taylor, how the 'politics of recognition' stayed the reformist hand of government. Infant marriage was, she argues, 'not only customary, it was far too strongly recommended by authoritative religious codes' for the state to contemplate intervention (Sarkar 2001). Huchi's and other similar cases merely reaffirmed the centrality of such brahminical norms as the cornerstone of the Hindu marriage system. British Indian courts were 'bound' to administer the incarceration of Hindu women within the citadel of the irrevocable Hindu marriage, now frozen by 'law'.

The position taken by the British government that 'Hindu' marriage was indissoluble and that divorce did not set a Hindu wife free to marry again was social engineering on a grand scale. Setting aside a few of the upper castes, most caste groups allowed women divorce and remarriage. Among the Devangada (or Devanga), a weaver caste, to which Huchi belonged, there were established customs of adult marriage and bride price (Thurston 1993 [1909]; Nanjundayya and Iyer 1931).[12] Evidence suggests a widespread custom of divorce involving the repayment of the bride price or refund of marriage expenses or payment of monetary compensation. Among certain groups, the second prospective husband was responsible for this payment (Sen 1999).

In the Hindu community in particular, but also in the nineteenth century in the Muslim community, there was considerable controversy over definition of marriage. British officialdom sought clear principles, which could be applied to marital disputes brought before colonial law courts. They were seeking, however, to draw lines in shifting sands. There were immense variations in customs across regions, religions, caste and class. Moreover, the line between transfer of women (marriage) and transactions in women (slavery) were not as clear as legal principles of freedom assumed. A range of cohabitation practices, prostitution, second and secondary marriages and concubinage were jumbled into understanding of marriage in the nineteenth century.

Despite the overwhelming weight of official opinion in favour of orthodox and brahminical interpretations of Hindu marriage, there were also contrary voices. Even within the government, there were officers who, without advocating an immediate executive or legislative intervention, remained unconvinced about complete non-interference in infant marriage. There were petitions against infant marriage, which argued it was not a religious but a social custom. There were cases before several high courts in the country in which shastric evidence was produced to show that a marriage prior to consummation could be regarded as a betrothal. Some petitions for divorce persuaded government to consider the possibility of a Divorce Act.[13] The Government of Bombay expressed the pious hope that 'the growing enlightenment of the Hindus may lead them before long to seek an alteration of the Hindu law regarding infant marriages'.[14] In 1881, Rivers Thompson anticipated more and more complications arising from infant marriages and foretold that 'some day' the Government would 'have to meet this difficulty', probably 'very soon'.[15]

The last two decades of the nineteenth saw two major legal developments on the issue of child marriage. Within four years of the notes written by Rivers Thompson, the Rukhmabai case began and went through various courts till 1888. Within and outside the courtroom, debate raged over the capacity of women to repudiate their child marriages. This case confirmed the Huchi decision, without the complication of conversion, and was thus to become an enormously significant legal precedent (Anagol 2005). With a few years came the Phulmoni case, leading to the age of consent controversy, which marked the passage to a phase of assertive cultural nationalism, defending and glorifying child marriage in the name of a revalorized 'tradition'. In Chapter 1 of this book, Mary John has discussed the historiography of these two cases.

The age of consent was more about age and less about consent (Singha 1998; Bannerji 2001; Pande 2020). Despite the compromises forced upon the colonial state, the Act succeeded in fixating upon age. This enabled digital age to become a fact in law (as was being done in parallel in other laws as well). Pande (2020) argues that the colonial state latched on to 'age' as a category for creating the juridical subject of the child. She takes this further to argue that age became an epistemic contract, enabling a conflation of a juridical category with the 'human' by technologies of the body. However, British Indian government made no effort to ensure the implementation of the registration of births, deaths and marriages. While age became increasingly important in law, there was no parallel initiative to enable determination of age, an incongruity that plagues implementation of various laws even today.

In conventional historiography, the social reform movement is considered to have ended with the age of consent controversy (1891). In this narrative, CMRA 1929 has been discussed somewhat in isolation. However, recent research shows that the 1920s witnessed numerous efforts to enact laws on family, marriage and property. These piecemeal reform initiatives led to the formation of the Rau Committee in the 1940s and major reform in Hindu law in 1955–56. The period of the 1920s to 1950s has been characterized as the 'second social reform' by Bhaswati Chatterjee (as Chakravarti) (2016). In Chapter 2, she has discussed the passing of the Sarda Act (1929) and its implications.

Eleanor Newbigin suggests that the second social reform was more about new men who wished to break away from the inter-generational patriarchal joint family and its authority. These were men of the new elite in professions or jobs and had their own independent income; they were creating wealth separate from the joint family and they wished to be able to secure this wealth for their children. The question of 'women's rights' became a proxy in battles between men (Newbigin 2013). Chatterjee suggests in Chapter 2 that women played a key role in the second social reform movement and were its chief beneficiaries. This included the CMRA 1929. Geraldine Forbes has argued that CMRA would not have been possible without the support of All-India Women's Conference. It was the one time in the inter-war period that women from across communities came together on a 'women's issue' (Forbes 1999).

Recent research also suggests the importance of investigating the intersection of questions of marriage and sex work. Ashwini Tambe (2009) raises the comparatively neglected question of age of consent with regard to non-marital sex, which was higher than that for marriage in India, reaching the age of 16 with CMRA 1929. International concerns over white slavery and trafficking succeeded in raising the age of consent for non-marital sex, particularly in the context of sex work, but nationalist focus on 'tradition' kept the age of marriage low. These relationships have been explored in Chapter 7 by Tinku Khanna and Juanita Kakoty. They show that marital and commercial exploitation of the sexual labour of the girl child are related phenomena.

In the decades after independence, there were drastic measures taken to 'eradicate' child marriage. Compared to the furore that attended interventions into marriage in the colonial period, these changes happened quietly. The bitterly-contested Hindu law reforms of 1955–56 introduced divorce and remarriage, monogamy for men and property rights for women (Parashar 1992; Agnes 2001; Sinha 2012) but did not stipulate age of marriage. Earlier, in 1949, CMRA had been modified, raising the age of marriage for girls to 15 from 14. In 1954, the Special Marriages Act set the minimum age for marriage for girls at 18 and for boys at 21. It was in October 1978 that the principle of adult marriage was generalized. The law was passed without a whisper of protest.

These new laws proscribing child marriage were not resisted, or even debated, since the practice had waned among the middle classes. Child marriage was now perceived as a problem of the poor and a development agenda. It was no longer linked to the assertion of social and cultural rights. Once the middle class ceased to practise child marriage or defend it in the name of 'tradition', the state was able to adopt a more interventionist role. State intervention, however, remained limited to passing laws; the scale of the problem held it back from actual implementation. Nevertheless, policy intervention against child marriage acquired new instrumentalist force with emerging consensus on population control and the need to reduce fertility rates. United Nations and other international agencies led perhaps this first global moment against child marriage.

POPULATION, DEVELOPMENT AND HUMAN RIGHTS

The twenty-first century has witnessed a new global moment in the campaign against child marriage with participation from various international agencies, including the UN. There was a resolution on child, early, and forced marriage adopted at the UN Human Rights Council in October 2013; another resolution at the UN General Assembly in 2014. At first, India rejected these moves and refused to sign these resolutions. However, India has the largest number of child marriages

in the world and has not been able to refuse to engage with
the question. The sustainable development goals 2016 have a
section devoted to child marriage.

How does South Asia figure on the global map of child
marriage? Child marriage is common among the world's
poorest countries. The highest prevalence rates are in South
Asia at 56 percent followed by various regions in Africa. The
highest child marriage is in Niger at 75 percent and in Chad
at 72 percent but the overall average in South Asia is higher
than in Sub-Saharan Africa. Child marriage rates are also high
in Latin America and the Caribbean, as well as the Middle East
and North Africa. Globally child marriage, defined as marriage below the age of 18, is more common for women. Within
South Asia, rates in Bangladesh are higher than in India but
the number of child wives in India is the largest in the world
(UNFPA 2012). The recent Indian Census 2011 reports 17
million children between the ages 10 and 19 married, which is
6 percent of that age group. The girls constitute the majority at
76 percent. This represents an increase of 0.9 million from the
previous Census of 2001 (Singh and Vennam 2016).

India ranks sixth among the top ten countries with high
rates of child marriage, especially among women, although
all recent studies are showing a declining trend. The pace of
decline is, however, much slower than desired. The median
age of marriage for women increased from 18.2 (2001) to 19.2
(2011); for men from 22.6 (2001) to 23.5 (2011). Behind these
national averages, however, hide great variation by states and
regions as well as across social and ethnic groups. For instance,
some adivasi communities have lower rates of child marriage.
Startlingly, the UNICEF 2014 study suggests that more boys
than girls are getting married before the legal age. Of course,
the legal age for men is higher than for women and there is
now some discussion as to whether the legal age for men and
women should be made the same, either 18 or 21.

The more dramatic decline in child marriage has been for
the age group up to 14 years. In the age group 16–17 there
has been very little change in the incidence of marriage. In

Bangladesh, for instance, marriage in this age group has actually increased by 35 percent, clearly because girls from a younger age cohort have moved up. There is now a concentration of child marriage in the immediately pre-adult age group (ibid.). This is one way of saying it; the other way to say it is that there is a steady increase in the age of marriage, though it has not yet reached 18 years for a significant proportion of the population. In India, there is noticeable increase in underage marriage up the age scale. If we take girls of the age group 10–14, only 3 percent are married and if we take boys in that age group, only 1.6 are married. If we look at the age group up to 19, then 20 percent girls are married and 5 percent boys are married. There is a tight clustering of marriage between 17 and 19 years (NCPCR Report 2011). These numbers bear out the basic argument made at the start of this introduction – that there is now very little by way of 'child' marriage; what we see is a persistence of early marriage. From 1990 onwards various data show that only 12 percent of Indian women who married before age 20 were younger than 15 at the time of marriage (Nirantar 2015: 7). Thus, the focus of legally 'child' marriage is actually on adolescents.

It has been mentioned already that scholarly research in the field of child marriage is woefully thin. What we have are a number of quantitative studies.[16] In India, statistical investigations of child marriage assume that there is some exactitude regarding age, which we have found utterly misplaced, especially in rural areas. This needs much more discussion than is seen in the literature. Imprecision apart, however, many recent studies have focused on consequences of early marriage on the overall development of girl and boy children. These range from making important life decisions, securing basic freedoms including pursuing opportunities for education, earning a sustainable livelihood and accessing sexual health and rights. There can be no doubt that child marriage involves profound physical, intellectual, psychological and emotional impact. For girls, it enlarges their fertility span, which almost certainly results in premature and multiple pregnancies and to a lifetime of domestic and sexual subservience. Poor health outcomes also involve malnutrition of mother and child and birth complications. So, child marriage adds to both higher infant mortality and maternal mortality (Statistical Analysis 2017). In Chapter 3 Elvira Graner has discussed some of these issues.

Among the very few full-length studies of child marriage, Jaya Sagade's book (2005) examines the question from the perspective of human rights. She explores the various laws against child marriage and the state's failure to implement them. She also charts the conflicts between personal laws, which led to a new law, Prohibition of Child Marriage Act (2006). Elvira Graner, Ishita Chowdhury and Utsarjana Mutsuddi have discussed this law and its implications in Chapters 3 and 4. PCMA for the first time made child marriage a cognizable offence and non-bailable. In October 2017 in a judgment, the Supreme Court extended the remit of this Act by making all sexual relations with minor girls illegal. The Court expressed great dismay at the alarming figure of 23 million child brides in the country, which meant that one out of every five marriages violated the law. As a result of this judgement, sexual intercourse with a minor wife now qualifies as rape.[17] This brings PCMA more in line with other legislation for the protection of children such as ICPS (Integrated Child Protection Act) and POCSO (Prevention of Child Sexual Offences Act). Taken together, the question of child sexuality has moved further into the domain of criminal law and these mark a new social moment in the construction of the 'child' in India.

RESEARCH PROJECT ON CHILD MARRIAGE AND METHODOLOGY

If we compare figures given by NFHS-3 and NFHS-4, we see that West Bengal has risen to number one position on child marriage within India at 40.7 percent, followed by Bihar at 39. At the other end, we find Kerala and Punjab at 7.6, Jammu and Kashmir at 8.7 and Himachal Pradesh at 8.6. There has been quite dramatic decrease in child marriage rates in Uttar

Pradesh, Rajasthan, Andhra Pradesh, Mizoram, Meghalaya
and Madhya Pradesh. The decline in West Bengal has been
very slow compared to these states, propelling it from rank
7 to rank 1. West Bengal does not have a high rate of child
marriage for men, nor does it report a high rate of marriage for
girls below 15. What it has instead is a high rate of marriage of
girls between 15 and 17. Within West Bengal, Birbhum, South
24-Parganas, Malda and Purba Medinipur reported 22 percent
incidence of child marriage among girls in the age group 10–17
years and Murshidabad and Nadia reported 19–20 percent.
This was the context for our project on child marriage, in
collaboration with the American Jewish World Service (2016–
2018) as described in the Preface.

Chapters 4, 5 and 6 are drawn from this project. It is thus
necessary to say a few words about the methodology adopted
for the study. We chose a qualitative study, based on in-depth
interviews of a small group of people, in a field already
dominated by sophisticated quantitative analysis. We chose to
do this in 7 districts, 6 in rural West Bengal (3 villages each)
and three localities in Kolkata city. This gave us 368 interviews.

A few words to explain the selection of the field: Some
districts of West Bengal have been identified, as just mentioned,
as having high rates of child marriage, these are Birbhum,
South 24-Parganas, Malda, Purba Medinipur, Murshidabad
and Nadia. Biswajit Ghosh has done considerable work on
Malda and various studies have included Murshidabad. In
order to select the districts, we chose 12 indicators. We chose
three variables mainly in two separate matrices: incidence
of under-age marriage of women, incidence of poverty and
levels of illiteracy. Incidentally, these three variables are
closely correlated with each other over different districts of the
state. We decided to take the incidence of underage marriage
as the common variable for both the matrices.

On this basis, we decided upon the following districts
to capture similarities as well as differences: Birbhum, South
24-Parganas, Kolkata, Jalpaiguri, Purba Medinipur, Purulia

and Murshidabad. Within each district, we chose three villages
from three separate gram panchayats under a single block.
Of course, we had to follow a different logic in Kolkata. We
took three different wards with very different characteristics.
We took two areas, which showed low incomes as well as
levels of education, such as Park Circus and Bagha Jatin. Then
we chose a middle-class area in south of the city, Bjoygarh/
Regent Estate. Initially, we had hoped also to include a similar
cluster in the north of the city but we ran short of time.

We were prepared to find that randomly chosen clusters
of neigbourhoods/villages within a district may not show the
average features of a particular district. Ideally it would have
been best to do a similar sort of exercise for selecting the village
clusters as we have done for the districts. But detailed data for
villages are difficult to get. Moreover, without some contacts
with local people, this sort of a survey is difficult to conduct.
Thus, we prioritized access in the final choice of the clusters.
After we chose the cluster of three villages and established
contact, we conducted a preliminary census in which each
household in the village was visited and asked whether there
had been any child marriage in (approximately) the last five
years. In some cases, we cross checked this information with
neighbours or school teachers or panchayat members. These
households were also categorized in terms of refugee settlers,
women headed households and according to land holding.

We organized one Focus Group Discussion (FGD) of about
30 persons in each district. In the seven FGDs we conducted,
we included school teachers, ICDS members, SHG members,
health workers, child grooms and brides, parents of child
grooms and brides, prospective child/early grooms and
brides, NGO workers and panchayat members.

It is important to mention a major limitation of the study.
The survey results did not show any substantial contrasting
features for the districts as was expected. This may be because
of our modes of selection and the decision to focus on households with an underage marriage in the last 5 years. The bulk

of our respondents turned out to be from landless or land-poor households. Our respondents include under-age brides (in a few cases underage boys who have been married as well), mothers (in a few cases fathers) and mothers-in-law of underage brides. The attempt has been to access the perceptions of both giving and receiving families in the context of women's underage marriage. There was an attempt to capture inter-generational change and this was facilitated by talking to mothers of under-age brides and grooms.

One aim was to explore the possibility of specific socio-economic characteristics of underage marriage that explains its persistence relative to other states. However, as will be clear from the papers in this book, the material threw up many questions far more interesting than simple causal relationships.

POLICY INTERVENTIONS: ERADICATING CHILD MARRIAGE

The causes and consequences of child marriage have been retold repeatedly. We have not found anything remarkable during our project that can be cited as new. Clearly, there are customs and traditions, which cannot be changed in the short term; the marriage system is universal and compulsory, and focused on the control of female sexuality; and there are questions of honour tied to the sexual protection of the unmarried daughter. There are other social dimensions, such as the poor quality of education in government schools, which fails to be an alternative for poor girls. There is a strong association between higher age at marriage and higher education level and vice versa. Various studies have shown that the highest dropout is at age 15 after Class 8, which is precisely the age which also shows the highest rate of early marriage.[18]

Since the causes of child marriage are so well known, in recent years there is less impetus for research and more demand for policy intervention. There have been a number of initiatives taken by governments at central and state level against child marriage. Some of these do not directly address the issue of marriage but take a circuitous approach. One group of 'schemes' are focused on reduction of child marriage. There is a great deal of optimism associated with the Integrated Child Protection Act, a flagship programme of the Ministry of Women and Child Development since 2009 and the Mahila Samakshya Programme, especially designed for women and children by the Ministry of Human Resource Development. It was launched in Kerala in 1998 with a campaign against child marriage and has had some degree of success. At the state level, we have programmes such as Deepshikha which was launched by UNICEF in 2008, in partnership with the Government of Maharashtra and local NGOs. It has had some success. *Mai kuch bhi kar sakti hu* [A woman can achieve anything] is an Indian trans-media initiative launched by the Population Foundation of India. 'Girls not Brides' is a global partnership of more than 350 civil society organizations from over 55 countries working to address child marriage. Its members are spread across Africa, Asia, the Middle East, Europe and the Americas. The group has been working towards mobilizing policy, financial support and programme initiatives to end child marriage.

The lesson from all these initiatives is that the key to preventing child marriage is through community mobilization. In West Bengal, there has been some social mobilization. The trigger appears to have been the Kanyashree scheme introduced by the government of West Bengal which aimed to incentivize families to continue girls' education. Chapter 4 discusses the scheme. In an unintended effect too, the scheme has mobilized teenage girls, potential child brides, against child marriage. This initiative is receiving considerable social support. In Chapter 8, Biswajit Ghose explores this new development in one district of West Bengal.

THE CHAPTERS

The first chapter by Mary John explores the history of child marriage in India, with an emphasis on analysing the historical literature for the colonial period. She makes the argument that 'child' marriage acquires significance in the colonial period within the discourses of social reform and nationalism. The second chapter by Bhaswati Chatterjee is historical rather than historiographical, which explores two moments, the Age of Consent Act of 1891 but more extensively the Sarda Act 1929 (CMRA). It explores the role of Hindu revivalism and the politics of demography behind reform efforts in the inter-war period. The third chapter by Elvira Graner explores law, policy and trends in child marriage in India. She challenges the usual causalities to argue that child marriage is co-incidental with other forms of denied citizenship rather than one being the cause of the other. The fourth chapter is written jointly by Ishita Chowdhury and Utsarjana Mutsuddi. This chapter examines the history of legislation with a focus on the PCMA and its implementation in six districts of West Bengal as well as the early stages of implementation of the Kanyashree scheme. It explores in some detail the widespread phenomenon of elopement we found in the field.

The fifth chapter sets out the employment argument to understand and explain why child marriage is declining else-where but persists in West Bengal. This chapter is contributed by Deepita Chakravarty. The author shows that among the fifteen major states of India, underage marriage of girls is rel-atively more prevalent in West Bengal. She argues that more than poverty and illiteracy, the lack of employment opportu-nities results in persistence of child marriage. Chapter 6 by Samita Sen and Anindita Ghosh continues this argument to show that the pattern of women's work in West Bengal and its folding within ideologies of domesticity is in tandem with early marriage.

Chapter 7 by Tinku Khanna and Juanita Kakoty proposes the notion of a 'Last Girl', the most marginal as defined by caste, class and region. She is vulnerable at the same time to marriage, sex work and trafficking. They argue that the absence (even shrinkage) of state's provision for welfare deepens these crises.

The book ends on a positive note. Biswajit Ghosh shows in Chapter 8 how young adolescent girls are now resisting child marriage. The cases he cites show a new mobilization in rural West Bengal, involving district administration and schools, which are attempting to implement PCMA. Moreover, Kanyashree has helped young school-going girls to come together to combat child marriage among their peers. This is as yet a small trend but it has transformative potential.

NOTES

1   Nayars, Nambudiris and many other communities of South India and Kashmiri Pandits of North India practised these kinds of marriages (Uberoi 1993).

2   While I say this, we found in our field in Kolkata (but not in the six rural districts) an argument among Muslims that Sharia allowed women's marriage at 15 years and it was legal, therefore, for Muslim 'women' to marry at that age. There is a debate about this, which crops up from time to time even in the context of national debates over Muslim law and marriage.

3   The 'story' was put together from the various petitions as well as the long written testimonies of some of the parties to the dispute. National Archives of India, New Delhi (henceforth NAI) Home Public September 1876 A73-78.

4   Ibid., Huchi's Petition, 6 Dec 1873.

5   Ibid.

6   Sir Henry Maine's speech to Legislative Council, 4 Nov. 1864. NAI Home Ecclesiastical August 1887 A15-17.

7   NAI, Home Department Ecclesiastical Branch, August 1881, A15–17.

8   Ibid., Letter from the Government of Bombay, No. 3282 dated 25 May 1881.

9   Ibid.

10 Ibid. Speech of 4 Nov. 1864. Quoted in the letter from the Government of Bombay.

11 Ibid. W. Stokes.

12 See entry for Devanga. It is worth noting that some of the descriptions of marriage ceremonies and other details are similar in Thurston's earlier work.

13 NAI Home Department, Ecclesiastical Branch, August 1881, A15–17.

14 Ibid. C. Gonne, Chief Secretary to Government of Bombay to Secretary, Government of India, 25 May 1881.

15 Ibid. Notes dated 15 July 1881.

16   There has been some effort to document child marriage, which has
     been an invaluable resource for this study. An UNICEF study (2005)
     entitled 'Early Marriage: A Harmful Traditional Practice' has been
     quoted extensively. An UNFPA report called 'Marrying Too Young:
     End Child Marriage' (2012) has also gained significant circulation.
     Another brief UNICEF study, 'Ending Child Marriage: Progress
     and Prospects' (2014) has also been quite influential in terms of
     providing quotable statistics.
17   https://www. 14emint.com/Politics/PRft3fAiTAnZj6KVZR3
     FHN/23-million-child-brides-in-India-Supreme-Court-expresses-
     di.html, accessed 17 September 2018.
18   According to NFHS-4, the reasons for early marriage of women
     may be attributed to the traditional system (27 percent), demand of
     dowry (16 percent), societal pressure (13 percent), safety and security
     concerns (10 percent), pressure from family members (10 percent),
     land ownership related issues (4 percent), economic hardship and
     poverty (2 percent) and others at 16 percent. https://factly.in/
     child-marriages-in-india-reasons-state-wise-analysis-child-abuse/,
     accessed on 25 April 2016 at 9:35 pm. The various studies in the
     book underline some earlier findings. Children from disadvantaged
     groups (by class, caste and ethnicity), particularly girls, are more
     likely to be married early; generally, girls from rural areas are twice
     as likely to be married before 18 but in West Bengal, urban child
     marriage rates are high; and girls enrolled in school at age 15 are less
     likely to be married ('A Statistical Analysis' 2017: 85–86).

REFERENCES

Agnes, Flavia. 2001. *Law and Gender Inequality: The Politics of Women's Rghts in India*. New Delhi: Oxford University Press.
Anagol, Padma. 2005. *The Emergence of Feminism in India, 1850–1920*. Aldershot: Ashgate.
Ariès, Philippe. 1960 [1962]. *Centuries of Childhood: A Social History of Family Life*. London: Cape.
Bannerji, Himani. 2001. *Inventing Subjects: Studies in Hegemony, Patriarchy and Colonialism*. New Delhi: Tulika.
Chakravarti, Bhaswati. 2016. 'The Second Social Reform Movement: Gender and Society in Bengal, 1930s–1950s', Unpublished Ph.D dissertation, Department of History, Calcutta University.

Chakravarti, Uma. 1989. 'Whatever happened to the Vedic Dasi? Orientalism, Nationalism and a Script for the Past'. In Kumkum Sangari and Sudesh Vaid, eds., *Recasting Women: Essays in Colonial History*. New Delhi: Kali for Women.

Forbes, Geraldine. 1999. *Women in Modern India*. Cambridge: Cambridge University Press.

Ghosh, Biswajit. 2011c. 'Child Marriage, Community, and Adolescent Girls: The Salience of Tradition and Modernity in the Malda District of West Bengal', *Sociological Bulletin*, Indian Sociological Society 60, 2 (May–August 2011): 307–26.

———. 2011b. 'Child Marriage, Society and the Law: A Study in a Rural Context in West Bengal, India', *International Journal of Law, Policy and Family* 25, 2 (2011): 199–219.

———. 2011a. 'Early Marriage of Girls in Contemporary Bengal: A Field View', *Social Change, Sage* 41, 1: 41–61.

Ghosh, Biswajit, and Ananda Mohan Kar. 2010. 'Child Marriage in Rural West Bengal: Status and Challenges', *Indian Journal of Development Research and Social Action* 6, 1–2 (Jan.-Dec.): 1–23.

Lal, Ruby. 2013. *Coming of Age in Nineteenth-Century India. The Girl Child and the Art of Playfulness*. Cambridge: Cambridge University Press.

Mani, Lata. 1998. *Contentious Traditions: The Debate on Sati in Colonial India*. Berkeley: University of California Press.

Nanjundayya, V., and L.K. Ananthakrishna Iyer. 1931. *The Mysore Tribes and Caste*, vol. IV, Mysore University.

National Commission for Protection of Child Rights (NCPCR) and Young Lives. 2017. *A Statistical Analysis of Child Marriage in India* based on Census 2011.

Newbigin, Eleanor. 2013. *The Hindu Family and the Emergence of Modern India*. Cambridge: Cambridge University Press.

Nirantar Trust. 2015. *Early and Child Marriage in India: A Landscape Analysis*. New Delhi: Nirantar Trust, Supported by American Jewish World Service.

Pande, Ishita, 2020. *Sex, Law and the Politics of Age: Child Marriage in India, 1891-1937*. Cambridge: Cambridge University Press.

Parashar, Archana. 1992. *Women and Family Law Reform in India: Uniform Civil Code and Gender Equality*. New Delhi: Sage.

Sagade, Jaya. 2005. *Child Marriage in India: Socio-Legal and Human Rights Dimensions*. New Delhi: Oxford University Press.

Sarkar, Sumit. 2007. 'Vidyasagar and Brahmanical Society'. In *Women and Social Reform in Modern India*, Sumit and Tanika Sarkar, eds. New Delhi: Permanent Black.

Sarkar, Tanika. 2001. *Hindu Wife, Hindu Nation: Community, Religion and Cultural Nationalism*. New Delhi: Permanent Black.

Sen, Samita. 1999. *Women and Labour in Late Colonial India: The Bengal Jute Industry*. Cambridge: Cambridge University Press.

———. 2009. Religious Conversion, Infant Marriage and Polygamy: Regulating Marriage in India in the Late Nineteenth Century', *Journal of History* 26: 99–145.

———. 2012. 'Crossing Communities: Religious Conversion, Rights in Marriage, and Personal Law'. In *Negotiating Spaces: Legal Domains, Gender Concerns and Community Constructs*, Flavia Agnes and Shoba Venkatesh Ghosh, eds. New Delhi: Oxford University Press.

Singh, Renu, and Uma Vennam. 2016. 'Factors Shaping Trajectories to Child and Early Marriage; Evidence from Young Lives in India', Working Paper 149, Young Lives, May 2016.

Singha, Radhika. 1998. *A Despotism of Law: Crime and Justice in Early Colonial India*. New Delhi: Oxford India Press.

Sinha, Chitra. 2012. *Debating Patriarchy: The Hindu Code Bill Controversy in India (1941–1956)*. New Delhi: Oxford University Press.

Sinha, Mrinalini. 2006. *Specters of Mother India: The Global Restructuring of an Empire*. Durham, NC: Duke University Press.

Tambe, Ashwini. 2009. *Codes of Misconduct: Regulating Prostitution in Late Colonial Bombay*, Minneapolis, MN: University of Minnesota Press.

———. 2019. *Defining Girlhood in India: A Transnational History of Sexual Maturity Laws*. Urbana, IN: University of Illinois Press.

Thurston, Edgar. 1993 [1909]. *Castes and Tribes of South India*. New Delhi: Asian Educational Services.

Uberoi, Patricia, ed., 1993. *Family, Kinship and Marriage in India*. New Delhi: Oxford University Press.

Viswanathan, Gauri. 1998. *Outside the Fold: Conversion, Modernity and Belief*. Oxford: Oxford University Press.

1

Some Historiographical Challenges in Approaching Child Marriage in India

Mary E. John

THE TWENTY-FIRST century is witnessing massive efforts globally to eliminate child marriage. There is a special focus on countries like India since we have the largest numbers of women in the world who have married before the age of 18. The Indian state is under pressure to further amend its laws on the age of marriage; organizations on the ground are addressing child marriage in various ways, and new studies, many of them sponsored by international bodies, are emerging.

Child marriage in India has a very special relationship to history. This needs to be understood both in a historiographical and a strictly historical sense. Is there a story in the first place and how can it be told? From precolonial times to the era of colonial rule, from the making of the new Indian nation to the first decades of the twenty-first century, child marriage throws up a distinct set of questions. There have been many phases and shifts from the nineteenth century, when child marriage repeatedly became the most controversial of issues, to the time after Independence when it recedes from the public eye, to the contemporary moment with its particular rekindling of focus. Here I would like to open up some early questions about history and region in relation to existing scholarship and writing on the subject.

Most current studies of present day trends of child marriage in India, be they demographic, statistical or qualitative in scope, begin with a short introductory historical section. They frequently evince an obligation to go back to pre-colonial if not pre-medieval times to look for the root cause of child marriage. It is not just that they suffer on many counts— whether by virtue of sweeping generalizations about Indian tradition, claims that child marriage was a response to the rape and abduction of unmarried girls by Muslim invaders in the medieval period, over hasty critiques of what nineteenth-century social reform may have been attempting in its time and place, and, all too frequently, patchy if not basically incorrect accounts of this history itself. There is a more fundamental problem in producing historical accounts when it comes to the Indian situation, which I shall try to explain below.

A FEW THOUGHTS ON THE PRE-COLONIAL PERIOD

The existing literature on the subject of child marriage in India leads me to believe that one can only begin an account of such a history in the colonial period, that is, from the early nineteenth century. In fact, I am tempted to go on to say that it is not possible to come up with a history from before this period in the first place. Was there a pre-colonial idea of childhood let alone of child marriage? When and why does child marriage become nameable as an issue? As we shall see, it is only under conditions of colonial rule that the child becomes a problem category and it is child marriage that grips the national imagination in the late colonial period. There is nothing in the existing literature to show either that there was a concept of child marriage in earlier times and even less that it was a matter to be questioned. Let me add that India is by no means alone here, because child marriage is taken for granted—or to put it differently, does not exist as an idea or a concern—in most parts of the world for a very long time.[1]

This brings me to the next crucial point. Many scholars have pointed out how, as a direct consequence of the experience of colonialism, there was a compulsion to trace some kind of ancient historical ancestry to the problems they were attempting to tackle. However, there is no robust data to reconstruct such a history in the first place, alongside having to acknowledge the obvious existence of a multiplicity of practices, all of which may have been in flux. So what one sees are either generic claims without providing the source from which they are taken, or an overwhelming reliance on certain brahminical texts in the existing literature (some examples will be provided shortly), but without the acknowledgement of the impossibility of providing anything like a history of marriage in India. Such accounts do a grave injustice by leaving out non-Hindu and non-scriptural pasts, apart from the very real intractabilities of interpreting scriptural sources themselves. So, the comments that follow should be understood in the spirit of these major caveats.

Given these preliminary but essential remarks, it should not be surprising to discover that child marriage hardly crops up in the literature on households and gender relations in the ancient period. Kumkum Roy has pointed out that while early Indian textual sources describe the ritualistic aspects of marriage in considerable detail, the epics (the *Mahabharata* and the *Ramayana*) focus on marriage for its critical social and political purposes, namely, the acquisition of new kin alliances between royal families (Roy 2014).

This is why I would suggest that there is a problem in some of the following efforts to actually come up with conceptions of childhood or child marriage that resonate with our contemporary concerns. Some developmental psychologists, for example, have tried to align ancient textual notions of the stages of life of a male brahmin (that is, infancy and childhood, *brahmacharya* translated as apprenticeship, the householder

and finally the stage of *sanyas* or renunciation) with modern
ideas of developmental psychology under the notion of 'Hindu
conceptions of life span development' (T. S. Saraswathi et al.
2011). Saraswathi, Datta and Mishra say that in such a 'Hindu'
conception, childhood stretches from infancy to about the age
of eight, followed by the phase of celibate apprenticeship till
18 years (or more), after which a man is to marry and start
a household, though it is not known where these age spans
come from. (The idea of stages of life is quite a widespread
notion in ancient cultures; see also Chapter 2; but these
cannot be narrowly mapped by age, since notions of strict age
were only introduced into modern societies.) They neglect to
mention that this is reserved not just for the twice-born upper
castes, but for upper-caste men. Moreover, we do not know
how common such ideas were, for whom and when. The soci-
ologist K. M. Kapadia appears to be quite unselfconscious in
his descriptions of the celibate state of brahmacharya in his
early work on *Marriage and Family in India* (third edition 1966).
Kapadia equates this stage with being a student, 'marked by a
rapid growth of the body, emotional instability, the development of the sexual functions and stimulation of sexual activities. It is a period of storm and stress, of impulsiveness . . . the
kind of life that was bound to withstand the storm of adolescence. It might be dubbed a repressed life, but there could be
hardly any talk of repression when . . . the body was disciplined
for a higher purpose in life' (Kapadia 1966: 29–30). There is no
reference to Freudian notions of repression nor that the idea of
'storm and stress' comes from the work of Granville Stanley
Hall, a founding figure in the psychology of adolescence in his
work of 1904, for whom adolescence was very much a modern
phenomenon.

Kapadia has a chapter on 'age at marriage' in which he cites
from various brahminical sources and writers to try and figure
out when marriages took place in ancient India, and whether
there were changes over time. A textual reference in the
Grihyasutras (700–300 BCE) to the consummation of marriage

within three days of the rites being performed compared to references in the Dharmasutras (300–100 BCE) that the right time to give away a daughter in marriage is when she is 'still naked' (i.e., pre-pubertal) makes him believe that marriage before puberty for Hindu girls cannot be firmly dated. But he is careful to add that such prescriptions need not imply that this was actual practice, which once again does not lead to any conclusions about trends or customs. Kapadia has other points to make: Since marriage was all about the transfer of authority over a woman, from the father to the husband, 'it should hence take place before a girl reached the age when she might question it' (ibid.: 142). Kapadia cites several texts, especially from the sixth century CE, that mention—in passing—marriageable ages for the girl of 8, 9 or 10 years, including statements that a brahmin who married a girl beyond this age would lose his caste, and her parents and brother would go to hell. He also believes that caste endogamy would have promoted early marriage, as the father of the girl would be on the lookout for a groom from within a relatively narrow field of selection. The husband was to be older, by anything from 3 to 10 years or more. It became a matter of prestige for girls to be sought after in marriage from a 'tender age', and with the passage of time, any departure was a matter of disapproval if not social disgrace. Kapadia then makes a huge leap from brahminical texts to cite major figures from the pantheon of social and religious reform in the nineteenth century who married very young girls: Ramakrishna Paramahamsa married a girl of six, M. G. Ranade a girl of eight and D. K. Karve a girl of nine (ibid.: 146). There is also a chapter on Muslim marriage but which is quite general in scope, mainly concentrating on polygamy and with no particular discussion on the Indian situation. Buddhist texts are never alluded to.

Textual references to the threatening nature of the sexuality of women—whether in the brahminic tradition or in stories coming from the Buddhist Jatakas—are better known and frequently referred to (Chakravarti 1993; Roy 2014). It does not take much to realize that such textual excesses about the uncontrollability of female sexuality would have been obvious and undisguised justifications for the need for strong measures of control, especially over those women most valued by virtue of their high status. And with procreation being central to the very meaning of being a woman, it would only further cement the surmize that early marriages were an unspoken norm, whether in religious texts or in the worlds of custom, and indeed that this is not at all surprising.

A brief look at a popular mythological figure like Sita would however indicate that we are on treacherous terrain if one were to make any attempts to come up with substantive notions of childhood and adulthood in pre-modern times. It may be true that two of the most popular heroines of the epics are remembered as adult women: Sita and Draupadi (Kumkum Roy, personal communication). But too much cannot be read into this. The anthropologist Irawati Karve quotes the following lines by the character Rama in an eighth-century Sanskrit drama *Uttara Rama Carita* (After the Rama Story) by Bhavabhuti, when Sita was about to be exiled in the forest by the King: 'the loved one was fed and clothed (in my family) since she was a child, in youth she was never separated from me and now I am handing her over to death like a pet bird to a butcher' (in Karve 1968: 73). Equally telling, according to Nabaneeta Dev Sen, is that the many later stories of Sita that were written or sung by women begin with Sita's birth, not Rama's. Dev Sen's project has been to collect these 'alternative *Ramayanas*' that range from sixteenth-century narratives by Chandrabati in Bengal and the Telugu writer Molla to the countless songs of village women across the country in contemporary times. So once again, a note of caution is required when we approach the numerous folk songs that she has interpreted from across present day rural India, where Sita is evoked as a foundling, an orphaned girl child. Such songs invariably go on to the travails of child marriage, with giving away songs lamenting the loss of her home and the hardships that await among the in-laws, including domestic abuse. Dev Sen quotes from a Telugu song sung by rural women in Andhra as follows: 'The tiny girl is only as tall as seven jasmine flowers . . . Such a child is being given away in marriage to Rama today.' (Dev Sen 2008: 585). Notice moreover, that Nabaneeta Dev Sen's many Sitas traverse not just the historical swathe from the sixteenth century to the contemporary but cut across quite distinct regions.

Irawati Karve, in her well-known treatise on *Kinship Organisation in India* (third edition 1968), also, without reflection, refers briefly to brahminical texts from early India in order to then discuss her well-known thesis about the huge significance of different kinship practices drawing from anthropological accounts of her own time. In patrilineal households where a girl came from an alien family, early marriage was a necessity, a matter of ensuring her loyalty (Karve 1968: 73). Karve's study of kinship patterns is well known for her discussions of the major divide between the North and the South. Northern India has exemplified marriage to a stranger with significant status differences between wife givers and wife takers; even the village of the bride is considered inferior to the village of the groom. Both girls and boys were generally married when they were children, with the girl remaining in her home, making occasional visits to the in-laws, and only moved permanently after her first menstruation with a 'gauna' ceremony (Karve 1968: 126–127). Compare this description with what she says about Dravidian practices in the southern parts of India. Marriage in the South was not about seeking new alliances but of strengthening existing bonds, often with permitted relatives. It does not symbolize separation from the father's house for the girl. The future husband is 'the cross-cousin and the playmate of his future wife, not her lord and master' (ibid.: 242). This raises an interesting set of questions. After all, in the South too, marriages have been strictly arranged by families and also at early ages, with no consideration of the desires of girl or boy. And yet, the tone adopted for the South by Karve in this classic text on kinship is one of comparative ease, naturalness, and even a certain egalitarianism compared to the relentlessly oppressive situation of the girl from the North. I raise this as a question not so much of how accurate this description of marriage practices in the South may be, but rather to show how it is the North that has occupied the standard position in anthropological discussions of kinship practices, whose very harshness makes the South seem so much better in contrast. Here age appears as less of a criterion than such claimed differences in marriage patterns.

This is not the most satisfactory way to begin an account of child marriage in India, given all the challenges that I have drawn attention to. Instead, we have to explore a modern entry point: the much cited social reform of women from the early nineteenth century.

THE COLONIAL PERIOD

It is surely remarkable that much of the social reform initiatives that centred on women during the long nineteenth century, were primarily about the girl child. However, till very recently, there has been next to no discussion of the idea of childhood in this history. Though such a history remains to written, some beginnings have been made. My own strategy has been to glean from existing research as to when and how age became as much of a problem as the status of women. Without doubt the institution of marriage came to be seen as being at the heart of what ailed Indian society in the eyes of the British colonial rulers, an opinion echoed by many Indians in the course of that century and beyond. We will see how this concern with marriage came to be indistinguishable from that of child marriage.

In her more lyrical account of 'coming of age in the nineteenth century', Ruby Lal has observed that she 'felt it necessary to reconceptualize the woman question as the question of the girl child/woman for a number of reasons' (Lal 2013: 36). In a world where women—whether young or old—could do nothing on their own (here she is citing James Mill's references to Manu), or, in other words, where women lived as lifelong dependents, the separation of a distinct stage called childhood was practically impossible. She emphasizes the namelessness of this imbricated condition where woman and child kept collapsing onto one another. Her resolution of the problem was to deploy the idea of playfulness gleaned from Urdu textual sources on the one hand, and an oral history of coming of age on the other (her book centres on the life memories of Azra Kidwai, born into an aristocratic Lucknow family in the early twentieth century) which offer Lal an opportunity to recover spaces beyond male control. This contrasts with other accounts considered below, which are dominated by all kinds of control. Rather than being in a state of namelessness, the child wife is inexorably talked about, fought over, contested, and becomes everyone's problem. The child/woman dyad is, moreover, a very critical site of slippage.

There are many strands, events and famous men (and thereafter many women) associated with a history so focussed on marriage and the girl child/woman. Feminists and scholars of social history have been quite active since the 1970s in making some of this history more widely available. A major shortcoming is the considerable unevenness in regional terms, though this is beginning to get redressed. As a result school textbooks across the country since at least the 1960s feature icons from colonial Bengal like Raja Rammohan Roy and Pandit Ishwarchandra Vidyasagar, while the achievements of Jotirao Phule in the western region of colonial Maharashtra are only now beginning to be better known.

BEGINNINGS IN COLONIAL BENGAL

The social reform period stretches from the late eighteenth century to the first decades of the twentieth century. It is during this period that we can track how child marriage became not just the name of a problem, but the biggest problem ailing

Indian society, able to capture all that was wrong about us as
a people. Two regions stand both together and apart in this
history, with prominent commonalities and differences: that of
colonial Bengal, on the one hand, and the western region of the
Bombay Presidency, now roughly the region of Maharashtra,
on the other. The critical difference between the two is the
centrality of caste in the western region, compared to the relative blindness towards caste in accounts dealing with colonial
Bengal.

Most historians begin their account of the period of social
reform in India with the long drawn out debate over the practice of sati or widow immolation in colonial Bengal between
the 1780s and 1830. According to one influential account, if one
looks closely at the three decades of controversy over whether
and how to ban sati, as the debates unfolded between British
colonial officials, Indian pandits and reformers like Rammohan
Roy, the woman herself does not feature in these discourses,
which are rather about whether sati as a practice is sanctioned
in ancient religious scriptures. This was a debate about religion
as scripture, not women (Mani 1989). The significance of Lata
Mani's study was to replace linear accounts of modernization
or the emergence of women's empowerment, with the frame
of a colonial discourse that relied on Hindu scriptural injunctions for any consideration of reform. (Indeed, in the light of
the discussion above on child marriage in pre-colonial times,
we have seen how this injunction to look for roots of contemporary practices in brahminical scriptural texts continues
unabated.) In a study concentrated on examining the complex
interpretative traffic between British officials and pandits over
what exactly the shastras permitted by way of widow immolation, Mani mentions how colonial representations typically
reinforced the victim status of such women by infantilizing
her. She was invariably rendered as a 'tender child' even
though their very own statistics challenged such a claim (ibid.:
32). When cases of sati were brought up and enumerated, it
would seem that sati was not a practice that affected the child

widow as much as the mature or older person, who was quite often in impoverished circumstances (Yang 1989). Though no details are provided, sixteen was set as the age below which sati could not be permitted, indicative therefore of the new connections that were now being forged between considerations of age and, quite possibly, an unprecedented notion of consent, one that somehow fell back on 'ancient tradition' in order to be authentic.

Sati was a very specific phenomenon undertaken by small numbers in certain parts of Bengal and to a lesser extent elsewhere, gaining hugely in global publicity because of the extreme violence associated with it. The less sensational practice of ritually enforced widowhood was much more widespread, certainly amongst upper castes. A very significant number of women in the Indian population were found to be widows, that is, seen to be no longer having the protection of a husband. As Janaki Nair has put it, the law against widow immolation may have 'saved them from the pyre, but condemned them to a living death' (Nair 1994: 61). Here, one can quite unambiguously see how ideas of the (girl) child came to be constructed through the plight of child widows, which grabbed the attention of reformers, especially those who may have never left their natal homes. In cases where the marriage had not been consummated, sexual innocence, the status of childhood and the loss of patriarchal protections could coalesce into a perfect symbol of victimhood. Widowhood was not just very common, but practically speaking a phase in the life cycle of women where husbands were older. In several instances where such men themselves died early, the wives left behind were little more than children. Brahminical laws decreed that widows remain chaste. As one commentator put it, 'Irrevocably, eternally married as a mere child, the death of a husband she had perhaps never known left the wife a widow, an inauspicious being whose sins in a previous life had deprived her of her husband, and her parents-in-law of their son, in this one' (Carroll 2007: 114–15). Lucy Carroll seems to be quite certain that not just enforced widowhood but also child marriage were purely upper-caste customs, confined to a minority (less than 20 percent of the population). As we shall see, others have not always agreed, nor is this entirely supported by historical evidence.

One strand in the history of child marriage in India therefore begins with the figure of the (upper-caste) child widow, and reform led by Ishwarchandra Vidyasagar in Bengal took the shape of demanding the legal possibility of her remarriage. Pandit Vidyasagar was as concerned with child marriage and girls' education, urging in 1850 that girls be at least 11 years old for marriage and boys 18. In 1861 the British declared in the just formulated Indian Penal Code that sexual intercourse to a girl below ten would be considered rape. While laws for widow remarriage were first proposed in 1837 it took till 1856 to be passed. Differences in caste practices do make an entry: one of the reasons for initial opposition was that 'such a law would lead the Hindus of upper castes and classes to be confused with the inferior castes and tribes among whom remarriage was common' (Nair 1996: 60). Others have pointed out that this law, for all its positive intentions, had unintended negative effects on precisely those castes and communities for whom remarriage had not been an issue. This is because the new law introduced certain provisions that effectively curtailed the more open remarriage practices among these non-elite castes. (Chowdhry 1993; Carroll 2007) In retrospect it might appear odd that the very practice of child marriage achieved some measure of acknowledgement first via its tragic outcome in the significant presence of child widows. But on further reflection this is quite understandable, given that child marriage per se had yet to attain the status of a problem. Since the widow had lost her patriarchally sanctioned source of protection, she could be viewed as an abjected figure, isolated and deprived for no fault of her own. The child widow thus invited considerable sympathy if not intervention, and the younger she was, the greater the identification with her plight. It took almost a century of social reform for child marriage itself to enter the fray of legislative action.

A much larger preoccupation that spanned several regions in colonial India, more so in the South, is that modern childhood is most closely entwined with ideas of education and schooling. Of course this is not at all confined to India. But what may be unique to the Indian situation is that colonial education introduced what became one of the most important aspects regulating a girl or woman's subsequent marriage, including her age at marriage. In the Indian context it was education that was decisive for affecting when a marriage takes place, whereas in other parts of the world it was work. More attention needs to be paid to the realm of education and its ramifications for thinking about changes in the institution of marriage. Matters relating to girls' education were for a long time as controversial as the more publicly fought over issues of marriage and widowhood. Because this is much less systematically explored, I am suggesting that further research is needed on the changing relationship between education and marriage both in the colonial context and thereafter.

In his study of western education in colonial India, Sanjay Seth has asked why the subject of female education was a matter of constant discussion when the actual numbers of girls and women in education was so miniscule, 'in staggering disproportion to the number of girls affected' (Seth 2007: 129). As late as 1882 there were just six girls in college, over 2000 in secondary schools, and 124,000 in mixed primary schools, mainly in the Presidencies of Bengal, Madras and Bombay. He goes on to say that by the end of the nineteenth century there was in fact widespread agreement in favour of the idea of women's education, but this did not result in a significant increase in numbers since women were burdened with being the bearers of Indian culture for the incipient nation (Chatterjee 1989), and, a western education was inappropriate for such women. These so-called obstacles however run considerably deeper, once the links with marriage are brought into the picture.

In the early years of social reform in the nineteenth century, the education of girls was not on the British colonial agenda. The British were concerned with using western education as a training ground for Indians who could be incorporated into the lower rungs of the administrative system, with English educated Indians being preferred for government appointments. Such Indians—it should be obvious—were entirely men. Wealthy Indians themselves took the first steps before the government stepped in, beginning with the establishment of the Hindu College in Calcutta in 1816. The first teachers to explicitly approach girls in their homes were missionaries or, more commonly, the wives of missionaries. Geraldine Forbes has discussed the specific interest in teaching women and girls, which led to their opening the first girls' schools where native Christian women were also brought in as school teachers (Forbes 1986, 1998). Thus was established the Calcutta Education Society for the promotion of girls' education, though families were initially hesitant to send their girls. Even the patronage of Indian gentlemen and the presence of Brahmin pandits on the staff did not suffice. Other regions of the country under colonial rule, notably western and southern India fared much better. The extensive documentation provided by S. Bhattacharya and his colleagues provides a more differential picture—it would be wrong to think that it was mainly colonial educators who took upon themselves the burden of women's education, with increasing initiatives coming from indigenous intellectuals, 'local notables' and 'monied people' (Bhattacharya et al. 2001: xxvii). Rekha Pappu has shown how social reformers emerged among both Muslims and Hindus, each addressing their own communities, privileging the education of their respective elites, looking for sanction in religious texts, and ultimately finding justification for regeneration through women's reform (Pappu 2015; Chakravarti 1998; Minault 1998).

A DIFFERENT FRAMING IN WESTERN INDIA

There has been as much scholarship if not more on western India than the better known Bengal example when it comes to social history more broadly, and questions relating to women's reform more specifically. However, for reasons that probably have to do with Calcutta being the seat of colonial power, Bengal has retained its dominance in histories of social reform. One of the interesting aspects of scholarship on the region that now falls broadly within the state of Maharashtra is that accounts of reform foreground structures of caste as much as those of gender, when discussing what ails Indian society. It is instructive to contrast otherwise very similar themes pertaining to women's status: the home and gender segregation, purdah and seclusion, the public/private dichotomy, marriage and bearing children and so on; in works dealing with Maharashtra (Kosambi 2007; O'Hanlon 1994; O'Hanlon 2014; Deshpande 2002; Chakravarti 1998) with those on Bengal (e.g., Chatterjee 1993; Sinha 1994; Sarkar 2001; Sarkar and Sarkar 2007). It is immediately clear that the problems of women in a region like Bengal are discussed in largely gendered terms (at least when it comes to its *bhadramahila* middle-class upper-caste woman), whereas in western India the story can only be told through the working of gender and caste together, and for all women, whether 'high' or 'low'.

One early sign of this difference can be vividly seen in the belated discovery of the pioneering efforts of Jotirao Phule and his wife, Savitribai. There is now a burgeoning literature on Phule including some translations of his writings, though equal attention has yet to be paid to the extraordinary life and work of Savitribai, who is unfortunately folded in as a 'wife' into accounts of the man who was the first to be called a Mahatma. Unlike Raja Rammohan Roy or Pandit Vidyasagar who came from upper-class and -caste backgrounds, Phule was born into an agricultural caste, a shudra. Thanks to having a father who was a building contractor, he was able to complete a school education. Phule's translator G. P. Deshpande makes the interesting comment in his introduction that while other reformers were influenced by 'the rather weak English branch of European liberalism' (Deshpande 2002: 3) Phule had read Thomas Paine's *The Rights of Man*. Phule established a school for *shudra-atishudra* (shudra and dalit) girls in 1848, the first of its kind anywhere in India. His father was shocked and, fearing a backlash from upper castes, threw both him and his new wife out of the house. Phule continued undeterred with other sources of support, from missionaries and the British state. Another school was opened in 1851 for girls from all castes. Many of his other actions, such as throwing open the family well to untouchables, were equally revolutionary, and not just for his time. Interesting, too, is that the terminology used by him and his followers was not that of social reform but rather of social justice. Phule's agenda in establishing the Satyashodak Samaj (truth-seeking society) was to promote a society that was egalitarian when it came to labour, gender and caste by resisting brahmin hegemony and abolishing shudra and dalit slavery.

Other scholarship on Maharashtra focusses on social reformers in cities like Pune and Bombay who appeared much closer to their Bengal counterparts, and were quite conscious of caste conventions, under upper-caste leaders like M. G. Ranade, R. G. Bhandarkar and others. Meera Kosambi has described the views of someone like Bhandarkar who sought to placate opponents to women's education by portraying it as a kind of 'patriarchal convergence'. Education was 'a window in the prison house' that would not disturb her place in the home or the discharging of household duties, a very limited modernising position (Kosambi 2007: 151). This is a harsher rendering of Partha Chatterjee's 'nationalist resolution of the women's question', whereby social reform was successfully contained by making the educated woman the bearer of Indian tradition in the cultural battle against colonial rule (Chatterjee 1989). The education of women had been strongly proscribed under brahminical norms: it was frequently said that to gain an education was to invite the worst fate of widowhood. Literate women (even daughters of pandits) were seen as potentially subversive by evading household control to engage in immoral relations with non-domestic men. Education lent itself to being contained within an evolving family structure for upwardly mobile newly educated men who needed literate wives. Kosambi quotes B. G. Tilak, the conservative and revivalist who, while sharply opposed to the liberal reformers on many issues, including that of child marriage, gave his sanction to a certain form of female education: training to become good wives and mothers, which allowed for primary schooling. She neglects to add that in his view, primary education was but a beginning; education is only fulfilled in the marital home, which he likened to a workshop where the actual training takes place. 'By the age of 15 or 16 years a woman should be well trained at housework and this training will never be available in a school as much as at home. *The marital home is the 'workshop' of female education'* (cited in Kosambi, ibid: 157; emphasis added). Only when they were assured that schools would pose no threat to the primary socialisation of the reproductive family form did they participate in promoting a limited form of education for women.

THE RAKHMABAI CASE

What then of the institution of marriage and the question of child marriage? The first major case relating to child marriage that became a matter of national and international controversy, inviting even the intervention of Queen Victoria herself, was the Rakhmabai case that unfolded in the 1880s. Much has been written about this case and from several perspectives (Heimsath 1964; Masselos 1998; Chandra 1998; Chakravarti 2005; Kosambi 2007). The Rakhmabai case is truly remarkable for several reasons. It pitted the colonial state and its British laws against the complex and multi-layered realm of so-called Hindu law, which encompassed both codified laws and caste based systems of adjudication. Rakhmabai herself was an unusual example of a woman who, though born into a shudra caste family whose traditional occupation was carpentry, had witnessed urbanization, upward mobility and the benefits of western education, thanks to the combination of financial security and liberal reformist ideas that characterized her larger familial context in Bombay. Yet, as was customary in those times (possibly also as a mark of taking on brahminical practices as an aspect of rising social status) she had been married in 1875 at the age of eleven to one Dadaji Thakur who, while staying with his maternal uncle, was expected to be groomed by way of education till the time was right for them to live together. However, this did not happen, as Rakhmabai in subsequent meetings found him incompatible and would not live with him. After various unsuccessful efforts, and rather than resort to caste adjudication, in 1884 Dadaji issued a legal notice for restitution of conjugal rights under British law, which was the year which saw the initiation of reform in the realm of child marriage. Rakhmabai refused to yield even when the judgement went against her; the matter went on appeal, with various aspects of Hindu law, British law and caste practice being drawn upon by opposing sides, until by 1888 a financial settlement was proposed whereby Dadaji relinquished his rights over her. During the court case Rakhmabai even took it upon herself to write two letters in English about her condition to the *Times of India* from which it is worth quoting:

> My English readers can hardly conceive the hard lot entailed upon Hindu women by the custom of early marriage . . . The treatment which even servants receive from their European masters is far better than falls to the share of us Hindu women. We are treated worse than beasts (cited in Kosambi 2007: 266).

Here was a case in which identifiably feminist protest was articulated using the most powerful analogies of colonial domestic servitude and animal cruelty to evoke maximum sympathy. While detractors could only see in Rakhmabai the baneful consequences of westernized education, hers was a case of a bad marriage to an undesirable man lower in status, yet sanctified both by Hindu and British law. It took until 1891 for the underlying question of child marriage in Hindu law to be subjected to some reform. But that moment belonged to yet another case, one that shook the public world of Calcutta.

THE AGE OF CONSENT CONTROVERSY

This section deals with what could, in retrospect be described as the processes that made possible the first major legislation concerning child marriage, namely, the Age of Consent Bill of 1891 under conditions of colonial rule. The story is a remarkably complex one, bringing in players from different regions of the country. It involved considerable controversy precisely because it pitted those who were prepared to approach the colonial state for change in matters of social reform, here having to do with consent to sexual intercourse (whether inside or outside of marriage) with those who believed that nationalist strivings demanded a break from this kind of petitioning to an alien state. This moment has been approached from different perspectives by scholars and continues to be a matter of ongoing investigation.

THE AGE OF CONSENT ACT

By the 1880s, as a consequence of widespread public debate, writing and networking across the subcontinent, reformers in the Bombay Presidency took up in earnest the issue of child marriage. It was not a Hindu but a Parsi, Behramji Malabari, who began the actual process of petitioning the imperial state with his 'Note on Infant Marriage in India' written in 1884, along with another note on enforced widowhood. Notice therefore the use of the term 'infant', not even that of 'child'. His Note draws on the common perception that traditional upper-caste Hindu marriages could be performed much before puberty (indeed even in infancy) through an alliance between families in which no notion of consent was even conceivable (which could also include the groom). However, such marriages were consummated upon reaching puberty through a second ritual: the *garbhadhan* or impregnation ceremony, after which it was common for the bride to move to the groom's house and begin her new life with all its attendant sexual, reproductive and household duties as wife and daughter-in-law.

Malabari's Note in 1884 referred to infant marriage as a worse evil than infanticide since it entailed life-long misery and for both the wife and husband: ill-health and disease, loss of studies for the husband, sickly children, 'a wreck of two lives grown almost old in youth' (cited in Kosambi 2007: 278). These arguments were used by many others in the subsequent campaign, ranging from Jotirao Phule to Pandita Ramabai (in her treatise *The High Caste Hindu Woman*) and also by a small number of the very first feminists of western India (Anagol 2007). Phule forwarded two Notes of his own, written in English. Interestingly, in his 'Note on Infant Marriage', Phule questioned the false universalism of the 'enlightened Hindu of Bengal' whose suggestions are 'not universal and applicable' to the 'ignorant shudra-atishudras', 'downtrodden aborigines' where a young wife could be worked harder 'than an American slave', a bridegroom's family ruined by indebtedness, or conjugal incompatibility due to early marriage end with the girl's suicide. While this certainly called for higher ages of marriage for both boys and girls, it also required change through a non-brahmin education (Deshpande 2002: 193–194). On the other hand, Phule went on to say, brahmin women suffer from the degeneracy of the brahminical institution of marriage, where a man is allowed every excess of polygamy and lust, while after his death, the wife must endure the severest strictures of widowhood, including being forced into prostitution to survive. Widows and widowers should both be allowed to remarry or both be prevented from doing so. Phule thus put forward a differential picture constituted by caste/gender/labour which was responsible not only for the direct victimization of the brahmin widow but also that of uneducated oppressed shudra-atishudra people with their own equally disastrous marriage practices. His views should also be seen as a corrective to those who believed that child marriage was only an upper-caste custom. He asked that the girl be at least eleven and the boy nineteen. In spite of his radicalism, this age gap would indicate how differently childhood was perceived even in his own thinking when it came to boys and girls. Malabari's Note demanded that the age of the girl be raised from ten to twelve years.

Scholars like Tanika Sarkar and Meera Kosambi have described at some length the enormous opposition this move invited; first in the western region by nationalists like Tilak and subsequently in Bengal. Opponents to raising the age saw this as a direct affront to shastric injunctions as well as to local caste practices, and castigated reformers for painting a grossly exaggerated picture of the evils of the Hindu custom of infant marriage. Indeed, their articulation went to considerable lengths to describe infant marriage as a marvellous Indian institution, the core of our culture, for which no apologies were required, least of all the intervention of an alien colonial state. The scriptures, it was said, made it clear that menstruation implied the death of the embryo and hence a marriage which took place after puberty would bring dishonour to the ancestors and family lineage. Puberty itself signalled the birth of a woman's sexual desire, which, it was also said, would be out of control if not already contained within the institution of a legitimate marriage. These undeniably caste-based sanctions could be redescribed such that ideas of female sexuality operated as a hinge between norms of *culture* in the form of religious sanction and *biology* represented by the female body at its first menarche. Sexual intercourse and the birth of children (especially sons) were mandatory duties that were entailed by marriage. These were the descriptions of the institution of Hindu marriage at the heart of the controversy, which reformers were prepared (to a certain degree) to question, but which had to be defended by those in opposition.

Sarkar has described how the Bengal Presidency was thrown into a frenzy of support for the anti-reformers, for whom the age of consent controversy crystallised into the birth of militant nationalism. Large numbers gathered in mass protest in public places, the first of its kind in colonial India. Alternate scriptural views that mentioned higher ages of cohabitation after puberty, newly evolving scientific conceptions of the female body, eugenic notions of breeding a stronger race of children, that is to say, other views of 'culture', 'nature' and moral entreaties were variously drawn upon by those in favour of reform.

According to Sarkar it was only the Phulmonee case of 1891 that dramatically ended the stalemate. Phulmonee was a young girl married at the age of eleven by most accounts to a man around thirty years of age. Sexual intercourse was so violent that she suffered from severe bleeding, leading to her death (Sarkar 2001). Some contemporary observers have anachronistically called it a fatal case of marital rape. (Given that the IPC of 1860 stipulated age 10 as the minimum age for sexual intercourse, the husband was finally let off.) Change happened at a different level. As Sarkar has gone on to elaborate, the dead body of Phulmonee caused the carefully crafted and aestheticized image of the doll-like infant wife celebrated by Hindu revivalists to collapse. After the Phulmonee case, several other cases involving injury or the death of child brides came to receive more attention, including news reports from different parts of the country.

In 1891 the Age of Consent Bill was passed which raised the age of consent for sexual activity on the part of a girl whether within marriage or outside of it from 10 to 12 years. Geraldine Forbes has commented that this was a compromise, since it did not prevent families from forming a marriage alliance at an earlier age, and then wait for its consummation when the girl was 12 (Forbes 1979: 410). Himani Bannerji in her careful analysis of the judgement has made the further observation regarding what consent actually amounted to here: Consent had little to do with notions of a girl's right to choose, this was rather about the right of legal guardians to alienate a woman's body to a man, whether as husband or client (Bannerji 2001).

Both the details of the Phulmonee case and the battles surrounding the passing of the Age of Consent Bill would imply that it is quite unclear what place if any can be accorded to notions of consent understood as women's agency in the passing of this Act. I would like to suggest that the Age of Consent Bill achieved something else: it should be seen as the *first critical moment* in the invention of *girlhood* in India, in which the question of *caste* that was so *central* in western India could be dissolved into that of a battle over *national culture*.

AGE AND GIRLHOOD IN THE WAKE OF THE AGE OF CONSENT BILL

Radhika Singha has offered a number of insights into how the Age of Consent Bill came to be focussed on age itself, when the colonial government had steered away from such a mode of approaching marriage till then. Much of the debate between officials, reformers and their many opponents rested on bringing together sexual intercourse within and outside marriage (i.e., the child wife and the prostitute) within the same law, and on the use of a puberty test or the onset of menstruation as a better 'fact' to assess readiness for sexual relations than age. Interestingly, however, the very 'facticity' of puberty suffered on two counts: first, medical officials believed that India's hot climate led to earlier manifestations of puberty than in Europe, and second, reformers added that puberty itself could be manipulated so to speak through an unnaturally early onset of sexual relations. Radhika Singha cites Dagmar Engels to show that ultimately the British were only keen to prove the 'superiority' of their race against the 'degeneracy' of the subject Indian population (in 1885 Britain had raised the age of consent for prostitution to sixteen). Singha makes the more significant point that it was precisely in the longer term interests of the reformers to make age alone their criterion:

> A uniform and higher age would detach the state of female minority both from the physical changes of puberty and from the life-cycle event of marriage, and put it more definitively

within the grasp of legislative enactment. The orthodox
accurately perceived the threat (Singha 2003: 24).

In other words, neither 'culture' (marriage rituals and scriptural
injunctions) nor 'nature' (puberty and menstruation) were to
determine girlhood. Rather, the more arbitrary question of age
(which need not bear any relation to social consciousness or
community practice) should be the basis, because it could lend
itself to further legal reform. This in turn called for setting up
a state apparatus to record dates of birth rather than a more
medicalized mode of regulation, as Janaki Nair has argued in
her study of Princely Mysore.

Ishita Pande is another scholar to have explored the question
of age in the history of social reform, if from a more critical
perspective. In her work on the child-wife (Pande 2012, 2013),
Pande argues that the status of the child has been largely taken
for granted in Indian historiography. The critical category that
circumscribed age in the colonial Indian context, she suggests,
was that of sexuality, and she even speaks of an age stratified
sexual system. This was exemplified in the Age of Consent
Bill, where even though the controversy was always being
discussed in terms of infant and child *marriage*, the form that
the Bill took was consent to *sexual intercourse*. In her essay on the
Age of Consent controversy Pande makes the same argument
as that of Radhika Singha but comes to a different conclusion.
Deliberating on how it is neither bio-medicine nor religious
scripture but age (a statistical artefact and not a reality) that
becomes the basis for deciding the break between the girl and
the adult woman (Pande 2012), she articulates her critique of
this dependence on age:

> The presumed universality and incontrovertibility of the
> 'child' defined exclusively with reference to chronological age,
> continues to obfuscate the use of age-categories and concepts of
> childhood...what, specifically, are the problems being tackled,
> above and beyond an assumed consensus on the need for the
> sexual protection of the digitally defined child? (2012: 223).

Sexual protection was certainly at the heart of the Age of Consent Act. At this moment then, girlhood came to be defined as the age prior to the onset of sexual relations (from which the girl child had to be protected by the force of criminal law), and by 1891 such age was identical whether it be for the consummation of marriage or for prostitution. However, it is unclear whether what was therefore set into law was a rigid age/sex system. Girlhood did not remain some kind of fixed category, precisely because questions of age not only changed but also diversified. Debates over marital and non-marital sex for girls (and to a lesser extent for boys) in the changed contexts of the first decades of the twentieth century rendered notions of girlhood unstable, subjected as they were to complex and contradictory forces that were international as much as local.

A further word about the consequences of the passing of the Age of Consent Act would be relevant. Tanika Sarkar has made the extremely important observation that for the generation of nationalists who had seen the failure of their efforts to anchor an emergent nationalism with the cultural symbol of non-consensual infant marriage, their subsequent move was to shift focus to a seemingly safer figure, that of the mother (Sarkar 2001). It is this symbol that becomes so central in subsequent debates and writings from the turn of the century, all the way to its contemporary revival as Bharat Mata/Mother India.

IN LIEU OF A CONCLUSION

I have tried to open up some of the challenges in thinking about child marriage in India historically, provisionally ending with the Age of Consent Act of 1891. I have been particularly critical of those who have attempted to provide a pre-colonial history of child marriage, when the very concept did not exist, and scholarship is more problematic than enlightening. I have further tried to demonstrate that child marriage becomes nameable during the colonial era when it turns into one of the most controversial issues for reformers and nationalists alike. It takes on regionally specific forms with caste as the most significant differentiator, while being connected through an agenda shaped by conflicted positions in relation to the imperial state and an incipient nationalism. By the time the first women's organizations are formed in the early twentieth century, child marriage has fully arrived in the public eye and indeed comes to acquire an enormous international reach. This marks a new moment in the history of child marriage in India, one that is taken up elsewhere in this volume.

This essay has been drawn from chapter one of my book Child Marriage in an International Frame: A Feminist Review from India *(Routledge 2021). I would like to take this opportunity to thank Shobhana Boyle, Ingrid Fitzgerald, Janaki Nair and Samita Sen for their careful and critical reading of this chapter.*

NOTE

1   For more on this, see Chapter 2 of my forthcoming book *Child Marriage in an International Frame: A Feminist Review from India* (Routledge 2021).

REFERENCES

Anagol, Padma. 2007. 'Rebellious Wives and Dysfunctional Marriages: Indian Women's Discourses and Participation in the Debates over Restitution of Conjugal Rights and the Child Marriage Controversy in the 1880s and 1890s'. In *Women and Social Reform in Modern India,* Tanika Sarkar and Sumit Sarkar, eds. Ranikhet: Permanent Black: 420–65.

Bannerji, Himani. 2001. *Inventing Subjects: Studies in Hegemony, Patriarchy and Colonialism.* New Delhi: Tulika.

Bhattacharya, Sabyasachi, et al. 2001. *The Development of Women's Education in India: A Collection of Documents, 1850–1920.* New Delhi, Kanishka with Education Research Records Unit, JNU.

Carroll, Lucy. 2007. 'Law, Custom and Statutory Social Reform: The Hindu Widows' Remarriage Act of 1856'. In *Women and Social Reform in Modern India*, vol.1, Tanika Sarkar and Sumit Sarkar, eds. Ranikhet: Permanent Black: 113–44.

Chakravarti, Uma. 2005. *The Life and Times of Pandita Ramabai*. New Delhi: Zubaan.

———. 1998. *Rewriting History: The Life and Times of Pandita Ramabai*. New Delhi: Kali for Women.

———. 1993. 'Conceptualising Brahmanical Patriarchy in Early India: Gender, Caste, Class and State', *Economic and Political Weekly* (henceforth *EPW*) 28, 14: 579–85.

Chandra, Sudhir. 1998. *Enslaved Daughters: Colonialism, Law and Women's Rights*. New Delhi: Oxford University Press.

Chatterjee, Partha 1993. *The Nation and its Fragments: Colonial and Postcolonial Histories*. Princeton, NJ: Princeton University Press.

———. 1989. 'The Nationalist Resolution of the Women's Question'. In *Recasting Women: Essays in Colonial History*, Kumkum Sangari and SudeshVaid, eds. New Delhi: Kali for Women: 233–53.

Chowdhry, Prem. 1993. 'Conjugality, Law and State: Inheritance Rights as Pivot of Control in Northern India', *National Law School Journal*, Special Issue on Feminism and Law, 1: 95–115.

Deshpande, Govind P. 2002. *Selected Writings of Jotirao Phule*. New Delhi: Leftword Books.

Forbes, Geraldine H. 1979. 'Women and Modernity: The Issue of Child Marriage in India', *Women's Studies International Quarterly* 2: 407–19.

———. 1986. 'In Search of the Pure Heathen: Missionary Women in Nineteenth Century India', *EPW* 21, 17: WS2–WS8.

———. 1998. *Women in Modern India*. Cambridge: Cambridge University Press.

Heimsath, C.H. 1964. *Indian Nationalism and Hindu Social Reform*. Princeton, NJ: Princeton University Press.

Kapadia, K. M. 1966. *Marriage and Family in India*. Delhi: Oxford University Press.

Karve, Irawati. 1968. *Kinship Organisation in India*. New Delhi: Asia Publishing House.

Kosambi, Meera. 2007. *Crossing Thresholds: Feminist Essays in Social History*. Ranikhet: Permanent Black.

Lal, Ruby. 2013. *Coming of Age in Nineteenth-Century India: The Girl-Child and the Art of Playfulness*. Cambridge: Cambridge University Press.

Mani, Lata. 1989. 'Contentious Traditions: The Debate on Sati in Colonial India', In *Recasting Women: Essays in Colonial History*, Kumkum Sangari and Sudesh Vaid, eds. New Delhi: Kali for Women: 88–126.

Masselos, Jim. 1998. 'Sexual Property/Sexual Violence: Wives in Late Nineteenth-Century Bombay'. In *Images of Women in Maharashtrian Society*, Anne Feldhaus, ed. Albany, NY: SUNY Press: 113–34.

Minault, Gail. 1998. *Secluded Scholars: Women's Education and Muslim Social Reform in Colonial India*. New Delhi: Oxford University Press.

Nair, Janaki. 1996. *Women and the Law in Colonial India: A Social History*. New Delhi: Kali for Women.

O'Hanlon, Rosalind. 1994. *A Comparison between Women and Men: Tarabai Shinde and the Critique of Gender Relations in Colonial India*. Madras: Oxford University Press.

———. 2014. *At the Edges of Empire: Essays in the Social and Intellectual History of India*. New Delhi: Permanent Black.

Pande, Ishita. 2012. 'Coming of Age: Law, Sex and Childhood in Late Colonial India', *Gender & History* 24, 1: 205–30.

———. 2013. ' "Listen to the Child": Law, Sex, and the Child Wife in Indian Historiography', *History Compass* 11, 9: 687–701.

Pappu, Rekha. 2015. 'Towards a Framework for Forging Links: Exploring the Connections between Women's Education, Empowerment and Employment', *Indian Journal of Gender Studies* 22, 2: 1–22.

Roy, Kumkum. 2014. *The Power of Gender and the Gender of Power*. New Delhi: Oxford University Press.

Saraswathi, T. S., ed. 1999. 'Adult-Child Continuity in India: Is Adolescence a Myth or an Emerging Reality?' In *Culture, Socialization and Human Development: Theory, Research and Applications in India*. New Delhi: Sage: 213–32.

Sarkar, Sumit, and Tanika Sarkar. 2007. *Women and Social Reform in Modern India*, vols. 1 and 2. Ranikhet: Permanent Black.

Sarkar, Tanika. 2001. *Hindu Wife, Hindu Nation: Community, Religion, and Cultural Nationalism*. Bloomington, IN: Indiana University Press.

Sen, Nabaneeta Dev. 2008. 'Alternative *Ramayanas*'. In *Women's Studies in India: A Reader*, Mary E. John, ed. New Delhi: Penguin.

Seth, Sanjay. 2007. *Subject Lessons: The Western Education of Colonial India*. Durham, NC: Duke University Press.

Singha, Radhika. 2003. 'Colonial Law and Infrastructural Power: Reconstructing Community, Locating the Female Subject', *Studies in History*, 19, 1: 87–126.

Sinha, Mrinalini. 1994. *Colonial Masculinities: The Manly Englishman and Effeminate Bengali*. Manchester: Manchester University Press.

Yang, Anand A. 1989. 'Whose Sati? Widow Burning in Early Nineteenth-Century India.' *Journal of Women's History* 1, 2: 8–33.

2

Child Marriage and the Second Social Reform Movement

Bhaswati Chatterjee

THE AGE OF Consent Act of 1891 addressed the issue of child marriage by enhancing the age of sexual cohabitation. The Act raised the age from 10 to 12 following the death of a young bride Phulmonee due to violent sexual intercourse by her husband Hari Maiti. This Act also represented the first step towards protecting girl brides from physical assault. Even before the growth of political agitation, child marriage was the issue on which the techniques of political mobilization and agitation were first elaborated and tested. However, with the Age of Consent Act, the consent of the individual became important and the woman became a legal subject. As argued by Tanika Sarkar (2001: 218), consent was made into a biological category, 'a stage when the female body was ready to accept sexual penetration without serious harm'. Therefore, it was her body that signified consent and enjoyed legal immunity.

The British imperial legislature, which passed this Act, had no Indian representation. The furore surrounding the Act discouraged the colonial state from intervention in social issues in the next decade or two. Social reform was quiescent. The scenario changed with the introduction of Indian legislators in the Central Assembly from 1919. Non-official Indian members began to take the initiative for reform; marriage and age of consent were their major priorities. A second phase of social reform started at the initiative of these reformers, hailing mostly from the western and southern regions of the country. The most important social legislation in this period was the Sarda Act, the first Act on marriage which affected all communities of India. It is also known as the Child Marriage Restraint Act 1929, which fixed the age of marriage for girls at 14 and for boys 18. While fixing a digital age,[1] the argument was that women's bodies biologically would be more receptive to sexual intercourse and pregnancy. Initially proposed for the Hindus only, as child marriage was also a problem for the Muslim community, the Sarda Act was applicable for both the communities. Subsequently the colonial government used extreme caution while applying this act. This law was followed by many others, especially for the Hindu community, which culminated in the Hindu Code Bill after Independence. I call this the 'second social reform movement'. The issues raised in the nineteenth-century social reform movement continued into the twentieth century, addressing marriage, property and family. The major difference being that social legislation was initiated by Indians instead of the colonial government (Chakrabarti 2016).

In the period 1920s to 1940s, Indian legislators addressed legal conditions of Hindu women to prove that colonized Indian society, particularly Hindu society, was not barbaric but a progressive society that could be improved further through reform. This was a self-civilizing mission. The nascent women's organizations were their main supporters and active agents of these reforms. It has been famously said by Lata Mani, that women were neither the subject nor the object but merely the site of the first social reform movement (Mani 1989). In the second social reform movement, women emerged at the forefront. From the early twentieth century, women began to intervene in myriad debates that related to questions of education, employment and, particularly, marriage laws. In the Age of Consent Act, the concept of 'consent' was individual; the demand to raise the age of marriage was a collective right asserted by these organized women during the Sarda Bill agitation.

In the 1920s, the controversy over *Mother India* by Katherine Mayo, published in 1927[2] forced the colonial state to renegotiate its own relationship with social reform. In an atmosphere of international criticism, conservative 'neutrality' on the part of the colonial government was read as reactionary obstructionism, while impending nationalist agitation from the late 1920s increased the need for political pragmatism (Major 2012). In the early 1920s, the Government of India repeatedly opposed bills on marriage or consent, reluctant to re-open controversial subjects, or even to allow individual Indian reformers to do so (Forbes 1979). This trend continued up to 1929 when at last the colonial government was compelled to pass the Child Marriage Restraint Act and the Gains of Learning Act.

Women's issues, especially familial and gender relations, continued to be the subject of bitter public controversies in the twentieth century. Age of consent, child marriage and widowhood continued to be a constant source of anxiety for Hindu society. Reformers addressed these issues through various means. Ishita Pande has pointed out that Sarda's earlier bills had 'sought to target child marriage within only those communities in which girl children were routinely married to much older men and subsequently spent most of their lives suffering from the (religion, caste, class and/or region-specific) incapacities that accompanied widowhood' (Pande 2012: 220). The native Indian states like Mysore, Indore, Kotah enforced legislation to prevent the marriage of older men with younger girls. Among the Indian states, Bombay took the lead. In 1927, though a private members Bill prohibiting the marriage of girls under 12 and boys under

16 was refused, the Bombay government itself introduced a Bill to prevent unequal marriages penalizing a marriage between a man above 45 and girls less than 18.

Thakurdas Bhargava's Old Men's Marriage with Young Girls Restraint Bill in 1930 addressed this age difference in marriage. The Bill was designed to stop unequal marriages, and penalized marriages of men of 45 years of age or over with girls below 18.[3] Sarda gave a notice of a resolution recommending the appointment of a committee to report inter alia on the question of penalizing marriage of a man over 40 with a girl below a certain age in communities in which widow marriage did not obtain.[4] The Age of Consent Committee in its report also stated that the evil of such disproportionate marriage was so great among some communities that they had earnestly asked for the prohibition to be recommended by legislation.[5] Sarda's Child Marriage Restraint Act was also designed to prevent child widowhood. According to the 1921 Census, less than 1.5 percent of 13.5 million Hindu girls under the age of 5 were either married or widowed (Major 2012: 169). There were 175 widows in every 1000 females and of these 148 were below 15; 93 out of 1000 girls between the ages 5 and 10 years; and 399 out of 1000 girls between the ages 10 and 15 years were married (Gulati 1976: 1225). The anxiety regarding widow's sexuality had not abated in the twentieth century. In this phase, however, reformers became hyper-anxious about religious conversions to Islam. Throughout the entire discourse of social reform, widowhood remained a major issue.

There were additional goads for social reform. There were anxieties about community identity in this period, fuelled by rising communalism. Hindu men became concerned about conversion and women's (self-)expulsion from the community fold. This motivated many reforms. The evils of child marriage leading to widowhood, absence of any right to property, unhappy marriages without exit within Hinduism, Hindu men's excessive polygamy, all these compelled many women to convert or abandon their community. It was felt that, in comparison to women of the 'Other' (especially Muslim) religion, Hindu women's social position was fragile and precarious. With the intermittent support of the Indian National Congress, a new generation of reformers sought to push the government into a fresh round of social legislation. The reformers propagated reform in every aspect of marriage right from the age of consent, child marriage, civil marriage, disparity of age in marriage, prohibiting polygamous marriages, inter-caste marriage and ultimately the right to divorce. From the 1920s, the All India Women's Conference (AIWC) played a vital role in creating pressure on legislators to bring in bills that would remove the legal disabilities of Hindu women. The reformers continued to appeal to the Shastras as had their forerunners in the nineteenth century. Reformers and their opponents argued in the name of Hinduism, the former wanted to strengthen the Hindu community, the traditionalists wanted to protect Hindus from reform.

TOWARDS AN ABOLITION OF CHILD MARRIAGE: INDIAN INITIATIVES

The age of consent controversy in the 1890s is often considered to be the end of the era of social reform, with emerging cultural nationalism resisting the intervention of the colonial state in matters designated as 'tradition' and to do with marriage, family, religion and women. The question of age at marriage remained in abeyance after the age of consent controversy for about twenty years. In 1919, Hari Singh Gour, a foremost advocate of social reform, produced a volume comprising about 1200 pages divided into 26 chapters containing a 'Hindu Code'. In Britain, under the influence of Bentham and Mill, codification was seen as a mechanism through which society could be improved and ordered. Gour noted that despite the policy of non-intervention in personal law, the colonial state had intervened sometimes in the direction of modernization, sometimes subverting customary and other rights. Since the colonial judicial system had to resolve disputes brought before it, both statutory and case law had a major collective influence on the Hindu legal system. Moreover, the heterogeneity of Hindu law, with regional and caste variations in customs and practices, necessitated codification for clarity. As the government's earlier attempts of codification had failed, he took the initiative.[6] In 1921, the Home Secretary declared that such initiative should be taken by non-official members rather than the government. Gour was elected to the Central Legislative Assembly the same year and he began to lobby for personal law reform as soon as he had taken his seat.

There had already been an earlier attempt at such an intervention. In 1914, V. S. Srinivasan had sought legal recognition of adult marriages for Hindu women. By then, it had become commonsense in some circles that Hindu law enjoined marriage before puberty. To counter this, Srinivasan sought to re-validate post-pubertal Hindu marriage. He introduced a Bill in the Madras Legislative Assembly to Declare the Validity of Marriages of Hindu Women after Puberty so that no marriage between Hindus would be deemed invalid by reason merely of the fact that the bride had, at the time of the marriage, attained puberty.[7] In 1922, Rai Bahadur Sohanlal also introduced an Age of Consent Bill in the Assembly to raise the age of consent both within and outside marriage to age 14 for Hindus in line with the Act of 1872 (Forbes 1979). Though Bombay and United Province gave strong support, Bengal gave an adverse opinion. The Bill was ultimately defeated.

Meanwhile the princely states of India led by Mysore and Baroda pioneered legislation against child marriage in India. Mysore passed the Infant Marriages Prevention Regulation of 1894 to stop marriages of girls under the age of 8 years (Basu 2001: 51). The Mysore government ignoring the opinions of the majority of representatives in the Assembly passed this Act. Marriage of young girls with old men was also opposed and this Act prohibited marriage of girls below 16 to men over 50. According to Janaki Nair, since the Act made marriages itself punishable, rather than consummation, the decision on 8 as the age of marriage was one that provoked least resistance amongst the upper castes (Nair 1996: 166). Though violation of the Act made the perpetrators criminals, the law did not challenge the marriage itself. Thereby it made the Act right in civil law but wrong in criminal law (ibid.: 168). The same state opposed the implementation of the Sarda Act forty years later. The princely state of Baroda, despite some opposition, passed the (Baroda) Early Marriage Prevention Act of 1904, which outlawed all marriages of girls below 9 years of age and demanded consent by a local tribunal for the marriage of a girl below 12 or a boy below 16 years. In 1918, the princely state of Indore prescribed 14 years for boys and 12 years for girls as minimum age for marriages (Kapadia 1972). Kotah in Rajputana promulgated a new Marriage Act with effect from 1 July 1927, prohibiting the marriage of girls under 12 and boys under 16, as well as of girls under 18 with men more than double their age and of unmarried girls over 18 with men over 45.[8]

A few months before the Act in Kotah, on 1 February 1927, Harbilas Sarda introduced the Hindu Child Marriage Bill and was vocal in the Legislative Assembly about the government's apathy regarding legislation on child marriage. When he encountered opposition, he reminded the government of its position that non-official members should bring Bills for social legislation. Despite the government's indifference, the Bill was sent for circulation for eliciting opinion throughout the country.

Meanwhile, Hari Singh Gour introduced a Bill in the Legislative Assembly in February 1924, which aimed at raising the age of consent from 12 to 14, both inside and outside the marital state. The Bill was referred to a Select Committee which made certain modifications and the amended Bill was circulated for opinion. However, in March 1925, when the Assembly came to vote on the bill as a whole, they voted that it should not be passed. Thereafter, the government undertook to introduce a Bill of their own, increasing the age of consent within marriage to 13 and outside it to 14 years. This Bill passed into law as Act XXIX of 1925.[9] By this Act, Sections 375 and 376 of the Indian Penal Code were amended.

Sir Hari Singh Gour was not satisfied with this and in the very next month after the Sarda Bill, in March 1927, he introduced a Bill with the object of raising the age of consent outside the marital relationship from 14 to 16 years, and creating a new offence of 'illicit intercourse' within marriage between 13 and 14 years, punishable with imprisonment up to two years, and also omitting the provision of the minor punishment for raping a wife between 12 and 13 years introduced by the Act of 1925.[10] The British government was concerned. Questions were raised in the House of Commons whether any representations had been received from the Women's Indian Association (WIA) urging the legislation, to which the government replied in the affirmative. Several associations, including the WIA, had written in support of the Bill, while traditionalists had opposed the Bill. The government was willing to appoint a committee but really wanted Gour to withdraw his Bill.[11] In direct contradiction of their previous statement, Sir James Crerar, discussing Sarda's bill, commented that they should regulate child marriage through a government measure, rather than a Private Member's Bill (Major 2012: 165).[12]

In the 1920s, both Harbilas Sarda and Hari Singh Gour attempted time and again to increase the age of consent and the minimum age of marriage. They spoke the language of social modernization and commanded the support of women's organizations of the period. They were also able to draw on international debates. League of Nations' Advisory Committee for the Protection and Welfare of Children and Young People in the third session from 2–7 May 1927 at Geneva had decided that fixing too early an age of consent was likely to encourage traffic in women and children and lead to the 'corruption' of young persons. They also recommended that the legal age of marriage reach an adequate standard.[13]

Katherine Mayo's *Mother India* (1927) exploded within the currents of these debates. It stirred international curiosity and controversy around the Indian marriage system. In various countries, including England, women's organizations wanted to know about the real condition of women in India and created pressure on the British government. Some of them were able to establish contact with leaders of the newly emerging women's organizations in India. Indian publicists vehemently opposed Mayo's claims. There was a rush of books and articles to denounce Mayo. By the end of 1927, there were three bills in the Central Assembly and in the Bombay and Madras Provincial Legislatures for fixing a minimum marriage age for boys and girls. The government turned down requests to introduce similar bills in Bengal and in the Central Provinces and Berar (Sinha 2006: 308).

Amidst the flurry created by Mayo's book, Sarda's Bill was referred to a Select Committee and on 25 March 1928 the government was compelled to appoint an Age of Consent Committee under the chairmanship of Sir Moropant V. Joshi to consider the volume of evidences from different parts of the country. The Select Committee changed the name of the Bill from the Hindu Child Marriage Act to the Child Marriage Restraint Act and extended it to all communities. It also recommended punishment by jail or fine; and recommended that the minimum ages be 18 for men and 14 for women. These recommendations were accepted but voting was postponed pending the report of the Joshi Committee. Originally appointed to throw light on Gour's Bill, this Committee had expanded its remit to the Sarda Bill (Forbes 1979).

Rameshwari Nehru was the first Indian woman member of this Committee to tour India. The Committee examined a large number of women witnesses in different parts of the country. To ascertain the opinions of women unable to appear and give evidence before the Committee, purdah parties were organized at some places; and there were meetings of women of different shades of opinions. Many villages were visited where women were examined. Views of women doctors were taken.[14] The Committee ultimately published its report on 26

August 1929 and recommended a separate law fixing the age of marriage for girls at 14 and boys at 18. Faced with these recommendations, the government decided to support Sarda's Bill. Sir James Crerar asserted

> We are convinced that the evil exists. We are convinced that the measure of Rai Saheb Harbilas Sarda is at any rate the first step in the direction of seeking a practical remedy. Where we find that evil, and where we find a promising remedy, we feel we must support what we think to be right. I trust a great of this House will agree in the view that this measure is one in the right direction, and it is their duty to support it.[15]

The traditionalist members of Hindu and Muslim communities were displeased. The proposal to exclude the Muslims by Maulana Shafi Daudi was defeated. With the support of the official members, the Bill was ultimately carried by 67 to 14 votes. The Bill also got the approval of the Council of State and became the Child Marriage Restraint Act of 1929 popularly known as the Sarda Act. It came into effect from 1 April 1930.

The Sarda Act was a major milestone, even though evidence suggests that its implementation was unsuccessful. According to Geraldine Forbes, it was in dealing with the Sarda Act that Indian women first made their presence felt as a pressure group to be reckoned with (Forbes 1979: 413). Eleanor Newbigin argues that women's role in the Sarda debates was used to reaffirm the progressive and egalitarian nature of what was in fact highly patriarchal reforms. For some decades, the family had been distanced from the state, the part of the realm of tradition in which the state did not intervene. Sarda Act signalled the return of the government into legislation on the domestic sphere. The Indian-led reform signified a willingness amongst Indian men to allow the state to intervene in home and family. However, the claims that Indian men rather than the colonial state were best able to secure the interests of Indian women served not to secure greater rights for women but to re-inscribe male authority in the family (Newbigin 2013). While advocating for the bill, Sarda also related it with nationalism. At the Assembly floor he argued that India's suitability to ask for self-rule depended on the condition of their womenfolk. He mentioned that people of England and America were watching how the Legislative Assembly of India was dealing with the Bill: 'Writers like Mayo and politicians like Mr. Winston Churchill have declared that India cannot be granted self-government so long as she tolerates and commits acts of oppression against girls of tender age.'[16]

Women's organizations wholeheartedly supported the bill. WIA sent a petition to the government supporting the bill which was discussed in the British Parliament. The government was forced to include one woman member in the Age of Consent Committee. AIWC was the most vocal. A standing committee dealt exclusively with child marriage and age of consent. They watched the progress of the Bills, co-ordinated and directed the activities of the provincial committees, and urged their views on the legislatures. AIWC through propaganda meetings and lectures, distribution of literature and posters, obtaining signatures, organizing a postcard campaign supported Sarda's bill and age of consent (ibid.).

A similar bill was also introduced in the princely state of Mysore by K. P. Puttanna Chetty, a member of the Mysore Assembly. Though the bill got 98 votes in comparison to eighty-seven, the Dewan announced that 'public opinion' had it that 'more harm than good was likely to accrue if such a penal measure was enacted as law' (Nair 1996: 178). As the Sarda Act was applicable to all communities, objection arose from the traditionalist sections of different communities. To satisfy traditionalist sentiment, soon after the Sarda Act was passed, the Government of India decided against its 'wholesale execution'. Local governments and administrations were secretly advised, by an order of the Viceroy's Executive Council in March 1930, to do little to advertise the act or to enforce its provisions when it came into effect.[17] As the Act came into effect, two types of Bills began to be tabled repeatedly on the floor of the House. First, there were attempts to repeal the Bill by Raja Bahadur G. Krishnamachariar, A. H. Ghuznavi, Dr. A. Suhrawardy, Pandit Satyendranath Sen, Khan Bahadur Haji Wajihuddin and Anwar-ul-Azim from 1931 to 1934. Second, there were Bills requiring amendments to its various provisions and exempting different groups:

(a)   Maulavi Muhammad Yakub's and M. K. Acharya's Bills to amend the Child Marriage Restraint Act, 1928, so as to exempt from its operation Nikah ceremony of Mussalmans and Marital Sacraments of Hindus which are not followed by consummation, 1929.

(b)   Child Marriage Restraint (Amendment) Bill by M. K. Acharya, 1929.

(c)   A.H. Guznavi's Bill to amend the Child Marriage Restraint Act so as to exempt Mussalman Marriages from the operation of the Act (lapsed), 1929.

(d)   Surpat Singh's Bill to amend the Sarda Act so as to permit marriages between boys of less than 18 and girls below 14 years of age, 1930.

(e)   K. V. Ramaswami Ayyangar's Bill to amend the Child Marriage Restraint Act so as to exempt brahmins and certain other castes and communities from its operation, 1930.

(f)   B. N . Misra's Bill to amend the Child Marriage Restraint Act so as to exempt brahmins from its operation, 1933.

(g)   Child Marriage Restraint Amendment Bill by Haji Wajiuddin for exclusion of Muslims from the operation of the Sarda Act, 1933.

As the government forbore from 'wholesale execution' or indeed any execution, Sarda Act soon became a dead letter. In a tone similar to the AIWC demands, Rai Bahadur Harbilas Sarda tabled another Bill in the Legislative Assembly in 1930 to treat offenders under the Act as first offenders and enlarging the scope of the discretionary powers under section 562 of the Criminal Procedure Code. A similar Bill was moved by M. S. Aney of Berar constituency which intended to make Child Marriage Restraint Act more educative than penal.

Several non-official members tabled bills to make Sarda Act more effective. In the Council of State, Lala Jagadish Prasad moved a resolution on 22 August 1934 recommending that steps should be taken to enforce the Act. He observed regretfully that the Act was being observed more in breach than in observance. M. G. Hallet, Home Secretary, however, defended the government's apathy. History, he argued, had proved that in such matters 'more haste means worse speed' and caution was better in matters of social reform. Lala Jagadish Prasad withdrew the resolution.[18] Around the same time, Rai Bahadur Raghuvir Singh moved a Minor Girls Protection Bill to protect girls under 14 being sold by parents or guardians to bridegrooms against their wishes. Sitarama Raju opposed the Bill on the ground that the Bill was unnecessary as the Sarda Act prevented the marriage of girls below 14. Law Member, N. N. Sircar, argued that the Bill was ill-conceived. Sir Henry Craik observed that though the object of the Bill might be laudable, it was impractical. The government being unsympathetic, Singh withdrew the Bill.[19] Amendments were also made to universalize the application of Sarda Act to prevent escape from the law by resorting to the Indian states or areas under French control. The amended Act passed in 1938 applied to 'all British subjects and servants of the Crown in any part of India', and to 'all British subjects who are domiciled in any part of India wherever they may be', in order to extend its scope and to include the British Indian subjects in the princely states, thereby preventing British subjects from hopping the borders to these states, or to French territories, to escape the provisions of the act (Pande 2012: 230).

AIWC was mobilizing the Congress to support the implementation of the Sarda Act. It was due to their propaganda that two Bills were tabled in 1935: Bhuvanananda Das's Child

Marriage Restraint (Amendment) Bill so as to make it more stringent and another by Lalchand Navalrai. AIWC wholeheartedly supported Das's Bill. They lobbied the public to form Sarda Act Enforcement Committees and to agitate for these amendments. Meanwhile, the Travancore Child Marriage Restraint Bill was introduced by T. Narayani Amma at the Travancore Durbar. Lakshmi N. Menon, Convener of the All India Sarda Act Sub-Committee, explained in the Travancore Assembly, that the bill should include the provisions of Das's Bill, otherwise it would be a dead letter like the Sarda Act. It was also lamented that a progressive state like Mysore refused to give permission to introduce a Bill in the local Legislative Council.

Throughout 1938, AIWC was creating public opinion in support of Navalrai and Das's amendments. The British Commonwealth League also extended their support in a letter to the London *Times*.[20] The gallery of the Assembly was filled with an audience of women when the debate started on the Bill on 10 February 1938. The government, apprehending war, was keen to keep the Congress on their side. The sponsor of the Bill was appreciative of the presence of women in the House to support the Bill and spoke of it as a measure of women's demand. The opponents charged the government with entering into an unholy alliance with the Congress. As the Bill came through the Select Committee, the Congress Party supported the Bill. Again with the help of official members and the European community, the Bill was ultimately passed on 31 March 1938 as Child Marriage Restraint Amendment Act, 1938.[21] Diwan Lalchand Navalrai's Bill for strengthening the Sarda Act was also passed in the Assembly the same year.[22] AIWC praised the passage of these amendments, which ensured that courts could issue injunctions against proposed child marriages, that offenders could be prosecuted, and that husbands had to make provision for the separate custody and maintenance of a child wife until she was of legal age (Ramusack 1981). This last provision was important for the protection of an illegally married child wife, who was not at fault.[23]

The issue of child marriage, however, remained. Even after Independence, Pandit Thakurdas Bhargava introduced a Child Marriage Restraint (Amendment) Bill on 25 August 1948 to raise the marriage age from 18 to 20 in the case of boys and from 14 to 15 in the case of girls. 'Despite the Sarda Act' Pandit Bhargava stated, 'at least 40 percent of the girls in the country, especially in rural areas were still being married below the age of 15. This was a serious crime.'[24] The Bill also addressed great disparity of age between women and men in marriage like his earlier bill in the 1930s. Supporting this clause, Ramnarayan Singh also wanted prevention of marriages between men above 45 and virgins of 'whatever age'. They might be allowed to marry widows, he suggested.[25]

Whether the bill should be made cognizable or not was much in debate. The Select Committee recommended that offences under the Act should be cognizable, bailable and non-compoundable. Pandit Thakurdas expressed his anxiety that unless imprisonment was made compulsory, the Act would become a dead letter.[26] Being cognizable meant the interference of police in 'social affairs' which was contested. Pattabhi Sitaramayya, a veteran Congress leader, endorsed the idea of a two-year interregnum before the enforcement of the Act. There was much support for the Bill. One of the reasons was that by passing this Bill, Indians could show the world that 'all bad customs were fast disappearing from the society'.[27] Dr. B. R. Ambedkar, then Law Minister, pointed out rightly, that in the absence of registration of births and deaths, age was difficult to prove in courts. The offences were thus better left non-cognizable.

Renuka Ray, a member of the AIWC and a Member of Parliament, welcomed the Bill on the ground of the health of the mother and nation-building.[28] Naziruddin Ahmed spoke of protecting girls up to 14 years of poorer classes as they had to earn their bread through manual labour. Some argued that for many poor parents, maintaining a daughter to the age of 14 was great economic stress. The Select Committee recommended stringent punishment for offenders. Not all agreed. Government nominee N. V. Gadgil argued that law should not precede public opinion, which should be allowed to grow gradually in favour of raising the marriageable age. Thakurdas was surprised at Gadgil's opposition and questioned how the marriageable age could remain 14 when 15 was the age of consent. A compromise was effected and the Bill was passed with certain important amendments. It raised the marriageable age of girls to 15 instead of 16, for boys it remained at 18. Though offences under the Act became cognizable, the police were not given powers to interfere.[29] Strong punitive measures were imposed. A man above 18 but below 21 who married a girl below the age of 15 could be sentenced to simple imprisonment for 15 days or a fine of rupees 1000 or both.[30] A man above 21 contracting a child marriage would face imprisonment of up to three months; in addition, they could be fined at the court's discretion. The guardians were also made punishable. Child marriage was regarded as a crime, where the 'digital' age became the determinant factor of the contravention of law. This process started from the Age of Consent Act 1891, where for the first time colonial legislation was based on digital age instead of biological age. This tradition has continued in the postcolonial period.

Pandit Thakurdas Bhargava also introduced another Bill at the same time to raise the age of consent from 16 to 18 for women in respect of extramarital offences under Section 375 of the Indian Penal Code, as the age of marriage had been fixed at 15. It was proposed that sexual intercourse by a man with his wife under 15 or with any girl under 16, with or without consent, should be considered rape.[31] As before, marital rape was excluded but a new offence called marital misbehaviour was introduced with different punishments according to the age of the wife (below or above 12 years).[32] The Bill was passed without amendment. The Act after receiving the assent of the Governor General came into effect from 15 July 1949.[33]

NEW SHASTRAS FOR OLD: MODERNITY AND NATIONALISM

'We want new Shastras', said AIWC leaders to Pandit Madan Mohan Malaviya, when he sought to lower the age of marriage for girls to 12, quoting Shastras to the deputation of the AIWC leaders at Delhi in 1928 (Forbes 1979: 415).[34] When the AIWC women called for 'new Shastras', they were making a new argument. They were questioning the accepted view that ancient Shastras rather than contemporary concerns was to be the basis of Hindu law. In many ways, this was a bold statement against, by then, nearly a century of the colonial state's efforts, complemented by that of Indian reformers, to establish Shastras as the repository of tradition and key resource for 'authentic' Hindu law and practice. Lata Mani has argued that both in the case of the abolition of sati and the enabling of widow remarriage, the focus had been on fashioning a scriptural tradition rather than remedying social injustice (Mani 1989). The main challenge came from women mobilized in new organizations, who refused to accept the principle of 'tradition' as enshrined in ancient texts as decisive of social arrangements and behaviour in the twentieth century. While adhering to the rhetoric of 'nationalism' and/or 'civilization' they put more stress on the intrinsic benefits of reform for women in terms of carefree childhoods, better education and improved prospect of happiness within marriage, lamenting the child-bride who 'robbed of her own girlhood and youth, is almost unaware of the many happiness for a cultured life'.[35]

Throughout the nineteenth century, shastric exegesis dominated reform efforts. The age of consent was no exception. Pre-pubertal marriage was sanctioned in the Shastras. The *garbhadhan* ceremony or the obligatory cohabitation between husband and wife was supposed to take place immediately after the wife reached puberty. Otherwise, the *pinda* or ancestral offerings served up by the sons would become impure. The digital age implemented in this Act interfered with this practice. However, the watered down Age of Consent Act that was passed in 1891 failed to satisfy the reformers. It did, however, have an important consequence; it not only placed the issue of marriage and consent on the public agenda for several decades, it also meant that the law and the state became invested in an individual woman's age of marriage and consummation.

Adjudication of the 'domestic' had started much earlier in the colonial period. As Radhika Singha argues, the British sought to narrow the range of public moral regulation of the Indian household. Whereas the enticement of an unmarried girl was punishable, so long as she was 'under the age of maturity' (15 years), no such exception was made for the married woman. Therefore, the husband had a lifelong right in the person of his wife in criminal law. While the 1819 regulation authorized the magistrate to punish the abductor of a married woman, whether she had gone willingly or not, the wife escaped any punishment and returned to her husband (Singha 1998: 147). The domain of the family was breached once again during this period. The age of a woman at the time of the consummation of her marriage could now be publicly questioned. Meanwhile, the British Indian courts upheld even draconian consequences of child marriage as in the case of Rakhmabai (see also Chapter 1). The issue did not disappear from public discussion, though there was no demand for new legislation in British India until Srinivasan's early attempt to validate adult marriages in Madras in 1914. The establishment of Indian legislatures after 1919 gave a new impetus to reformers, who once again turned to law as a means of eradicating what they considered a 'social evil'. This also gave the colonial government power to intervene in the domestic sphere. After 1891, the family had been distanced from the state. Newbigin, as stated earlier, has pointed out that the Sarda Act re-inscribed male authority by enabling Indian men to undertake family reform (Newbigin 2008).

Rai Bahadur Harbilas Sarda, who succeeded 15 years after Srinivasan, in pushing through a law against child marriage, had said that his prime concern was child widowhood (Table 2.1). His concerns were not dissimilar to those of

TABLE 2.1: On Girls Experience of Marriage and Widowhood

	Girls under the age 5	Between the ages 5 and 10	Between the ages 10 and 15	Total
Married	218,463	2,016,687	6,330,207	8,565,357
Unmarried	19,938,007	20,782,275	9,961,195	50,681,477
Widowed	15,139	102,293	279,124	396,556
Total	20,171,609	22,901,255	16,570,526	59,643,390

Source: Report of the Age of Consent Committee, 1928–1929, Calcutta, Government of India, Central Publication Branch, 1929, p. 94.

nineteenth-century reformers, but focused more sharply within the framework of nation and modernity. The immediate concern was quality and quantity of population; the physical and mental growth of the young, men and women, as well as infant mortality, maternal mortality and morbidity.[36] The law regarding the age of consent had been in existence for three decades by that time, but the Age of Consent Committee said 'There is little evidence in the Census figures to suggest that the practice of infant marriage is dying out'.[37]

Taking the age period 10–15, where the density of marriages was the greatest, in 1891 the year of the passing of the Age of Consent Act, the number of unmarried girls out of every thousand was 491 whereas in 1921 it became 601.[38] In 30 years, the percentage of unmarried girls had risen only by 11 percent, which did not engender hope of speedy improvement. AIWC, supporting Sarda's Bill, appealed to the Age of Consent Committee that many mothers wished to marry their daughters at a later age. They were afraid of social ostracism, and both the parents would welcome legislation, making a later age the law. Moreover, they repudiated the suggestion that a later marriage age might bring immorality. They stated that under the present circumstances there were, in many households, young widows were looked after and the same would apply to young girls.[39]

The 'new Shastras', often at loggerheads with the old, shaped the contours of the Legislative Assembly debates.

The position derived from the old Shastras was questioned by the reformers as well as the women's organizations. Gour, aware that his bill on Age of Consent would be seen as an infringement of the doctrine of sacrament, limited its scope and adopted the line of least resistance. He merely argued equity. The members of AIWC were more virulent in their attack against the concept of sacrament. They raised their voice against arguments grounded on shastric injunctions again and again, but especially during the debates on divorce for Hindu women. Some of them challenged the role of Shastras behind marriage. Sarojini Mehta, an AIWC member, said further:

> How is Hindu marriage a sacrament? There is no divine agency working behind the marriage. The marriage is brought about absolutely by human efforts and material circumstances. The only considerations at a marriage are dowries, ornaments, festivities and gaieties. How is a marriage performed under such circumstances a sacrament . . . Shastras were written thousands of years ago by selfish Brahmans who had no consideration for woman or for anyone except themselves. No weight need be given to their opinion. Shastras were not written for all time. No book could be written for all time.[40]

Sarda himself adhered to the principle of women's organizations and stated

> The women of India do not talk of Shastras; they do not bother themselves about the effect of marriage on their prospects in the next world. They are practical and think of this world, and they want their sufferings in this world should come to an end (Major 2012: 175).

Another member of the AIWC, Malatibai Abhyankar went further to question religion and the authenticity of dharma, which was the basis of the premium placed upon the Shastras. She argued that since there was no one holy scripture in

Hindu 'religion', the Shastras were deemed as equivalent. The problem was of course that Shastras were many and often contradictory and this facilitated reform either to find contrary voices within the Shastras as Vidyasagar did or to deny their significance altogether as a source of religious law binding on social practice.

She further argued that 'dharma is regulated by society and if certain things do not suit society, the latter has got the right to change it as it wants. Only it requires sufficient popular support and then it becomes a law which in its turn becomes Dharma. Dharma can be changed at any time according to popular ideas'.[41] Questioning the double standard of the Shastras that expected total allegiance of women in a marriage, whereas men were left free, she suggested that the institution of marriage should be based upon contract. In the mid-1930s, she insisted on a law of divorce for Hindu women rather than await social awareness.[42]

For the women's organizations, one major issue was education. AIWC at its first conference at Pune emphasized education. The age of marriage and education were linked as cause and consequence. On the one hand, raising the age of marriage would enable education; on the other, a focus on education must raise the age of marriage. Moreover, they argued, raising the age of marriage would reduce the number of child widows. They also advocated the abolition of purdah to enable spread of women's education. They supported Gour's Bill with a deputation to the Legislative Assembly to convey 'its demand on this vital subject'.[43] Education was sometimes seen as the magic bullet that would redress all social disabilities; education alone could lead Indian women 'to proper realization of rights and duties' both at home and in the nation (Forbes 1979: 415). Sarala Ray at the presidential address of AIWC conference of 1931 argued that only education would bring awareness to women of the many evils of child marriage.[44]

AIWC demanded that at least two women should be nominated to the Legislative Assembly, where issues regarding

women and children were debated. With mothers as legislators, it was argued, the health of the nation was bound to be
raised. In 1934, the AIWC, disappointed with the ineffective-
ness of the Sarda Act and the proposed India Act, asked the
government to appoint an all-India commission to consider
the legal disabilities of women. AIWC published a pamphlet
entitled 'Legal Disabilities of Indian Women: A Plea for a
Commission of Enquiry' authored by Renuka Ray, legal secretary of AIWC. She argued that legal change would both
alleviate the suffering of individual women and allow India
to join the modern and progressive states of the world (Forbes
1998). Ray wanted new personal and family law that would
make women independent and fully equipped to participate
in public life.

During the legislative debates of the twentieth century, one
major question was whether girls should be married before
attaining puberty.[45] In 1914, V. S. Srinivasan argued that it
was true that some Smritis such as those of Parasara, Yama
and Samvarta disapproved post-puberty marriages. However,
others such as Manu, Gautama, Yajnavalkya, Baudhayana and
Vasistha, allowed it. *Grihyasutras* which were of equal authority
with the Smritis and of higher value as evidence of early
custom, seemed to contemplate only post-puberty marriages.
Sarda too succumbed to the lure of shastric arguments. He
argued that no Shastras, ancient or modern, enjoined that a
girl must be married before she attained puberty. It was being
argued that post-puberty marriage, far from being forbidden
by the Shastras, had their clear sanction and was at one time
the prevalent custom. Reformist men wished to educate their
daughters and reduce the chance of widowhood and argued
strongly for later marriages.

For women such as Sarojini Mehta, the question of gender
equity was as important as a national and religious identity
routed through ancient scriptures. Many of the men reformers also followed this line. Even if it were to be accepted that
marriage was a sacrament, was it so only for women? Dr. G.V.
Deshmukh questioned whether marriage could be regarded

as a 'unilateral' sacrament. For a marriage two parties were required and if marriage was a sacrament, it ought to be a sacrament for both of them. If the traditionalists argued the in translatability of *vivaha*, he turned the tables on them by making a similar argument: *vivaha* was a *samskar* not a sacrament. To translate *samskar* as sacrament was misleading.[46]

MARRIAGE AND THE BOUNDARIES OF COMMUNITY

Mrinalini Sinha (2006) suggests that while the abolition of sati represented the project of colonial modernity, the Child Marriage Restraint Act represented the project of nationalist modernity in late colonial India. That child marriage was a deterrent to the growth of a Hindu nation was argued in 1891 during the Age of Consent debates. More than child widowhood, child marriage became the central issue in the campaign that stressed physical weaknesses and moral degeneration (Forbes 1979). Vidyasagar's argument had rested on the belief that child marriage was detrimental to the health of women and consequently detrimental to the health of the nation. It was the weaknesses in the Indian social fabric that had led to colonial rule (Nair 1996). At the National Social Conference, Dr. Mahendralal Sircar, President of the Conference, in 1887 spoke of the evils of child marriage:

> The Hindu race consists at the present day....by virtue of this very blessed custom, of abortions and premature births.... every man and woman born of parents of such tender years as 10 or 12 for a girl and 15 or 16 for a boy must be pronounced to be either an abortion or a premature birth. And are you surprised that the people of a nation so constituted should have fallen easy victim under every blessed tyrant that ever chose to trample them? (Heimsath 1964: 167).

These arguments gained in strength in the twentieth century. In the 1920s, Geraldine Forbes points out, the age of consent was discussed in the League of Nations and age of marriage became crucial to political and social modernization. Even Gandhi suggested 16 as the minimum age for marriage and claimed that prohibition on early marriage would protect girls from premature old age, prevent Hinduism from sanctioning the birth of weak, rickety children, help curb man's lust, and help develop man's capacity for self-sacrifice (Forbes 1979). Annie Besant, one of the founders of the Women's Indian Association, regarded child marriage as a custom which sapped the vitality of the nation and the future of India depended on its reform (ibid.).

Thus, the reform of child marriage became linked to nation-building. Sarda also argued that the Act he proposed would help women in India develop physically and mentally: 'so long as these evils exist in this country, we will have neither the strength of arm nor the strength of character to win freedom' (ibid.: 412). The most common argument was that child marriage resulted in early consummation and early motherhood and the race was weakened (ibid.). M. R. Jayakar, the proposer of the Hindu Gains of Learning Bill urged immediate consideration of Sarda's Bill.[47] Motilal Nehru, the leader of the Swarajist Party in the Legislative Assembly, wrote on the eve of the vote on the Sarda Bill: 'We are today on our trial before the civilized nations of the world, and the measure of the Assembly's support to the Sarda Bill will be the measure of our fitness to rank among those nations' (Sinha 1999: 208). Sarda's Bill became equivalent to regeneration of Hinduism. As S. Srinivasa Iyengar put it, 'we who stand up for Hinduism have a duty to see that Hinduism promotes the growth of a virile race of men and an efficient race of girls who will become the mothers of a greater India' (Major 2012: 173). Civilizing Hindu marriage customs was thus inextricably linked to political progress and to positioning India as an equal among 'civilized' nations.

Indeed, colonial opposition to reform was now interpreted as an attempt to delay Indian development towards self-government. 'How long, Sir, shall we then allow this canker to eat into the vitals of our race?' said Sarda, 'Shall we stand by and see the race sink below the point when regeneration and resuscitation become impossible?'[48] Emphasizing the binary between tradition and modernity, Ramananda Chatterjee also wrote in the *Modern Review*:

> The abolition of child marriage and child mortality and the raising of the Age of Consent within and outside marital relations would tend to make Indians a physically, intellectually and morally a fitter nation. But British bureaucrats have all along been very unwilling to help Indian social reformers in effecting these reforms by direct and indirect legislation. They had no objection to abolish Suttee, probably because it was mainly a question of humanity; the abolition of Suttee was not expected to promote the building up a stalwart nation. But the abolition of child marriage, etc., is directly and almost directly a political as well as a social remedy. So, in these matters our British bureaucratic friends fall back upon the cant of neutrality and non-interference in religious and socio-religious matters.[49]

That abolition of child marriage was a step towards modernity, a vital criterion to become an independent nation. Sarda stressed upon social reform as a foundation for political action and 'the abolition of child marriage will be the principal item, must be taken in hand along with the pursuit of political reform'.[50] Presenting his Bill, Sarda quoted Abraham Lincoln, 'A nation cannot be half free and half slave'. These connections were, however, not without detractors. By stressing on the international ramifications in the hostile post-Mayo scenario, Sarda invited the criticism of those such as Amar Nath Dutt, who warned the Assembly not to be 'misled by the hypnotism of words such as "progress," "advance," "emancipation" and "twentieth century" into thinking that the path of civilization must be following the footsteps of western nations'. He argued that India's superior civilization rested upon Hindu tradition and this bill was guilty of 'setting at naught our ancient ideals of marriage.' Sarda being the author of *Hindu Superiority*, he alleged, had given up his respect for the ancient ideals and aligned himself with the 'westernizers' in an attempt to foist a false modernity in India (Major 2012: 174).

Sir Hari Singh Gour also drew on a western paradigm. He argued that marriages had to be sanctioned by the state and not religion: thus civil marriage rather than personal law would be the touchstone of Indian modernity. A marriage in India had to be valid outside it, which required registration by the state rather than adherence to obsolete religious customs, whether in Hinduism or Islam. The focus was on India's status within the world community and marriage, strangely enough, became its index. Bhupendranath Basu, H. S. Gour, M. R. Jayakar, Harbilas Sarda and Dr. G. V. Deshmukh made repeated efforts to stress on national unity among various religious communities. For instance, by trying to amend the Special Marriage Act of 1872, these reformers attempted to prove marriage was a contract rather than a sacrament. The laws of marriage should, they argued, promote Indian unification and nationalism without interfering with an individual's religion. As an addendum, there was also the question of modern ideas of social justice. These reforms were considered far ahead of their time and rejected.

The two towering figures in the Second Social Reform Movement were Hari Singh Gour and Harbilas Sarda. Gour married out of community and converted and thereby became a target of traditionalists whenever he initiated or supported reform. Sarda was a more difficult figure to combat by the same tactics. He wrote *Hindu Superiority: An Attempt to Determine the Position of the Hindu Race in the Scale of Nations* (1906), in which he extolled Hindu superiority in culture and civilization. An Arya Samajist, he propagated a return to a 'Golden Age'. The superiority of the Aryans was constantly demonstrated in Dayananda's work by denigrating Islam and Christianity. Arya Samaj played a crucial role in the creation of Hindu nationalism. The Hindu Mahasabha, founded in 1915 as a pressure group within Congress, was led largely by

Arya Samaj members, and it became a major vehicle of Hindu nationalism (Jaffrelot 1999).

The reform effort of the twentieth century was an offshoot of political ramifications. Peter van der Veer (1999) argues that the theme of Hindu Superiority, both in spiritual and racial terms, was the Hindu answer to the mobilization of Muslims in the political arena in the twentieth century. There was an obsession with the growth of the Muslim population and the stagnation or decline of the Hindu population. While upholding the spirit of Hindu superiority, the Hindu intellectuals of nineteenth century neglected Indian Muslims. By 1920s, this changed drastically when the 'threat' from Muslims in electoral and demographic terms became central to Hindu politics. The British started the Census from 1872 and by 1901, the British policy designers planned to control the embrace of Hinduism by extracting the tribal population from its fold (Sinha 2017: 11). Prior to 1911 Census, the Superintendent, E. A. Gait, issued a circular that laid down a set of parameters to differentiate between the other sects and the Hindus. In response, Col. Upendra Nath Mukherji of Calcutta wrote 'Hinduism and the Coming Census', where he stated, 'It will break into two communities those that hitherto have been regarded as one. What is going to happen next, where is this going to end?' (ibid.: 17). The 1911 Census Report stated that 'forcible conversions are now a thing of the past, but nonetheless there is a steady migration towards Islam'.[51]

Meanwhile, in 1909, Col. Mukherji published a series of articles in the *Bengalee*, an English daily edited by Surendranath Banerjea, which was later published as *Hindus: A Dying Race*, which influenced many tracts and publications of the Hindu Mahasabha. He stressed on the need for social reform among the Hindus. In 1912, he fuelled a phobia about Hindus being swallowed up in the next 420 years in a personal meeting with Swami Shradhanand, who became convinced enough to begin the work of reconversion of Hindus from Islam and Christianity. Shradhanand wrote an influential book entitled,

Hindu Sangathan: Saviour of the Dying Race in 1926. Muslims were portrayed as excessively fertile and militant. Quoting the 1911 Census Report he wrote:

> The greater reproductive capacity of the Muslims is revealed by the fact that the proportion of married females to the total number of females aged 15–40 exceeds the corresponding proportion for Hindus. The result is that Muslims have 37 children aged 0–5, while the Hindus have only 33. Since 1881 the number of Muslims in the areas then enumerated has risen by 26.4 percent while the corresponding increase for Hindus is only 15.1 percent (Sinha 2017: 28).

The social reform programme of this period followed from this logic of competing communities. The reformers argued that some reforms in Hindu society were essential for unity, cohesion, even survival. The growth of population and, in broader terms, social empowerment itself, could only be achieved by producing a single collective body of Hindus (ibid.). In this politics of inter-community competition and intra-community consolidation, marriage became an important issue because it was an instrument for drawing boundaries and reproducing both identity and difference.

CONCLUSION

The second social reform movement of the twentieth century revolved round Hindu women. While the basic structure of Hindu society was never questioned, reform was initiated to prove India a progressive nation where women's rights were established. As Geraldine Forbes argued, it was never the intention of the reformers to give women equal rights. Regarding Sarda Act, they were more committed to its symbolic utility than to actually improving women's lives (Forbes 1979). The failure to include a provision for the registration of births and marriages was a glaring hole in the legislation, making it difficult to prove violations. Prosecutions under the Act were rare; between the Act coming into force on 1 April 1930 and 31 August 1932, there were 473 prosecutions and 167 convictions (Major 2012: 183). Even after Independence, child marriage remained a problem. Hindu Marriage Act of 1955 laid down a minimum age of 15 for girls and 18 for boys.

Though women's organizations struggled for equal rights, there was ambivalence among members about the precise meaning of the term *equality*. These concerns were in interplay with the growing political demands of the Muslim League and a phobia about decreasing number of the Hindus. As communal anxiety grew, attention of male reformers was drawn to the vulnerabilities of Hindu women; they became anxious to retain women within the Hindu fold and to be able to control their sexuality. In Bengal, some reformers emphasized the ills of child marriage, leading to child maternity and poor health as the causes behind the deterioration of numbers of the Hindus. To create a monolithic Hindu society, some variety of practices within Hinduism had to be sanctioned, in law if not within brahminical tradition.

In the logic of competitive communalism, however, the 1930s also found Muslims addressing the question of marriage and law. Thus, two important pieces of legislation reshaped Muslim personal law in India. The Moslem Personal Law (Shariat) Application Bill by H. M. Abdullah in 1936 which became the Application of Shariat Act, 1937, was a landmark reform in the history of Islamic law in India.[52] The logic was that the application of the Shariat would protect the interest of the women as guaranteed in Islam as laws of inheritance that drew on the concept of joint family property were discriminatory against women. An amendment of this bill was later introduced in 1942 which was known as The Muslim Personal Law (Shariat) Application (Amendment) Bill by Qazi Muhammad Ahmed Kazmi. He also introduced the Dissolution of Muslim Marriages Act 1939 which was a major step forward. By these interventions, the Muslim League sought to unify Muslims and strengthen their political base, as well as the religious hold over the community and seek to retain women within their community.[53] According to the Shariat, on apostasy a Muslim marriage stood dissolved. Muslim women, who felt trapped within oppressive marriages, used this provision and opted for religious conversion to dissolve their marital ties. The Act sought to arrest this trend by providing Muslim women a statutory right to divorce within their own religion, thus retaining them within the Islamic fold. Though both these Acts were politically motivated, they did also enhance the legal position of Muslim women. A variety of women's organizations supported these measures.

The women's organizations were demanding a total over-haul of Hindu law with respect to marriage and property. They demanded a law commission to investigate the matter rather than piecemeal reforms, though they also gave full-throated support to every reform that came to the table. What was unique was that even the Muslim women sup-ported them in their venture for a long time. Women legisla-tors such as Muthulakshmi Reddi, Radhabai Subbarayon and Lilavati Munshi brought bills to improve the legal condition of Hindu women and played the role of reformers. AIWC and other women's organizations created a consciousness for social change and initiated a leading role. Though their legal activities affected a small section of society, yet they were concerned about women in other sections of society and also adopted various social welfare programmes like protecting the women miners, women's condition of labour and maternity benefit act.

After independence, child marriage became associated with poverty. Yet, states and reformers have hesitated to apply draconian legislation to fix what is universally regarded as a problem. As Flavia Agnes has shown, none of the laws against child marriage declares such marriages void. This is because of the ideology of Hindu marriages being sacramental and the grave social implications such a move would have on children born of such unions (Agnes 2013). Thus successive laws against child marriage, beginning with the CMRA, have been more a rhetoric or an aspiration than a legal mandate.

NOTES

1   Digital age is age as represented by a number. The Hindu conservative opinion was that marriage should be immediately consummated after the first menstrual flow through the *garbhadhan* ceremony. The legislative intervention by the colonial government fixed a particular age for marriage.

2   Katherine Mayo, an American journalist in her polemical book *Mother India*, 1927, attacked Hindu religion, society and culture. Based on her exposé of some of the horrific conditions under which women in India lived in the early twentieth century — poor sanitation, unsafe childbirth, rampant illiteracy, and malnutrition — Mayo argued that Indians could not be trusted with political autonomy or independence from the British. The conjoining of the social and political allowed Mayo to demand that the colonial state carry on ruling India, as Indians did not have the ability to rule themselves, given their treatment of 'their' own women. However, her pro-imperial arguments produced a dramatic backlash from Indian nationalists and women's organizations.

3   National Archives of India (NAI), New Delhi, Home Judicial, 1930, F.No.77/30.

4   Ibid.: F.No.58/30.

5   Report of the Age of Consent Committee, 1928–29, Calcutta: Government of India, Central Publication Branch 1929.

6   Various Law Commissions had been set up to study the case of codifying Hindu Law. The first such committee was formed in 1832 and was followed by a second in 1853. The findings of these two commissions stipulated that legislating personal law was beyond the mandate of the government and even if such powers could be exercised it would stunt development of Hindu Law. A third and fourth commission was set up in 1861 and 1875 respectively but they all declared the task to be impossible.

7   Nehru Memorial Museum and Library, New Delhi [NMML], S. Muthulakshmi Reddi Papers, File No.8.

8   NAI, Home Judicial, 1930, F.No.77/30.

9   Ibid.: 1927, F.No.730/27.
10   Ibid.
11   Ibid.: 1927, F.No.797/27.
12   Major argues 'Governments are invariably held responsible in the end for all legislation, whether they have promoted it themselves or merely acquiesced in it. If any odium is incurred it will inevitably fall on the Government and we may as well have the merit'. (2012: 165).
13   NAI, Home Judicial, 1927, F.No.809/27.
14   *Indian Annual Register (IAR)*, 1929, vol. II.
15   Ibid.
16   Har Bilas Sarda, *Speeches and Writings* (Ajmer: Vedic Yantralaya, 1935).
17   Secret telegram, March 23, 1930, NAI, Home Judicial, 1930, F. No. 181/1/30.
18   *Indian Annual Register*, 1934, vol. II.
19   Ibid.
20   *Modern Review*, 1936, vol. I
21   *IAR* 1938, vol.I.
22   *IAR*, 1938, vol.II.
23   NMML, AIWC Papers, F.No.1.
24   *Amrita Bazar Patrika,* 5 April 1949.
25   Ibid.
26   Ibid.
27   Ibid.
28   *Amrita Bazar Patrika*, 26 August 1948.
29   *Amrita Bazar Patrika*, 5 April 1949.
30   *ABP*, 25 June 1949.
31   Ibid.
32   *ABP*, 4 December 1949.
33   Ibid, 25 June 1949.
34   Kamalabai Lakshman Rao, a member of the AIWC from Madras on the women's delegation that met the leaders of the All-India Parties Conference in Delhi when confronted by orthodox leaders quoting Shastras against the Sarda Bill, uttered 'We want new Shastras' as cited in Sinha (1999).
35   *Stri Dharma*, December 1927: 22.
36   Sarda, *Speeches and Writings.*
37   All India Women's Conference Library, Deputation of the AIWC to the Age of Consent Committee, AIWC Annual Report, 1928.

38 Ibid.: 96.
39 AIWC Library, Deputation of the AIWC to the Age of Consent Committee, AIWC Annual Report, 1928.
40 AIWC Library, AIWC Seventh Annual Conference, AIWC Annual Report, 1933: 77–78.
41 AIWC Annual Report, 1934: 118–19.
42 AIWC Annual Report, 1934.
43 NMML, AIWC Papers, microfilm.
44 NMML, AIWC Papers, F.No.1.
45 NAI, Home Judicial, F.No.946/29.
46 NAI, 1939, F.No. 28/9/38-Judl. and K.W.
47 *IAR*, 1929, vol.II.
48 Sarda, *Speeches and Writings*.
49 Ibid.
50 Ibid.
51 The Census Report 1911: 121.
52 WBSA, Home Judicial, File No. J. 1-A-24 of 1936.
53 WBSA, Home Judicial, File No. J.1-A-17 of 1938.

REFERENCES

Agnes, Flavia. 2013. 'Controversy over Age of Consent', *Economic and Political Weekly* (henceforth *EPW*) 48, 29 (20 July).

Basu, Monmayee. 2001. *Hindu Women and Marriage Law: From Sacrament to Contract*. New Delhi: Oxford University Press.

Chakrabarti, Bhaswati. 2016. 'The Second Social Reform Movement: Gender and Society in Bengal 1930s–50s', Unpublished Ph.D thesis, Department of History, University of Calcutta.

Forbes, Geraldine. 1979. 'Women and Modernity: The Issue of Child Marriage in India', *Women's Studies International Quarterly* 2, 4: 407–19.

———. 1998. *The New Cambridge History of India Women in Modern India*. Cambridge University Press, Cambridge.

Gulati, Leela. 1976. 'Age of Marriage of Women and Population Growth: The Kerala Experience', *EPW* 11, 31–33, Special Number: Population and Poverty (Aug.): 1225–34.

Heimsath, Charles H. 1964. *Indian Nationalism and Hindu Social Reform*. Princeton, NJ: Princeton University Press.

Jaffrelot, Christophe. ed. 1999. *The Hindu Nationalist Movement and Indian Politics, 1925 to the 1990s*. New Delhi: Penguin.

Kapadia, K. M. 1972. *Marriage and Family in India*. Calcutta: Oxford University Press.

Major, Andrea. 2012. 'Mediating Modernity: Colonial State, Indian Nationalism and the Renegotiation of the "Civilizing Mission" in the Indian Child Marriage Debate of 1927–1932'. In *Civilizing Missions in Colonial and Post Colonial South Asia: From Improvement to Development*, Carey A. Watt and Michael Mann, eds. London: Anthem: 165–89.

Mani, Lata. 1989. 'Contentious Traditions: The Debate on Sati in Colonial India'. In *Recasting Women: Essays in Colonial India*, Kumkum Sangari and Sudesh Vaid, eds. New Delhi: Kali for Women.

Nair, Janaki. 1996. *Women and Law in Colonial India: A Social History*. New Delhi: Kali for Women.

Newbigin, Eleanor. 2008. 'The Hindu Code Bill and the Making of the Modern Indian State', Unpublished Ph.D thesis, Trinity College, Faculty of History, University of Cambridge.

———. 2013. *The Hindu Family and the Emergence of Modern Indian Law, Citizenship and Community*. Cambridge: Cambridge University Press.

Pande, Ishita. 2012. 'Coming of Age: Law, Sex and Childhood in Late Colonial India', *Gender & History* 24 (April): 205–30.

Ramusack, Barbara N. 1981. 'Women's Organizations and Social Change: The Age-of-Marriage Issue in India'. In *Women and World Change. Equity Issues in Development*, Naomi Black and Ann Baker Cottrell, eds. Beverley Hills: Sage: 198–216.

Sarda, Harbilas. 1935. *Speeches and Writings of Harbilas Sarda*, Ajmer: Vedic Yantralaya.

Sarkar, Tanika. 2001. *Hindu Wife, Hindu Nation: Community, Religion And Cultural Nationalism*. New Delhi: Permanent Black.

Singha, Radhika. 1998. *A Despotism of Law. Crime and Justice in Early Colonial India*. New Delhi: Oxford University Press.

Sinha, Mrinalini. 1999. 'The Lineage of the Indian Modern: Rhetoric, Agency and the Sarda Act'. In *Gender, Sexuality and Colonial Modernities*, Antoinette Burton, ed. New York: Routledge: 207–21.

———. 2006. *Spectres of Mother India: The Global Restructuring of an Empire*. New Delhi: Zubaan.

Sinha, Rakesh. ed. 2017. *Is Hindu a Dying Race: A Social and Political Perspective of Hindu Reformers of Early Twentieth Century*. New Delhi: Kautilya.

Veer, Peter van der. 1999. 'Hindus: A Superior Race', *Nations and Nationalism* 5, 3: 419–30.

3

Governing Child Marriage in India: The Protracted Reform Process

Elvira Graner

CONCERNS ABOUT CHILD marriages in India have quite a pronounced history, dating back to the late nineteenth century (see Chapter 1). It is apparent that for the past decades, there has been a gradual shift to address child marriage from a human rights perspective. Early debates about child marriage were closely linked to public discussions about the need for legislation to ban it, triggered by a rather tragic case. Back in 1890 a young girl in Bengal had bled to death at the tender age of 11 years and 3 months, after her husband had 'consummated' their marriage. This case was debated not only in India but worldwide, both politically and academically (Roy 1888; Sagade 2005; Yadav 2006; Human Rights Law Network 2005; Goswami 2010). It finally brought about the first-ever legislation to regulate the age of marriage, although it was to take several decades to enact the law. In 1929, the Indian Legislative Assembly passed the Child Marriage Restraint Act. While the Act initially set the marriage age at 14 for girls two amendments in 1949 and 1978, first increased the age to 15 and later onto 18. Based on these two amendments, the last girls who could have been married without violating Indian law were those born in the mid to late 1970s. This Act remained the core legal document until the Child Marriage Prohibition Act 2006 was promulgated. The new Act set in place a highly elaborate legal framework, allowing for the annulment of marriages conducted by under-age partners, both brides and grooms. While the previous Act had only allowed for legal action within one year of getting married, this was now linked to reaching maturity. The plight of Laxmi Sargara from Rajasthan or Santa Devi Meghwal from Gujarat caught the attention of the international media (see NBC 2012; Sieczkowski 2012; *The Economist* 2011; and *Economic and Political Weekly,* Editorials 2013 and 2014). The latter girl had been married as a child and was forced to move in with her husband when she was 16 (Dhillon 2015; Roberts 2015). After initially complying with her parents' wish and with cultural traditions, at age 18 she approached a local NGO in order to obtain legal support to void her marriage. Supported by a local child rights campaigner, Kriti Bharti, she said, 'I couldn't face being treated like a parcel to be picked up by a man I didn't care for' (Dhillon 2015: 1), became a striking slogan. Kriti Bharti had already made headlines in 2012 for obtaining India's first-ever annulment of a child marriage, for Laxmi Sargara (see *EPW* editorials 2013, 2014; Roberts 2015; Sieczkowski 2012).

I address child marriage from a vantage point of governance studies. It largely draws from a joint research project during an assignment at UNFPA in New Delhi and the Tata Institute of Social Sciences (TISS) in Mumbai, during summer–autumn 2015, and up-dated in 2017, while based at the International Centre of Advanced Studies: Metamorphoses of the Political (ICAS: MP). Following a brief introduction about some core figures, it briefly summarizes current debates about different concepts of governance, elaborates on the complex legal reform process and portrays the core features of child marriage. This is followed by analysing patterns of under-aged motherhood and access to reproductive health services, questioning what are often addressed as causalities. A core argument is that child marriage often goes hand in hand with other forms of denied citizenship, such as the lack of birth registrations and birth certificates.

1 INTRODUCTION: FIDDLING WITH NUMBERS

When comparing child marriage across the globe, India is usually listed among the bottom 30 countries, although the country ranges mid-field within this group in terms of actual rates (Nguyen and Woden 2012; UNFPA 2013; 2019; UNICEF 2005; 2017; Tewari 2014). Nevertheless, the 'staggering figures' (Plan Asia Regional Office 2012: 19) of young girls who get married in India are of high concern, not only nationally but also globally. Worldwide, the percentages of early marriages and early pregnancies are highest in Sub-Saharan African countries (some even at 35–51 percent) whereas the South Asian scenario is characterized by rather 'moderate' rates (at about 20–35 percent, UNFPA 2013). In India it is of high political concern because of the country's vast numbers of adolescents and youth. The *Population Census 2011* reported a total of 253.2 million adolescents (aged 10–19), that is, a cohort of about 25 million (and thus about 12–13 million girls) for each single-year age group (GOI and UNFPA 2014: 11). As a consequence, among the world's under-aged brides, about every third one is from South Asia (Singh 2017; UNFPA 2013; 2017; UNICEF 2017).

When assessing the total numbers of under-aged marriages, the latest *Population Census* 2011 documented that in the four years preceding the Census, nearly 6.5 million marriages of under-aged adolescent girls/women had been performed (GOI 2014; see also Singh 2017; Young Lives 2017). This figure is equivalent to more than 1.6 million per year, or nearly 4,500 each single day, thus 3 per minute. To emphasize this scenario, a young mother from India was chosen as an iconic representation and cover page for UNFPA's *State of the World*

Population 2013, focussing on 'Motherhood in Childhood' (UNFPA 2013). Even if these figures had dropped to half by 2015–16, as suggested by some recent sources, then a further 800,000 to 900,000 girls across India would have become child brides. Again, this would be equivalent to approximately 2,200 to 2,300 adolescent girls a day, or one to two every minute. In addition, India not only has the third highest rate of under-aged married girls in South Asia, but also, a matter of grave concern, a high rate of girls who marry at an age of less than 15 (Plan Asia Regional Office 2012). Again, given their absolute numbers, India ranks first, or rather bottom, among all Asian countries.

A second major concern is the rather slow rate of decline. A standard global indicator for assessing human development in general (education, health and other indicators) is to assess rates among the 20–24 age group and compare these different cohorts over time. The most comprehensive national source, the National Family and Health Surveys (NFHS-3 and NFHS-4), indicates that the rates for child marriage stood at 47 percent for the contemporary cohort in 2005–06 (see IIPS and GOI 2007: 163; see also UNFPA 2012: 23), with rather slow declines during the 1990s, that is, at a time when legislation had banned child marriage for more than a decade. Overall, annual declines had stagnated at a rate of about 0.5 percent since 1992–93 (at 54 percent; ibid.), and only slowly increased to about 1 percent (see Fig. 3.1). If so, it would have taken another 15 to 30 years to reach any politically acceptable single-digit figure of less than 10 percent, which would be the mid to late 2030s or 2040s.

Of even greater concern are the pronounced regional and social disparities within India (see section 4). Thus, it is primarily the states in northern India, where overall human development indicators are much lower than in most other parts of the country and where social disparities are paramount. Overall, these states are characterized by significant gender disparities, in terms of health, education, or overall gender empowerment, and by lagging behind both the Millennium Development Goals (MDGs) and the Sustainable Development Goals (SDGs)

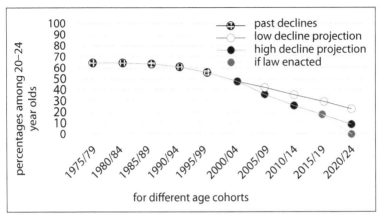

FIGURE 3.1: Past Rates and Different Projections for Declines in Child Marriages (among Women)

(UNDP 2015), as will be elaborated in detail (see section 4). Among social groups, it is both the lowest and the second lowest wealth quintiles that are particularly at risk.

2 (RE-)DEFINING GOVERNANCE

Ideas of governance and good governance have been at the core of citizen-friendly policy implementation over the past decades, both at the global and national levels. A crucial aspect of the term 'governance' is that it is applied both as an analytical concept but also a normative one, the latter often specified as 'good governance' (or its antonym 'mal-governance'; see Islam and Asaduzzaman 2008). As a recent discourse, it is prominent across many fields of social sciences, particularly in sociology and political science, and partly also in development studies. At a conceptual level, Bevir defined governance as 'a broader concept of ruling than government [and] the product of changes in the state' (2012: 12). From the vantage point of political theory, Peters (2011a) specifies the need for 'focusing more explicitly on how the public sector, in conjunction with private sector actors or alone, is capable of providing direction to society and economy' (63). This orientation has also led several authors to apply a metaphorical use of the term, relating it to steering a boat, as its Latin meaning suggests (65). As will be elaborated in the following section the legal reform process of drafting new legislation against child marriage can be seen as a model case of strengthening governance.

When portraying the archaeology of the term 'governance', Sørensen and Torfing point to its steadily growing influence (ibid. 2018: 203) but claim that the term was 'on a bumpy road from enfant terrible to mature paradigm' (ibid.). In recent years, some authors even attribute some degree of ubiquity to it (Bevir 2012), although such a wide application has also come at a cost. Thus, Sørensen and Torfing raise concerns that this ubiquity makes the term 'notoriously slippery' (2018: 204), although they also point to a 'gradual gravitation . . . towards a common understanding'. Agreeing rather on the first point, Peters even addresses the danger of 'stretching the meaning beyond all utility' (2011a: 63). Thus, he counter-argues that 'the several versions of governance theory. . . make the approach to appear incoherent and excessively open' (66). Nevertheless, he attributes a high potential to it as an 'organizing framework' (62) for political science, contributing to political theory. By pointing out 'the importance to place the behaviour of individuals into the broader context of governance' (ibid.), Peters argues that the concept 'enables the discipline, that is, political science, to recapture some of its roots' (64; see also ibid; 2011b), by shifting away from individual behaviour.

Similarly, when defining governance, Sørensen and Torfing (2018: 205) conclude that it is a 'lens to analyse the complex processes through which collective goals are formulated, adjusted and achieved'. As many other authors, they point out the strength that it 'allows us to study new ways of governing, new institutional arenas and new types of actors' (ibid.). Accordingly, they also argue about 'the need to study the complex processes through which a plethora of public and private actors interact to define problems, set goals, design solutions and implement them in practice' (ibid.). The setting of goals is also a crucial feature for Peters (2011a). Based on what he characterizes as a 'functionalist argument' (65), he defines successful governance by including the following four activities, namely: *(i)* goal selection; *(ii)* goal reconciliation; *(iii)* implementation; and *(iv)* feedback and accountability. Besides these 'basic functions' he also adds the need to investigate into decision-making, resource mobilization, implementation and adjudication. The latter, in particular, is of core relevance for the current research project.

Implicitly, such an approach has close links to institutional theory, addressing how different players are engaged when re-negotiating new rules. In this regard, the arguments provided by North (1990, 1995) are important, that '[players] have an interest in changing the rules of the game, in their favour' (1990: 5ff). Thus, North points out the need to understand that 'institutions are not necessarily or even usually created to be socially efficient; rather they are created to serve the interests of those with the bargaining power to create new rules' (1995: 18). Similar ideas about the need to address conflicts and reconciling different ideas are also important for Bevir who addresses a 'plurality of stakeholders' (2012: 23). Overall, he adds that the concept of governance is more hybrid than the state-government, as it is acting through different relations. In line with ideas from the World Bank (see below) he emphasizes close links to networks and markets, and organizations working together in contracting out and delivering services (ibid.). He also points out that governance is multi-jurisdictional.

Based on its normative meaning, a core feature of governance is the setting in place transparent and inclusive policies that regulate the rights and duties of all core stakeholders, vis-à-vis the state and vis-à-vis each other. As a normative concept applied by development partners, (good) governance had been addressed by DFID as a core strategy in their 'Why Governance Matters' back in 2006. It was also attributed a prominent position for UNESCO's 'Education for All (EFA) Monitoring Report 2009' and more recently for the World Bank's *World Development Report 2017*. In 2009, the EFA report epitomised the role of governance, titled 'Overcoming Inequality. Why Governance Matters'. For them, core criteria were how priorities are set and how resources are mobilized, allocated and managed (UNESCO 2009). In a later report they added 'ensuring that the necessary resources . . . are managed in a transparent and accountable manner' (2010: 35). For the World Bank, it is imperative to strengthen governance by paying more attention to 'the complex network of actors and interests' (2017: 3). Yet, based on their rationale, the private sector is given quite some prominence, as outlined in the chapter 'Governance for Growth' (137ff).

When elaborating on interlinkages between governance and policies, both Fukuyama (2013) and Peters (2011a and 2011b) address some important aspects. When applying this aspect to policy reform processes, they both point to the urgent need not only to understand policies as an outcome of reform processes, but also to address re-negotiation processes. In addition to this crucial argument, Fukuyama (2013) elaborates a few critical aspects specifically for assessing policies. Defining governance as 'a government's ability to make and enforce rules, and to deliver services' (ibid.: 350), he adds a vital concern about measuring policy outcomes, a crucial argument also for this research project. In contrast to many other scholars, he attributes the form of government a less important role and questions 'the current orthodoxy . . . that democracy and good governance are mutually supportive' (ibid.). When pointing out 'the poor state of empirical measures' (347) he suggests four different types of measuring governance: *(i)* procedural measures; *(ii)* capacity measures; *(iii)* output measures; and *(iv)* measures of bureaucratic autonomy.

When Fukuyama elaborates on these four criteria, he voices strong reservations about measuring outputs. Thus, he argues that 'attractive as output measures sound, there are several big ... and decisive drawbacks' (355). His reasoning is based on policies for education and health, where he argues that '[these] are not simply the consequences of public action; the public sector interacts with the environment around it and the society it is dealing with' (ibid.). As a consequence, he points out that 'the public sectors produce primarily services which are notoriously hard to measure' (ibid.). Generally, these arguments are quite crucial for assessing policies, and those about abolishing child marriage in particular. Overall, changing patterns of governance and policy reform processes can, and, indeed have, sparked off a comprehensive legal reform process. Yet, the actual implementations and indicators for measuring these are much more complex and difficult to define. Thus, banning child marriage and analysing implementation and success of this legislation by analysing declining rates could capture only a part of the success, and Fukuyama's concerns are fully applicable. On the other hand, this also asks for searching for and defining a more appropriate proxy variable. One option for such a proxy can be the issuing of core administrative documents, as will be elaborated later. This comprises core administrative procedures, such as undertaking birth registrations and issuing birth certificates, since these are fundamental prerequisites for marriage registrations.

Thus, the ideas about governance are crucial when analysing policy reforms. Such an analysis needs to investigate the rules and regulations that are being put in place and are being (re-)negotiated, by the government as well as by other core agents–stakeholders. It is a crucial argument that while (re-)formulating such legislations and policies, regulations either change or perpetuate the power positions of important stakeholders. What is crucial to understand is how the government defines its own role, vis-à-vis other core agents, in this case, vis-à-vis minor citizens and their parents (and local bureaucrats). As will be elaborated in the next section, such a shift in governance has taken place when reforming the legislation for banning child marriage in India.

3 (RE-)NEGOTIATING THE LEGAL FRAMEWORK
OF CHILD MARRIAGE

Policies and legislations are core documents that define the relationship between the state and its citizens. Usually both policies and legislations can be seen as a crucial indicator to assess the commitment from the side of the government towards specific fields of state responsibilities. As outlined above, from the vantage point of governance studies, these need to be understood as outcomes of complex and multi-layered (re-)negotiation processes among core stakeholders. This section will briefly introduce the core conventions and legislations, and portray the legal reform process(es): how successive Indian governments have (re-)defined the parameters for marriage, and thus their role vis-à-vis their adolescent and youth population. As briefly summarized above, the Prohibition of Child Marriage Act 2006, has set in place a highly elaborate legal framework, and can rightfully be addressed as a crucial milestone in banning child marriage. It was the outcome of a lengthy process of negotiations, including a public interest litigation (PIL) initiated by a national NGO. Two additional Acts of high importance for child marriage regulating the administration of civil data are the Registration of Birth and Death Act (1969), as well as its latest reform, the Registration of Births, Death and Marriages Act 2013.

At an international level, the Universal Declaration of Human Rights (Article 16) states that 'marriages shall be entered into only with the free and full consent of the intending parties' (UN 1949; see also HRLN 2005; Gonsalves 2005: 7). More specifically, child marriage is being addressed in the United Nation's Convention on the Rights for Children (CRC, UN 1989) and the Convention on the Elimination of All Forms of Discrimination Against Women (CEDAW, UN 1979). While signing these two conventions in reverse order (CRC in December 1992 and CEDAW in 1993 only), the Indian government insisted on including a rather apologetic position that seriously casts doubts on its contemporary commitment on tackling child marriage. Thus, it stated that 'the Government of the Republic of India declares that, though in principle it fully supports the principle of compulsory registration of marriages, it is not practical in a vast country like India with its variety of customs, religions and level of literacy' (quoted from Sagade 2005: 145; for an overview see Table 3.1). This politically vague position was only changed in 2013, when the Registration of Births, Deaths, and Marriages Act was passed. By following state-level legislations from Goa (1961) and Maharashtra (1998) this again was a crucial shift in governance, also aiming to reduce regional disparities.

The 1929 Act was only repealed in 2006, when the current Prohibition of Child Marriage Act 2006 was finally promulgated,

TABLE 3.1: International Conventions and National Legislations Addressing Child Marriage

	Year	Policies and Acts	Brief outline
1	2013	Registration of Births, Deaths and Marriages Act	Amendment of the 1969 Act, including the registration of marriages
2	2013	National Policy for Children	Incl. Child Marriage
3	2006	Prohibition of Child Marriage Act	Repealed Child Marriage Restraint Act (CMRA) 1929–1978
4	2004	Prevention of Child Marriage Bill	revised the CMRA of 1929, punishments substantially increased (by factor 100), institutional reform (Child Marriage Prevention Officers)
5	1998	Maharasthra Registration of Marriage Act 1998	Following the Goa Registration of Marriages Act 1961, registrations were made compulsory (state-level only)
6	1993	GOI signs UN CEDAW (1979)	Adds limitation for civil registrations
7	1992	GOI signs UN CRC (1989)	
8	1978	Amendment of the Child Marriage Restraint Act	Minimum age was increased, to 18 for girls — 21 for boys (from 15 and 18, respectively)
9	1969	Registration of Births and Death Act	Need for registration of all births and death within 21 days or one year
10	1955	Hindu Marriage Act	Regulates marriages for Indian Hindu, and Jain
11	1949	Amendment of the CMRA	Minimum age of girls was increased from 14 to 15
12	1929	Child Marriage Restraint Act (CMRA)	Minimum age was set at 14 year for girls
13	1927	'Sharda Bill' (Sarda Bill)	Bill to restrain the solemnisation of child marriages

after quite considerable re-negotiations. The history of this legal reform process is quite illustrative for demonstrating a new understanding of governance, by strengthening the role of civil society, and NGOs in particular. Thus, the first step of the reform process was a Public Interest Litigation (PIL) filed in April 2003 by an association of lawyers called the Forum for Fact Finding, Documentation and Advocacy (FFDA) (for a detailed account see HRLN 2005: 91ff and Sagade 2005). The PIL had been triggered by what FFDA captured as follows 'a shocking instance of mass child marriages in the state of Chhattisgarh was brought to everyone's notice' (HRLN 2005: 101), where the NGO had been alerted by a UNICEF survey about the Akha Teej festival. As a follow up of the UNICEF study, FFDA initiated a series of studies among several tribes in Odisha and Chhattisgarh, where they documented more than 10,000 marriage within a few weeks.

One crucial piece of information was the ambivalent role of some government officials ('sarkari babus'; ibid.: 93). They had instructed the tribal communities to mention their ages as 18 and 21 for girls and boys, respectively (ibid.). The petition documents a rather harsh assessment of the role of government officials: 'the indifference of the administration and indeed the encouragement given to child marriage is in breach of the Children Marriage Restraint Act' (94). Thus, in spite of being a clear violation of their duties as 'civil' servants, the contemporary legislation did not allow for any form of prosecution. An additional argument provided by FFDA was based on human rights, that 'such an apathy is also in breach of the Convention on Rights of Children and the CEDAW' (ibid.). In some cases, 'child marriages are merely a camouflage for servitude and sexual abuse of the girl child' (ibid.). If so, then these are in gross violation of the Indian Constitution: Articles 21 (violation of right to life), Article 23 (bondage and beggar) as well as Article 32 that makes the officials liable for prosecution (ibid.).

The PIL then brought about a first draft of the revised legislation. Interestingly, its original version still had a rather vague and non committal title: the 'Child Marriage Prevention Bill 2004' (GOI 2004). Human Rights groups insisted on a consultative process that was held in July 2004, 'Child Marriages in India. The Way Forward' (HRLN 2005), which 'attempted to bring various issues related to child marriage into public deliberation' (ibid.: 101). The six presentations held included a critical review of the 1929 Act (Bhat 2005), an outline of health-related issues, by MAMTA as well as from the side of the Population Council (Santhya et al. 2010). In addition, various programmes addressing child marriage were outlined by ICRW (2005: 179ff).

For highlighting legal responses, Human Rights Law Network also presented responses from seven state governments to the PIL that had been filed earlier (Menon 2005: 165ff). These affidavits had been submitted by Tripura, Goa, Punjab, Maharashtra, Madhya Pradesh, Chhattisgarh, and Bihar (HRLN 2005, 104ff and Menon 2005: 165ff), reflecting a cross-section of views regarding how different state governments perceive their role vis-à-vis their citizens. Thus, while the state government of Goa pointed out that they were following Portuguese law, the state of Maharashtra reported that they had made registration compulsory since 1999, based on the 'Maharashtra Regulation of Marriages Bureau and Registration of Marriages Act 1998' (HRLN 2005: 97ff). The latter state was also the first to appoint a new type of officer in the form of a 'Child Marriage Prevention Officer' as marriage registrars at the gram sevak level in 2003 (ibid.). This crucial institutional change was later on adopted as a model at the national level (see below).

The Prohibition of Child Marriage Act was finally published in the Gazette, *Bharat ka Rajpatra* in January 2007, with immediate effect across the country. As mentioned above, it made a few fundamental changes to the previous Act and its two Amendments (see Table 3.2). First, the title of the Act already indicates a much stronger commitment from the side of legislators to aim at a universal ban of child marriages,

TABLE 3.2: Major Changes from the Prohibition of Child Marriage Act 2006

No.		Child Marriage Prevention Act 1929–78	Prohibition of Child Marriage Act 2006
2(a)	Minimum ages	had been revised to 18 and 21, respectively (in 1978)	No changes
3(1)	Legal status of marriage	could be anulled	Every child marriage, whether solemnised before or after the commencement of this Act, shall be voidable at the option of the contracting party who was a child at the time of the marriage
3(3)	Legal claims	up to one year after the marriage	The petition under this section may be filed at any time but before the child completes two years of attaining majority
9	Amounts for legal fines	₹1,000 ₹/person	₹100,000/person and – or 'rigorous imprisonment'
11 (1)	Persons for legal actions	Grooms – parents	including parents, in-laws, civil servants, and religious leaders; 'all parties who negligently fail to prevent a child marriage from being solemnised'
16(A)	Institutional reform	–	Child Marriage Prohibition Officers

Source: Based on GOI, 2006.

a crucial change from the original Bill of 2004. Second, the short period of only one year allowed for legal appeal to annul the marriage, which had existed in the previous Act, has been substantially increased and, above all, its rationale has been changed. Thus, the Act not only allows for a two-year period for appeal, but it also guarantees that this is based on reaching majority age, and not on the time of marriage. From a human rights perspective, this has been a highly needed change, given that some of the marriages are conducted among young adolescents (10–14), or even younger children.

Third, the Act introduces comparatively draconic penalties that strongly aims at discouraging future child marriages, both in terms of prison sentences as well as fines (see Table 3.2). The latter have been increased to ₹100,000 per case, from the previous fines of merely ₹1,000. As argued before, it should be noted that the fines had been quite substantial in the original Act in 1929, but had never been adjusted to inflation for a nearly 70-year period (Graner 2020: 161). Imprisonment has been increased from one month to a maximum of two years for all parties, although women are still exempted from imprisonment. At the same time, for men, all offences are non-bailable. While allowing for annulling these marriages, the Act safeguards the status of children born during these marriages, and rests the decision for custody with the court. Similarly, married women who annul these marriages, are eligible for financial support from the side of the husband and/or his family, and are also guaranteed the right of residence until they re-marry. The Act also defines a clear regulation about the 'gifts exchanged', and regulates that these need to be returned.

Fourth, one of the major changes introduced by the 2006 Act was an institutional innovation, in the form of a Child Marriage Prohibition Officer, following a law passed in Maharashtra in 1998. Thus, Section 16 of the Act outlines that 'an officer or officers to be known as the Child Marriage Prohibition Officer having jurisdiction over the area or areas specified in the notification' (GOI 2006: 16(A)). These can be assisted by any 'respectable member of the locality with a record of social service or an officer of the Gram Panchayat or Municipality or an officer of the government or any public sector undertaking or an office bearer of any non-governmental organization' (16 B). Their duties are quite comprehensive, including *(a)* to prevent solemnization of child marriages by taking such action as he may; *(b)* to collect evidence for the effective prosecution of persons contravening the provisions of this Act; *(c)* to create awareness of the evil which results from child marriages; and *(d)* to sensitize the community' (16 A).

Last but not least, a major shift in governance was not only limited to changes at the administrative and institutional level. The Act also provided crucial changes in regard to substantially widening the field of potential offenders. Thus, while parents and their children had been the main targets of legal prosecution during the entire twentieth century, the new Act also turns a critical eye on several other parties engaged in allowing minors to get married. Besides government officials and politicians, this also defines a critical role for religious leaders, who could be prosecuted. Above all, not only does it criminalize active roles in permitting child marriage but also penalizes those who played passive, non-interfering roles. This indeed widens the range for legal prosecution and thus governance, in the maximum possible way. It will be highly interesting to witness how such a challenging regulation will be implemented among the different religious communities, in the years to come.

4 (RE-)ASSESSING CHILD MARRIAGE IN INDIA: REGIONAL AND SOCIAL DISPARITIES

A few core features will be highlighted in this section, followed by a critical assessment about links between child marriage and health. Besides the overall high numbers of about annually one million newly wedded brides until at least the early 2010s, as mentioned earlier, a second core issue of concern are the low rates of decline. Third, there still are vast regional and even higher social disparities. Generally, one of the core methodological approaches for assessing changes for several aspects of human development are diachronic analyses based on the age cohorts of 20–24 year olds. For doing so, two of the most comprehensive data sets are the decennial Population Censuses and the National Family Health Surveys (NFHS). The latter have been conducted at regular intervals, in 1992–93, 2005–06 and 2015–16, and have been analysed (and visualized) in depth (see also Graner 2015 and 2020).

Based on NFHSs, the rates of under-aged marriages had initially only slowly declined among 20–24-year-old women, but later on quite substantially. While rates were about 60 percent for this cohort in 1975–79 (women born 1950–54), they declined to 54 percent in 1992–93 (IIPS and GOI 2007:163), and further to about 46 percent by 2005–06 (among those born 1980–85; IIPS and GOI 2007: 166). Thus, during the 1980s until the early 2000s declines had staggered at about 0.5 percent a year, and if rates had continued to decline at this slow rate, then child marriages in India would have been prevalent even in the 2050s, or beyond. Based on rates of annual declines of 1 percent, a projection made in 2015 assessed the contemporary level (2015–16) at about 34 to 38 percent (Graner 2015: 54). Yet, even at these increased annual rates of decline, to reach any politically acceptable single-digit figure would take another 15 to 30 years, that is, not before the mid to late 2030s or 2040s (see Fig. 3.1).

Interestingly, the latest NFHS (2015–16) Report does indicate that such a drastic decline has taken place, although the data seem to be inconsistent. Thus, among the 20–24 age group (those born 1990–95) only 26.8 were married under-age, a figure also quoted in the latest 'State of World Population Report' (UNFPA 2019: 160; for the period 2006–17). Critically, among those 6.6 percent were at an age younger than 15 (GOI and IIPS 2017: 165).

If correct, then annual rates of decline would have increased to about 1.5 and more recently even to nearly 2 percent. If so, this would document an extremely encouraging picture. However, figures for older cohorts grossly undercut the ones from previous reports. While there are only minor inconsistencies for younger cohorts (44.4 percent, i.e., 2.6 percent

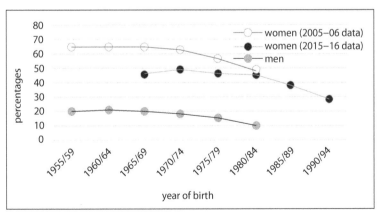

FIGURE 3.2: Ratios of Under-Aged Marriages in India
(by Year of Birth and Gender)

less), discrepancies are vast among older cohorts, where the new survey reports merely 48.6 and 46 percent, respectively, for those born 1970–75 and 1965–69 (165), whereas previous surveys had documented rates of over 60 percent (see Fig.3.2). Similar inconsistencies also exist for median ages of first marriages for different wealth groups (see below).

What is also of great concern is that not only are national figures alarmingly high, there are also grave regional and social disparities. Accordingly, the situation in some of the states, and particularly the most populous ones, are alarming. Based on NFHS-3 data, many of the northern states in 2005–06 still had early marriage rates ranging between 55 and 61, as for instance, Jharkhand, Bihar, Rajasthan, Andhra Pradesh as well as Madhya Pradesh. Again, within these states, Young Lives identified the most critical districts (Singh 2017 and NFHS-3).

In addition, Uttar Pradesh (UP) with its high population of adolescents needs to be seen as a further critical state, not so much in terms of actual rates but rather in terms of overall numbers. In UP, the Population Census of 2011 documents a total population of 23 million adolescents aged 15–19, plus 25.8 million aged 10–14 (GOI and UNFPA 2014: 11). Thus, even at comparatively 'low' rates of about 35–50 percent, this implies that more than 5–8 million girls could have been married by now in Uttar Pradesh alone, and thus nearly accounted for numbers equivalent to the next two states, Bihar and West Bengal. This issue is confirmed by data about adolescent mothers (see Fig. 3.3 below).

When considering more recent data, states can be grouped into three categories. A first group are the states that have had low rates of child marriage for quite some time, and have thus seen low declines (such as Kerala, Delhi, Sikkim and Uttarakhand). A second group are states that have successfully managed to more or less drastically reduce the rates of child marriages, such as Tamil Nadu, Andhra Pradesh, and Maharashtra. Lastly, in the bottom eight states rates are still lingering at a high level, of 32.6–43.6 percent, the latter

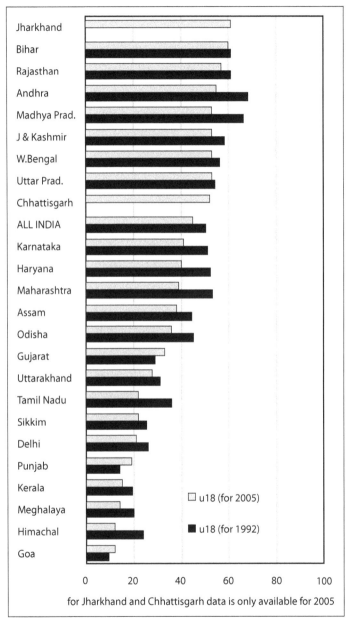

FIGURE 3.3: Regional Disparities of Under-Aged Marriages in India
for 1992–93 and 2005–06 (Based on NHFH-3 and NFHS-4)

including West Bengal with the country's highest value (GOI
and IIPS 2017: 167). Again, while Uttar Pradesh has much
lower rates (at 22.5 percent), actual numbers of marriages have
also remained of national concern (ibid.).

In addition to regional disparities, social disparities are
statistically highly significant, even stronger than for education (Graner 2020: 165). Based on NHFS 2005–06 data, median
ages of marriage for different wealth groups ranged from 15.5
for the lowest wealth quintile to 21 for the highest one for
women born 1975–79 (IIPS and GOI 2007: 164). Promisingly,
median ages had gone up significantly by 2.4 years for women
in the highest wealth group, within 20 years. Thus, while in
2005–06 among wealthier women the median age was 18.5 for
those aged 45–49 (born 1955–1960) it increased to 20.9 among
those aged 25–29 (Fig. 3.4). Comparatively, median ages for
women from the lowest and second lowest wealth groups
not only have been substantially lower (at 15), but have
increased to 16 and 16.8, respectively. This indicates a clear
violation of the legislation that had increased the minimum
age of getting married to 18 in 1978. Again, NFHS-4 data document quite a different scenario, both for younger cohorts as
well as for older ones. Based on these data, no wealth group
and age cohorts were reported as getting married at an age
below 17, not even from the lowest wealth quintile and for

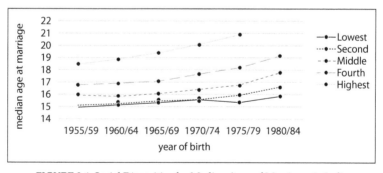

FIGURE 3.4: Social Disparities for Median Ages of Marriages in India
(for 2005–06)

older groups (see Fig. 3.4). As argued before, these data are difficult to interpret and urgently need to be cross-tabulated with other surveys and studies.

5 (RE-)ASSESSING MATERNITY AND ACCESS TO REPRODUCTIVE HEALTH

Needless to say, child marriage has a strong negative impact upon both education and (reproductive) health. For the latter, India's high rates of adolescent pregnancies go hand in hand with the world's highest maternal mortality rates (MMRs). Again, while actual rates are 'moderate', it is rather the overall numbers that are of high concern (see, for instance, ICRW 2010; Lal 2013; MAMTA 2006; Moore et al. 2009; Raj 2010; Sagade 2005; Salvi 2009; Santhya et al. 2010; Save The Children 2004; Sethuraman et al. 2007; Singh et al. 1994; WHO 2006; 2011; 2012; as well as UNFPA 2014; 2019). Worldwide, India holds a rather sad first position in maternal deaths. Back in 2013, among all maternal deaths globally, nearly 50,000 cases occurred in India alone, accounting for 17 percent of all cases (UNFPA 2014; Barnagawala 2014). While again overall population figures can partly explain this highly unfortunate position, neighbouring China, if reported accurately, has levels that are nearly one tenth, at less than 6,000 mothers (ibid.). By 2016, maternal mortality rates had declined to 174/100,000 (UNFPA 2017: 120), a figure still quoted in the latest *World Population Report* (see UNFPA 2019: 154). The latter report indicates some lack of precision, ranging between 139–217/100,000 (ibid.); accordingly, these figures show about 35,000–54,000 annual deaths (extrapolated from about 25 million annual births).

Generally, analysts tend to establish close links of causalities between maternal mortality rates and the young ages of mothers. I question such a simplistic and partly misleading correlation, addressed as 'causalities versus correlations' (Graner et al. 2015: 75ff). I argue that rather than the actual ages of these young mothers, high death rates are due to the lack of access to vital public health services and facilities. As has been portrayed above, child marriage has a strong social bias, and is predominantly prevalent among socially disadvantaged groups. As will be documented, a similar pattern of vast social disparities is also prevalent for access to public (or other) reproductive health facilities. As a result, until today, pregnancies and deliveries have remained a highly risky issue for many mothers from socially disadvantaged communities and under-age ones in particular (UNICEF 2005; 2017).

When assessing early motherhood during the early millennium, the NFHS documents that in 2005–06 of all women, women aged 20 to 24, 22 percent had given birth while still minors (IIPS and GOI 2007: 94). Within a single decade, these figures have significantly declined to 9.3 percent by 2015–16. If correct, this implies annual rates of decline at more than 1 percent, and thus demonstrates a laudable success. On the other hand, even in 2015–16 it documented 1 percent of mothers who were younger than 15 (GOI and IIPS 2017: 96). When carrying out a trend analysis for older cohorts, ages at first births have been quite high. Based on NHFS-3 (IIPS and GOI 2007: 91) there is a strong pattern that median age at first birth has decreased across the different age groups. In spite of a few inconsistencies, declines were from 20.2 years among the 45 to 40 year olds (those born during the 1960s), to about 19.6 years among younger age groups (those born during the 1980s). Strangely, the youngest cohort again had a median age of 19.9.

Similarly, the NFHS also documents that the share of women or girls who had given birth at the age of 15, had decreased along the past two decades, from 5.9 to 5.3 and 4.6 percent for the age groups 45–49, 40–44, and 35–39, respectively. However, among the younger age groups (20–24, 25–29 and 30–34), percentages of early motherhood (aged 15) had been slightly higher (at 5.8 and 5 percent), although again lower for the youngest group (3.4 percent). Yet, inconsistencies remain and could indicate some errors while either enumerating or analysing. For 2015–16, NFHS confirms these lower values. For women aged 25–29 (a cohort older than the one usually used as standard indicator) median ages in rural areas are 21 years and 23 in urban areas. Yet, again social disparities among different wealth groups are persistent, at 20.3 years for the lowest and 24.4 years for the highest groups (ibid.: 83).

As elaborated for several core indicators, regional disparities for early pregnancies are also quite high. Thus, for the early 2000s, percentages of adolescent motherhood were highest in Jharkhand, at approximately 27.5 percent, with more than 20 percent of adolescent girls who had already given birth, and 7 percent contemporarily pregnant (see Fig. 3.5). Two other states with critically high values are West Bengal (at 25.3 percent) and Bihar (at 25 percent). In terms of overall rates, other states that fall into the 'bottom 10' group are three in the Northeast (Tripura, Assam and Arunachal Pradesh, at 18.5, 16.4 and 15.4, percent respectively). While Uttar Pradesh ranked only 12th in regard to rates, the state nevertheless needs to be assessed among the critical states, due to its enormous population size (at 14.3 percent; see Fig. 3.5). Again, by 2015–16 these rates have drastically declined, if data are correct.

As portrayed in the sections above, regional and social disparities are paramount for all development and health indicators. In 2005–06, under 5-year mortality rates were still nearly triple for the lowest wealth group, when compared to the highest one at 35 versus 105/1000 births (see Fig. 3.6). Disparities were slightly lower, but still high, for IMRs, at about factor 2.5. By 2015–16 mortality rates had declined to 50 /1000 at the national level, and IMR to 40.7 /1000 (GOI and IIPS 2017: 190). For the latter, social disparities ranged from 18.7 to 46.7 /1000, for the highest and lowest wealth quintiles, respectively (ibid.).

As argued above, access to health facilities are extremely important for safeguarding safe motherhood. Due to lack of data about teenage (under 18) motherhood, the following analyses will be based on births in general. Overall, there are

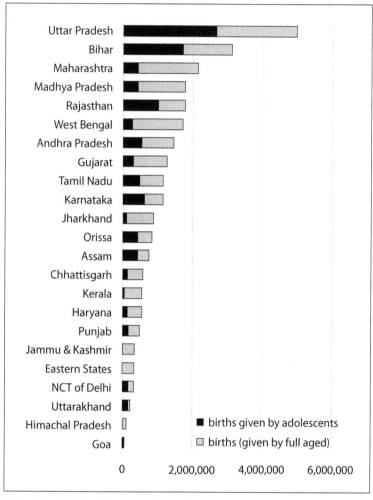

FIGURE 3.5: Regional Disparities for Under-Aged Mothers (Assessment for 2011)

vast disparities for several indicators. As the two most critical ones, the places of deliveries and attendance during birth have been analysed in more detail. In addition, the whole package of pre-natal and post-natal care is also vital, for both mothers and newborns. Again, there are vast regional and social disparities,

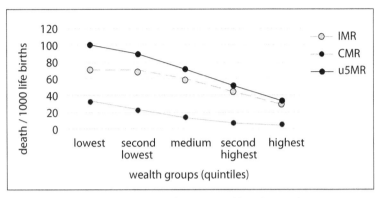

FIGURE 3.6: Social Disparities for Core Health Indicators for 2005–06
(IMR/CMR/u5MR)

IMR infant mortality rates
CMR child mortality rates
U5MR mortality rates of children under the age of 5 (ie. IMR plus CMR)

and accessing services is particularly difficult in most of the northern states and among low wealth families.

Access to institutional deliveries at either public or private hospitals shows a rather promising trend overall. Based on the vast number of nearly one quarter of a million births between 2010 and 2015, the NFHS-4 documents that births at health facilities have increased to nearly 80 percent. Naturally, institutional births went along with a drastic decline of deliveries at home, from 51 percent in 2005–06 to only 18 percent in 2015–16 (see GOI and IIPS 2017: 228). On the other hand, these changes occurred primarily for higher wealth quintiles, whereas deliveries at home still accounted for a substantial number of births for the lowest two wealth quintiles (at 35 and 21 percent, respectively; ibid.). Nevertheless, since 2005 there have been substantial changes even for lower wealth groups, when deliveries at home had still accounted for 76 percent, compared to an average of 51 percent for all women (IIPS and GOI 2007: 235). Women from higher wealth groups had their deliveries mainly at private hospitals (60 percent), a place quite unlikely for women from the two lowest wealth groups (at 8 and 14 percent, respectively). Interestingly, access to public hospitals showed much lower disparities (at 34 versus 60 percent, but only 50 percent for the lowest wealth quintile; see Fig. 3.7 below).

In terms of health outcomes, when assessing dangers due to complications, women from lower wealth groups were thus nearly tenfold as exposed as those from the highest wealth quintile. Similarly, when analysing assistance at deliveries, these have gradually changed, even within the last decade. In 2015–16, a substantial proportion of women from the lowest wealth groups were assisted by doctors (32 percent), mainly at public hospitals. Thus, disparities between women from different wealth groups had significantly declined (at 81 percent for the highest wealth group).

Unfortunately, the latest NFHS-4 Report for 2015–16 does not provide critically important data about regional disparities for deliveries. In order to portray some disparities, the prevalence of ante-natal care (ANC) services will be taken as proxy indicator, assuming that these two parameters have strong correlations. Again, overall there has been a rather promising trend of better access to services, including ante-natal check-ups, with 83.6 percent of women utilizing these services (GOI and IIPS 2017: 215). Yet, while among the southern states Karnataka has the lowest utilization rates, with 11 percent women not using the services, these rates are much higher across nearly all northern states. Besides the eastern hill region

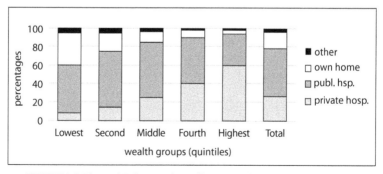

FIGURE 3.7: Place of Deliveries for Different Wealth Groups (for 2010–15)

(with Nagaland at 53.7 percent), many other northern states also only have middle-digit figures, at 22–44 percent, the latter for Bihar (ibid.). While 5 percent amongst the highest quintile do not access ANCs, amongst the poorest group it rises to 34 percent (ibid.). Reasons for avoiding these services are usually that expenses are too high (24.4 percent) or that women (and often their husbands) do not think these are necessary (24.8 percent; ibid.: 224).

Not surprisingly, there are strong correlations between infant mortality rates (IMRs) and access to public health services. At a national average of 40.7/1000 births, IMRs in different states range between top-level values in Kerala (at 5.6) and the bottom 10 states, where IMRs range between 29.5 and 63.5 (ibid.: 197). Since the latter value is for Uttar Pradesh, this could imply deaths of annually approximately 30,000 infants (based on 5 million births).

As argued above, when addressing (reproductive) health from a vantage point of governance, it is a fundamental policy decision, where and under which conditions and costs, such services are being offered. Similarly, it is a core policy decision to empower women to be in a position to access these services, and also to be in a position to decide to do so, rather than leaving such decisions to other family members.

6 GOVERNING CITIZENSHIP: INDIA'S (UN-)REGISTERED ADOLESCENTS

As elaborated in the previous sections, the Indian government aims at abolishing child marriage and has substantially stepped up its strategies and legislations to do so. Besides passing the Child Marriage Prohibition Act in 2006, strictly prohibiting such marriages, they also have passed, as mentioned earlier, the Right to Education Act 2006, in order to comply with fulfilling the global Education for All Policy, as well as the MDGs (Millennium Development Goals) and now the Sustainable Development Goals (see UNESCO 2010ff; UN

2015). The core argument here is that a fundamental prereq-
uisite for achieving these critical and ambitious goals is to
establish and document full citizenship for the country's entire
young generation, by rigorously registering all newborn children. In the critical group which needs this assistance most
are those born into underprivileged families, whose parents are
highly likely not be in a position to safeguard these rights
for their daughters (and sons) on their own. This section will
provide a brief summary about the legal regulations, as well
as showcase the low level of implementation in several states.
The latter is particularly ironical when compared to the prominence and political endeavour that has gone into the issuing
of aadhaar cards.

Generally, this argument has also been voiced by the
Indian government. In their publication on 'Vital Statistics
of India based on the Civil Registration System' the Ministry of
Home Affairs (MHA) stated that 'registration of birth is a right
of the child and is the first step towards establishing their
identity' (GOI–MHA–ORG 2014: 1). They also add that these
registrations are 'essential for socio-economic planning and
also to evaluate the effectiveness of various public related programmes' (ibid.). On the other hand, statistical data document
that implementation is lagging vastly behind, and it is particularly the under-privileged who, until today, have remained
excluded. Taking up Fukuyama's argument about the difficulties to measure policy outputs for assessing governance
(see section 2.), one vital proxy variable for assessing the state
of citizenship (and thus governance) are the registration and
provision of birth certificates. Assessing whether marriages
are taking place among minors or among citizens who have
reached the legally defined minimum age can logically only be
based on the provision that both parties are willing to, but also
capable of, disclosing their correct ages. In addition, registration for elections and thus voting rights are also fundamental
to exercise citizenship.

As mentioned above, India has a worldwide unique demographic pattern, of more than a quarter million adolescents

(253 million in 2011; GOI and UNFPA 2014: 11), that is, annual cohorts of roughly 25 million newborn children. As briefly elaborated earlier, for administrative officers this implies shouldering a massive task, and mastering this was assessed impossible back in 1993, when signing the UN's CEDAW. However, the vast developments that have taken place in the IT sector worldwide have provided a completely different technological infrastructure, particularly when considering India's substantial contribution in advancing these. Thus, in the new millennium, maintaining such an up-to-date administrative data base, for both birth and marriage registrations, should not be considered a task too complicated. At the same time, only once this can be mastered, retro-fitting of vital demographic data will no longer be technically possible and thus verifying child marriages can be done consistently.

While the legislation for the Registration of Birth and Death Act was already set in place in 1969, implementation had been negligible for decades, to put it mildly. This Act has recently been amended (2013), and now also includes the registration of marriages. Yet, in many states across the country, neither the original legislation nor the amendment has been implemented at any meaningful scale. As a sad consequence, even for the current generation of adolescents and youth, birth registrations and birth certificates in many states have remained the exception rather than the rule, in some states at less than 50 percent, as documented by both Census 2011 and NFHS-3. Besides state-level disparities, rural-urban disparities had been pronounced, along with social disparities. Overall, by 2015–16 registrations have tremendously increased (see below), if data are correct, although social disparities are still pronounced.

The Registration of Births and Death Act 1969 clearly regulates the time framework of these reporting and also defines the responsible persons and officers. All births and deaths need to be reported within 21 days, and birth certificates need to be issued, exempt from any fees. When reported 21 to 30 days after the events, then a late fee needs to be paid, and when reported only after one month but within one year, then affidavits need to be produced. Once this period has elapsed, the registration can only be done with the permission of a First Class Magistrate. In addition to these clear guidelines, the Registration of Births and Death Act also defines responsibilities for various other agents. Thus, the head of any household is responsible for reporting, but the Civil Registration System attributes a crucial role to local authorities, as well. Similarly, public servants in health institutions (hospitals, nursing homes, health centres) as well as midwives and other para-medical persons who have attended a birth 'are duty bound to notify the registrar' (ibid.: 4).

In spite of this clear-cut legislation, the registration of births is yet to be seen as a core civil duty by either parents or civil servants in many states across the country, in spite of substantial changes. When assessing birth registrations, the government in 2014 pointed out that registrations had reached 21.8 million in 2011, compared to only 8.4 million in 1982 (GOI–MHA 2014: 5). Yet, while claiming that the level of registration had reached 83.6 percent in 2011, assessments based on NFHSs data are substantially lower, and stood at only 41 percent for 2005–06, and 80 percent in 2015–16. If correct, this documents increase of about 4 percent annually, and, assuming linear growth, rates in 2011 would have been around 60 percent. Birth registrations over the past three decades (from 1982 onwards) show a particular pattern, with a considerable decline during the late 1990s until the early 2000s. Overall, increases had been about 2 to 6 percent during most of the 1980s and early 1990s, and increased to about 10–20 percent, more recently. These latter increases could be interpreted as successful political campaigns for registration, but possibly also include 'children' at any age, particularly new voters prior to (state) elections. Thus, it is crucial to note that registrations are always gross data, and thus distortions are vast. Net registrations of actual newborns are likely to be substantially lower than these official data suggest.

Above all, NHFS data for 2005–06 documented that the registration of births had extremely high regional disparities. In addition, urban-rural disparities were also extremely high in most states. Birth registrations, at least until the mid-2000s, had remained by and large an 'urban affair'. Not surprisingly, the states with the lowest registrations by-and-large correspond to those states where human development indicators are quite low, and where child marriage has remained highly prevalent. Thus, back in 2005–06 only a few states had certificates issued to more than 80 percent of the population, namely, Goa, Kerala and Tamil Nadu. For other states, such as Gujarat and Maharashtra, rates were high in urban areas only. In many other states, birth certificates were issued to only 50 to 60 percent of the population. The 'Bottom Five' states of (not) issuing birth certificates in 2005–06 were Bihar, Uttar Pradesh, Jharkhand, Rajasthan, and Madhya Pradesh. States that fell substantially short of registrations of birth, were Chhattisgarh, Bihar, and Uttar Pradesh, at 55.1, 59.8 and 64.9 percent, respectively (see Fig. 3.8).

Several critical states had registrations of less than 40 percent in rural areas, and some even less than 20 percent, including Rajasthan, Uttar Pradesh, Jharkhand, and Bihar. Similarly, social disparities have been substantial, as is apparent when analysing wealth groups (see Fig. 3.9). Thus, only the two highest wealth groups had a high access to this core service, whereas among the two lowest groups, only one-third and one-fourth, respectively, had at least registered their children's birth. Whereas registrations had gone up promisingly by 2015–16, both the regional and social disparities remain. Thus, even in 2015–16 a minority from the lowest wealth group (40.7 percent) had been registered and held certificates. Sadly, this clearly indicates that fully documented citizenship has remained a privilege for the upper wealth groups.

Why bother about these data, at all, you might ask? The answer is fairly simple: it is these young girls and boys who will reach their early and mid teens in the current decade.

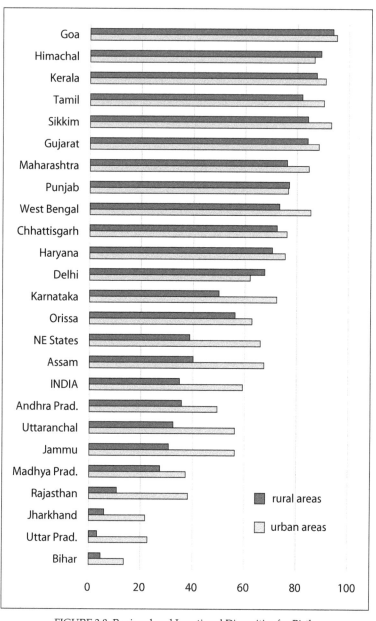

FIGURE 3.8: Regional and Locational Disparities for Birth
Registrations (for 2005–06)

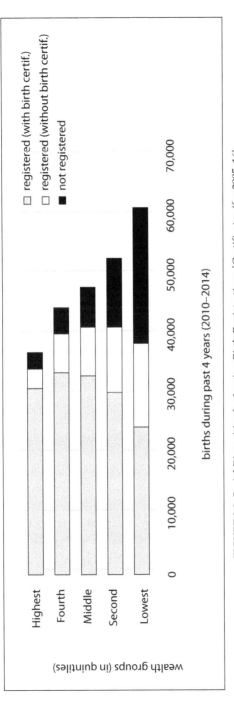

FIGURE 3.9: Social Disparities for Issuing Birth Registrations/Certificates (for 2005–16)

And whether or not their births have been registered, has a strong causality as to whether or not they are likely to engage in child marriage. And when considering governance and Fukuyama's argument about the challenges to implement both education and health policies, the registration of births and the issuing of birth certificates should not face such difficulties.

7 CHILD MARRIAGE IN INDIA: SOME AFTERTHOUGHTS

Aiming at abolishing child marriage is a political imperative for any government that has signed the UN's Declaration of Human Rights and/or other relevant Conventions. For compliance, the Indian government has initiated a comprehensive legislation reform process over the past decades. Besides prohibiting new child marriages, and allowing for annulling existing ones, this also includes the need to register all marriages, as well as all births. Yet, as elaborated in detail, policy makers, administrators, and the judiciary are still struggling with fully implementing these legislations. As a result, child marriage has remained a prevalent phenomenon in several Indian states, and particularly among socially disadvantages groups. As argued in this chapter, this lack of implementation needs to be addressed not only as a lack of governance but as a form of denied citizenship.

When categorizing child marriage in this way, perpetrators can be identified both within the family (parents and in-laws) but also within the state and its administrators. Parents have usually (been) married as children themselves, and thus many among them may fail to understand the importance of banning child marriage. On the other hand, the Indian government and judiciary have by now fully followed international conventions of defining child marriage as a violation of human rights. As a logical consequence, in cases of conflict, the state needs to take up its role as a protector vis-à-vis minors. Such a protection is particularly important for those young people who need to rely on public assistance, since their parents are

highly unlikely to be in any position to safeguard (or understand) their constitutional rights, both for education and for
not being married off as children.

While generally, most scholars emphasize the important
links between child marriage and human development indicators, such as education, access to health services, or poverty
in a broader sense, this chapter shifts the analysis to a more
fundamental approach. Without questioning the importance
of these parameters above, it establishes a link between child
marriage and denying young citizens their fundamental right
to be registered, and to receive birth certificates. At the policy
level, such a shift in argument is quite significant. While child
marriage is extremely complex to tackle, the registration of all
births is a comparatively simple administrative procedure. At
the same time, it is a vital and crucial precondition not only for
defining under-age marriage but for establishing citizenship.
Only once this has been accomplished, the state is in a position to take up its constitutional mandate to protect children
(and adolescents) from human rights offences, such as child
marriage.

Once this step has been accomplished, global visions of
childhood no longer remain as 'mission impossible'. Yet,
visions such as UNICEF's State of the World's Children (SWC)
2015 'Reimagine the Future' (UNICEF 2014), or 'Adolescence:
An Age of Opportunity' (UNICEF 2011) also need to explicitly address children's rights, as has been done in the SWC
2014, 'Revealing disparities, advancing children's rights'
(UNICEF 2013). As a consequence, it was also added as one of
the targets of the UN's Sustainable Development Goals (16.9;
see UN 2015). This comprehensive rights approach will finally
guarantee the status of the next generation as future citizens,
with full entitlements to access a range of different public services, including the future right to vote. Thus, once reaching
majority the next generation can then contribute to further
strengthen the policy and legal framework for their families'
and the country's next generation.

REFERENCES

Please note web access for publications prior to 2015 are all August/September 2015; for later publications January-March 2019. All tables and figures compiled by author.

Bevir, Mark. 2012. *Governance. A Very Short Introduction*. Oxford: Oxford University Press.

Bhat, Arpana. 2005. 'Child Marriage Restraint Act'. In *Child Marriages and the Law in India*, Human Rights Law Network, eds. New Delhi: HRLN, 139–41.

DFID. 2006. *Why Governance Matters*. London: DfID.

Dhillon, A. 2015. 'Child Marriage in India Finally Meets Its Match as Young Brides Turn to Courts', *The Guardian*. May 27; http://www.theguardian.com/global-development/2015/may/27/india-child-marriage-annulment-brides-go-to-court

Economist. 2011. 'Child Brides. For Poorer, Most of the Time'. *Economist* (28 Feb). http/: www.economist.com/blogs/dailychart/2011/02/child_brides 94, 15: 7.

EPW Editorials. 2013. 'Will Child Marriages Ever End? '*EPW* 48, 44: 9.

———. 2014. 'Not Made in Heaven'. *EPW* 49, 51: 8.

EPW Letters 2013. 'Child Marriage', *EPW* 48, 52: 4–6.

Fukuyama, Francis. 2013. 'What Is Governance?' *Governance* 26, 3: 347–68.

Gonsalves, E. 2006: 'Foreword'. *Child Marriages and the Law in India*. Human Rights Law Network, New Delhi: HRLN: 6–8.

GOI and IIPS. 2017. *National Family Health Survey-4*. New Delhi/Mumbai: GOI and International Institute for Population Sciences.

GOI. 2011. *India Human Development Report*. New Delhi: Oxford University Press and GOI/Planning Commission; http://www.iamrindia.gov.in/ihdr_book.pdf

GOI/MHA/Registrar General. 2014. *Vital Statistics of India. Based on the Civil Registration System 2011*. New Delhi: GOI.

GOI. 2001. 'Convention on the Rights of the Child. First Periodic Report'. New Delhi: Ministry of Human Resource Development/Department of Women and Child Development.

GOI/Ministry of Law and Justice. 2006. *Right to Education Act 2006*. New Delhi: Bharat ka Rajpatra/India Gazette.

———. 2007. 'Prevention of Child Marriage Act 2006'. New Delhi: Bharat ka Rajpatra/India Gazette (18 Jan.).

———. 'Registration of Births and Death Act. Amendment for Registration of Marriages'. New Delhi: Bharat ka Rajpatra; http://www.prsindia.

org/uploadsmedia/Registration%20of%20births%20and%20deaths/
REegistration%20of%20Births%20and%20Deaths%20(Amendment)
%20bill,%202012.pdf
———. 1949. 'Amendment to the Child Marriage Restraint Act'.
New Delhi: Bharat ka Rajpatra/India Gazette.
———. 1969. 'Registration of Births and Death Act'. New Delhi: Bharat
ka Rajpatra/India Gazette.
———. 1978. 'Amendment to the Child Marriage Restraint Act'.
New Delhi: Bharat ka Rajpatra.
———. 2004. 'The Prevention of Child Marriage Bill'. New Delhi: Bharat
ka Rajpatra/India Gazette.
GOI/MWCD. 2011. 'Report on CEDAW' (Convention on the Elimination
of All Forms of Discrimination against Women). New Delhi: GOI;
www.wcd.nic.in/cedawdraft20nov2011.pdf
———. 2012. 'National Strategy Document on Prevention of Child
Marriage'. New Delhi: GOI. http://www.khubmarriage18.org/sites/
default/files/207.pdf
GOI and UNPFA. 2014. *A Profile of Adolescents and Youth in India*.
New Delhi: GOI and UNFPA.
Government of India. 2014. *Population Census 2011*. New Delhi: GOI.
http://censusindia.gov.in/
Goswami, Ruchira. 2010. 'Child Marriage in India. Mapping the Legal
Trajectories'. Kolkata: Sanhati; http://sanhati.com/excerpted/2207/
Graner, Elvira. 2020. 'Governing Childhood in India. The Uphill Battle
to Abolish Child Marriage', *Studies on Sociology of Childhood and Youth*
35, 35–57.
Graner, Elvira, S. Parasuraman, Nishi Mitra et al. 2015: *State of Adolescents
and Youth in India 2015. Early Marriage and Adolescent Pregnancy*.
Mumbai/New Delhi: TISS and UNFPA (internal report).
Human Rights Law Network (HRLN). 2005. *Child Marriages and the Law
in India*. New Delhi: HRLN.
IIPS and GOI/MHFW. 2007. *India. National Family Health Survey-3*.
Mumbai: IIPS and GOI. http//:www.dhsprogram.com/pubs/pdf/
FRIND3/FRIND3-Vol1AndVol2.pdf.
Indian Legislature. 1929. *Child Marriage Restraint Act 1929*. Indian Gazette
Act NO. XIX (October 1st, 1929).
International Center for the Rights of Women (ICRW). 2014. *Too
Young to Wed. Education and Action towards Ending Child Marriage.
Policy Solutions*. Washington, DC: ICRW; www.icrw.org/files/

publications/Too-Young-to-Wed-Education-and-Action-Toward-Ending-Child-Marriage.pdf

———. 2005. 'Child Marriage and Development Programme'. In *Child Marriages and the Law in India*, Human Rights Law Network, eds. New Delhi: Human Rights Law Network: 139–141.

———. 2010. *New Insights on Preventing Child Marriage. A Global Analysis of Factors and Programmes*. Washington, DC: ICRW; https://www.icrw.org/files/publications/New-Insights-on-Preventing-Child-Marriage.pdf

Islam, Nurul, and Asaduzzaman, eds. 2008. *A Ship Adrift. Governance and Development in Bangladesh*. Dhaka: CPD.

John, M.E. 2011. 'Census 2011. Governing Populations and the Girl Child'. *EPW* 46, 16: 10–12. https://www.unfpa.org/sites/default/files/resource-pdf/UNFPA_Publication-39866.pdf

Lal, B. Suresh. 2013. 'Child Marriage in India. Factors and Problems', *International Journal of Science and Research* 4, 4: 2292–97; www.ijsr.net/archive/v4i4/SUB1536991.pdf

MAMTA. 2005. 'Early Marriage and Early Pregnancy in India'. In *Child Marriages and the Law in India*, Human Rights Law Network, eds. New Delhi: HRLN, 143–60.

Menon, Pratibha P. 2005. 'State Responses to the Petition'. In *Child Marriages and the Law in India*, Human Rights Law Network, eds. New Delhi: HRLN, 139–41.

Moore, A. M., et al. 2009. *Adolescent Marriage and Childbearing in India. Current Situation and Recent Trends*. Washington, DC: Guttmacher Institute. http://www.guttmacher.org/pubs/2009/06/04/Adolescent MarriageIndia.pdf

NBC. 2012. 'Indian Baby Bride Wins Annulment'. NBC (April 25). www.worldnews.nbcnews.com/_news/2012/04/25/11394397-indian-baby-bride-laxmi-sargara-wins-annulment-in-landmark-case?lite

Nguyen, Minh Cong, and Quentin Wodon. 2012. *Global Trends in Child Marriage*. Washington, DC World Bank; http://www.ungei.org/files/Child_Marriage_Trends3.pdf

North, D.C. 1990. *Institutions, Institutional Change and Economic Performance*. Cambridge: Cambridge University Press.

———. 1995. 'The New Institutional Economics and Third World Development'. In *The New Institutional Economics and Third World Development*, J. Harriss et al. London/New York, 17–26.

Peters, B. Guy. 2011a. 'Governance as Political Theory', *Critical Policy Studies* 5, 1: 63–72; https://doi.org/10.1080/19460171.2011.555683

————. 2011b. 'Response to Mark Bevir and Benjamin Krupicka, Hubert Heinelt and Birgit Sauer. *Critical Policy Studies* 5, 4: 467–70; https://doi.org/10.1080/19460171.2011.629131

Plan Asia Regional Office. 2012. 'Asia Child Marriage Initiative (ACMI). Eliminating Child Marriage'. Bangkok: Plan Asia Regional Office (PARO).

Plan Asia Regional Office and ICRW. 2013. *Asia Child Marriage Initiative: Summary of Research in Bangladesh, India and Nepal.* Bangkok: PARO; http//:www.planinternational.org/files/Asia/publications/asia-child-marriageinitiative-summary-of-research-in-bangladesh-india-and-nepal.pdf

Plan International. 2011. *Breaking Vows. Early and Forced Marriage and Girls' Education.* London: Plan International; http://www.plan-uk.org/resources/documents/Breaking-Vows-Early-and-Forced-Marriage-and-Girls-Education/

Raj, A. 2010. 'When the Mother Is a Child. The Impact of Child Marriage on the Health and Human Rights of Girls', *Archives of Disease in Childhood* 95: 931–35. http://adc.bmj.com/content/early/2010/10/07/ad3c.2009.178707.full.pdf

Roberts, Helen. 2015. 'Baby Bride Who Wed at One and Divorced at 18 Marries Again', *Daily Mail* (21 Oct.); http://www.dailymail.co.uk/news/article-2274350/Baby-bride-Laxmi-Sargara-marries-second-time.html#ixzz3i7r5cuSc

Roy, Raj Coomar. 1888. 'Child Marriage in India', *The North American Review* 147, 383: 415–423. www.jstor.org/stable/25101631

Sagade, Jaya. 2005. *Child Marriage in India: Socio-Legal and Human Rights Dimensions.* New Delhi: Oxford University Press.

Salvi, Vinita. 2009. 'Child Marriage in India: A Tradition with Alarming Implications', *The Lancet* 373, 9678: 1826–27.

Santhya, K.G., et al. 2010. 'Associations between Early Marriage and Young Women's Marital and Reproductive Health Outcomes: Evidence from India', *International Perspectives on Sexual and Reproductive Health* 36, 3: 132–39.

Save the Children. 2015. *The State of the World's Mothers: Urban Disadvantage.* Westport, CT: Save the Children.

————. 2014. *WINGS 2014. The World of India's Girls.* New Delhi: Save the Children. http://resourcecentre.savethechildren.se/sites/default/files/documents/wingsreportpdf.pdf

————. 2004. *The State of the World's Mothers.* Adolescent Mothers. Westport. CT.: Save the Children. www.savethechildren.org/atf/cf/{9def2ebe-10ae-432c-9bd0-df91d2eba74a}/SOWM_2004_final.pdf

Sen, Samita. 2009. 'Religious Conversion, Infant Marriage and Polygamy: Regulating Marriage in India in the Late Nineteenth Century', *Journal of History* 26: 99–145.

Sethuraman, K., et al. 2007. 'Delaying the First Pregnancy: A Survey in Maharashtra, Rajasthan and Bangladesh', *EPW* 44 (3 Nov.): 79–89.

Sieczkowski, Cavan. 2012. 'Indian Child Bride, Laxmi Sargara, Has Marriage Annulled After Marrying at One-Year-Old', *International Business Times* (April 26). www.ibtimes.com/indian-child-bride-laxmi-sargara-has-marriage-annulled-after-marrying-one-year-old-693198.

Singh, Renu. 2017. *A Statistical Analysis of Child Marriage in India*. Oxford: Young Lives.

Singh, Susheela, et al. 2014. *Adding It Up: The Costs and Benefits of Investing in Sexual and Reproductive Health 2014*. New York: Guttmacher Institute and UNFPA.

Sørensen, E., and Torfing, J. 2018. 'Governance on a Bumpy Road from Enfant Terrible to Mature Paradigm', *Critical Policy Studies* 5: 203–24.

Tewari, S. 2014. 'At 240 million, India Has a Third of Child Marriages in the World', *Hindustan Times* (12 Aug.12). http://www.hindustantimes.com/india-news/at-240-million-india-has-a-third-of-child-marriages-in-the-world/article1-1251139.aspx

United Nations. 2015. *Transforming Our World. The 2030 Agenda for Sustainable Development*. New York: UN.

UN Women. 2015. *Progress of the World's Women. Transforming Economies, Realizing Rights*. New York: UN Women. http://progress.unwomen.org/en/2015/pdf/UNW_progressreport.pdf

UNDP. 2014. *Human Development Report: Sustainable Development*. New York: UNDP; www.hdr.undp.org/sites/default/files/hdr14-report-en-1.pdf.

UNESCO. 2010. *EFA Global Monitoring Report: Reaching the Marginalized*. Paris: UNESCO; www.unesdoc.unesco.org/images/0018/001865/186525e.pdf

UNESCO. 2009. *EFA Global Monitoring Report. Overcoming Inequality. Why Governance Matters*. Paris: UNESCO. ; www.download.eiie.org/docs/IRISDocuments/Education/EducationForAll/Global MonitoringReport2009/2009-00090-01-E.pdf

UNFPA. 2005. State of World Population. *The Promise of Equality*. New York: UNFPA. www.unfpa.org/sites/default/files/pub-pdf/swp05_eng.pdf

———. 2012a. *State of World Population. By Choice, Not by Chance*. New York: UNFPA. https://www.unfpa.org/sites/default/files/pub-pdf/EN_SWOP2012_Report.pdf

————. 2012b. *Marrying Too Young*. New York: UNFPA. http://www. unfpa.org/sites/default/files/pub-pdf/MarryingTooYoung.pdf

————. 2013. *Motherhood in Childhood. Facing the Challenge of Adolescent Pregnancy*. New York: UNFPA. www.unfpa.org/sites/default/files/ pub-pdf/EN-SWOP2013-final.pdf

————. 2019. *State of World Population 2019*. New York: UNFPA. www. unfpa.org/sites/default/files/pub-pdf/EN-SWOP19-Report_FINAL-web.pdf

UNFPA/ICRW/ AusAID and AFPPD. 2010. *Child Marriage in Southern Asia. Policy Options for Action*. Bangkok: UNFPA. www.icrw.org/ publications/child-marriagesouthern-asia.

Unicef. 2001. 'Early Marriage: Child Spouses'. *Innocenti Digest*, 7. http:// www.unicef-icdc.org/publications/pdf/digest7e.pdf

————. 2005. *Early Marriage. A Harmful Traditional Practice. A Statistical Exploration*. New York: unicef. http://www.unicef.org/publications/ files/Early_Marriage_12.lo.pdf

————. 2010. *Progress for Children: Achieving the MDGs with Equity Number 9*. New York: unicef. www.unicef.org/publications/fi les/ Progress_for_Children-No.9_EN_081710.pdf

————. 2011. *The State of World's Children. Adolescence. An Age of Opportunity*. New York: unicef. www.unicef.org/adolescence/files/ SOWC_2011_Main_Report_EN_02092011.pdf

————. 2012. *Child Marriage in India*. New Delhi: unicef. http://www. unicef.in/Itstartswithme/childmarriage.pdf

————. 2013a. *The State of the World's Children 2014. Revealing Disparities, Advancing Children's Rights*. New York: unicef; www.unicef.org/ gambia/SOWC_report_2014.pdf

————. 2013b. 'Deepshikha: Educating and Empowering Adolescent Girls in Remote Communities'. New Delhi: unicef (unpublished document).

————. 2014a. *The State of the World's Children 2015. Reimagine the Future. Innovation for Every Child*. New York: unicef. http://www.unicef. org/publications/files/SOWC_2015_Summary_and_Tables.pdf

————. 2014b. *Improving Children's Lives Transforming the Future. 25 Years of Child Rights in South Asia*. New York: unicef.

————. 2014c. *Ending Child Marriage. Progress and Prospects*. New York: unicef. www.unicef.org/media/files/Child_Marriage_Report_7_17_ LR.pdf

————. 2017. *Ending Child Marriage in India*. New Delhi: UNICEF India.

USAID. 2005. *Ending Child Marriage and Meeting the Needs of Married Children. The USAID Vision for Action*. Washington, DC: USAID. www.pdf.usaid.gov/pdf_docs/pdacu300.pdf

WHO. 1993. *The Health of Young People. A Challenge and a Promise.* Geneva: WHO.

———. 2006. *Married Adolescents. No Place for Safety.* Geneva: WHO.

———. 2011. 'The Sexual and Reproductive Health of Younger Adolescents: Research Issues in Developing Countries'. Background paper for a consultation. Geneva: World Health Organization. http://www.who.int/reproductivehealth/publications/adolescence/rhr_11_15/en/index.html

———. 2012. *Adolescent Sexual and Reproductive Health. Global Research Priorities.* Geneva: WHO.

World Bank. 2004. *Attaining the Millennium Development Goals in India. How Likely and What Will It Take to Reduce Infant Mortality, Child Malnutrition, Gender Disparities and Hunger- Poverty to Increase School Enrollment and Completion?* Washington, DC: World Bank/ Human Development Unit. https://openknowledge.worldbank.org/bitstream/handle/10986/8627/318460rev.pdf?sequence=1

———. 2007. *World Development Report. The Next Generation.* Washington, DC: World Bank. http://www-wds.worldbank.org/external/default/WDSContentServer/IW3P/IB/2006/09/13/000112742_200 60913111024/Rendered/PDF/359990WDR0complete.pdf

———. 2014. *Understanding the Economic Costs of Child Marriage.* Washington, DC: World Bank. www.worldbank.org/en/topic/education/brief/understanding-the-economic-impacts-of-child-marriage

———. 2017. *World Development Report 2017. Governance and the Law.* Washington, D.C.: World Bank.

World Health Assembly. 2012. *Early Marriages, Adolescent and Young Pregnancies.* Geneva; WHO; http://apps.who.int/gb/ebwha/pdf_files/WHA65/A65_13-en.pdf

Yadav, K. P. 2006. *Child Marriage in India.* New Delhi: Adhyayan Publ.

Young Lives 2017. *Incidence of Child Marriage. New Findings Form the 2011 Census of India.* Policy Brief 32. Oxford: Young Lives.

———. 2013. *Delivering the MDGs in India. Targeting Children's Nutrition and Education.* India Policy Brief No. 3 New Delhi: Young Lives; http://www.younglives-india.org/files/policy-papers/mdgs-targeting-children-nutrition-and-education

4

Love and Law: Understanding Child Marriages in Rural West Bengal

Ishita Chowdhury and Utsarjana Mutsuddi

THE SOCIAL REFORM movement in nineteenth-century Bengal raised a number of questions regarding the marriage system in India, especially with respect to Hindus. In these discussions, child marriage was identified as a widespread social problem, which needed to be eliminated. There was by no means a consensus on this. The so-called orthodox opinion in the province, and later 'cultural nationalists', upheld the virtues of child marriage, arguing that it uniquely fitted in with Hindu customs and values. Over time, the spread of education raised the age of marriage for women of the higher castes and middle classes, especially in urban India. Paradoxically, communities, which had previously been tolerant of adult marriage, if not actively encouraging such practices, began to give their women in marriage at progressively younger ages. By the time of independence in 1947, child marriage was becoming a problem associated with the 'rural poor'. In fact, however, the spread and extent of child marriage even today indicates that it is in practice among the urban as well

as the rural poor. Despite repeated attempts at legislative interventions, the rate of child marriage in India is still 27 percent,
with the country ranking sixth in child marriage across the
world. At present, within India, West Bengal has the highest
rate of child marriage, despite its well-deserved reputation as
a pioneer in social reform in the nineteenth century. We will
address some of the questions that arise from the dissonance
between law and practice, which allows the persistence of the
custom: On the one hand, it has been given the status of a 'tradition' bound in religious and community identity; on the other,
there is a general and growing consensus that early marriage is
pernicious both for the youth or adolescents on whom it is
imposed and for society at large.

The attempts to outlaw child marriage began in the colonial
period. After independence, a series of laws and schemes
have been formulated to tackle this 'menace'. The first legal
intervention was in 1891; the attempt by the colonial state to
enact an age of consent law caused considerable controversy
and is regarded as the beginning of what Tanika Sarkar terms
'cultural nationalism'. She has drawn our attention to ways
in which the question of child marriage became implicated in
colonial law (Sarkar 2001). The next major intervention was
the law restraining child marriages passed in 1929, this time
on Indian initiative. The Child Marriage Restraint Act is also
known as Sarda Act after Har Bilas Sarda, who championed
this controversial legislation. It prohibited marriages of girls
below the age of 15 years and of boys below the age of 18. Later,
in 1949, an amendment to this Act was introduced according
to which the minimum age of marriage for girls became 15
years and the minimum age of marriage for boys was raised
to 20 years.[1]

The law remained in force till 1978, when it was amended
and the marriageable age for girls was raised to 18 years
and for boys to 21 years. In 2006, the old law was repealed and
the focus was shifted from mere restraining of child marriages

to that of prohibition. The new law, known as Prohibition of Child Marriage Act 2006 (PCMA), has far stricter measures than earlier. Even so, the law has failed to curb child marriage. The law retains the minimum age for marriage of women as 18 years and for men as 21 years. Census 2011 reveals that one out of every three girls is married before she reaches the legal minimum age of 18 years. In fact, more properly 'child' marriage (or 'infant' marriage as it was termed in colonial India) shows a stubborn persistence: 78.5 lakh girls (2.3 percent of all women or girls who were ever married or were married in 2011) were married before 10 years. The Census data also show that 91 percent of all married women were married by the age of 25 years. The state of West Bengal (as earlier mentioned, which is now at number one in the incidence of child marriage) ranked among the top four states in 2007–08, according to the National Family Health Survey (NFHS). A later NFHS (2015–16) reveals that the child marriage rate is still 40.7 percent in West Bengal with 46.3 percent in rural areas.

Let us try to understand the application of PCMA in rural West Bengal from material collected through a field survey.[2] We have found considerable awareness about the legal age for marriage among rural communities and, equally, a persistent attempt to circumvent the law. We focus on discrepancies between law and custom, and also the confusion regarding contrary provisions in personal laws. Moreover, the assumption in most laws against child marriage is that the 'child' is given in marriage by parents/guardians. But it is also found that young people (at ages below the legal minimum for marriage) also exercise their agency in this matter, often eloping against the wishes of parents. In West Bengal, such elopements seem to be accepted and lead to formal marriage, which is a contrast to North India, where elopements seem to invite violent sanctions from family and community. Finally, an analysis is offered on the Kanyashree Prakalpa in West Bengal and its effectiveness in curbing child marriages (see also Chapters 2 and 8).

THE LEGAL FRAMEWORK

In 1927, Rai Sahib Har Bilas Sarda introduced the Hindu Child Marriage Bill. He defended his Bill in terms of its many benefits for women and he appealed to the growing nationalist movement in the country, arguing that the eradication of such an evil was a precursor to freedom. Sarda's bill was referred to a Select Committee, which suggested that it be changed from Hindu Child Marriage Bill to Child Marriage Restraint Bill (henceforth CMRA) and be applicable to all communities. They further recommended that the punishment for an infraction of the law be imprisonment or a fine, that the minimum ages be 18 for men and 14 for women. In the assembly, 77 persons voted in favour of it and only 14 voted against it, causing it to come into effect from 1930.

CMRA did not declare child marriages to be illegal or invalid; it did not say anything about the status of marriage or the rights of the parties once they were married; rather, it laid down simple punishments like imprisonment of 3 months and/or fine of ₹1,000 if the Act was violated. The data on marriage in the Census of 1931 suggests that the Act was a failure. The number of wives under 15 increased from 8.5 million to 12 million and husbands under the age of 15 also rose from 3 million to more than 5 million. The number of wives under the age of five had quadrupled. Historians have attributed this sudden escalation to an attempt by parents to marry off young children before CMRA came into effect (Ghosh 2011). Until its amendment in 1978, the CMRA had no discernible impact on marital behaviour. The persistence of child marriage in India showed that neither law nor 'development' was very effective in a wholesale raising of the age of marriage. It was felt, increasingly, that more concerted action from the state was necessary; moreover, a number of social ills were attributed to child marriage. For instance, the gender gap in health and education were felt to be because of child marriage. Need for a much stronger law was felt and thus, in 2006, a new law was passed, which sought to 'prohibit' child marriages rather than merely 'restrain'. The Prohibition of Child Marriage Act 2006 (henceforth referred to as PCMA) came into force on 11 January 2007 and was implemented in West Bengal in December 2008.

The features of this law have already been discussed in some detail by Graner (Chapter 3). To recapitulate briefly for the discussion to follow:

(a) The minimum age for marriage for men and women continues to be 21 and 18, respectively.

(b) The Act has for the first time declared child marriage voidable. Despite subsequent changes, a child marriage is not void by default. A contracting party who was a 'child' at the time of the marriage has the option to nullify the marriage within 2 years of attaining majority. There is a provision for the return of all valuables, money, ornaments, and gifts made in marriage upon nullity. According to Section 12, a marriage is null and void if there is force or deceit or trafficking involved in the marriage.

(c) The Act allows for maintenance from the husband or his parents for the girl till her remarriage. The court may also make a suitable provision for her residence until her remarriage. As all children born from the marriage are declared legitimate, the Act further allows for appropriate orders for custody of children from such marriages.

(d) All the punishments for contracting a child marriage have been enhanced. The punishment for a man over 18 years of age is rigorous imprisonment up to two years or with a fine up to ₹100,000 or both. A similar punishment is prescribed for anyone who performs, conducts, directs, or abets any child marriage. The same punishment is also prescribed for anyone who solemnizes or promotes such a marriage. No woman can however be punished with imprisonment. The Act also makes all offences cognizable and non-bailable.

(e) The Act further allows for injunctions to prohibit child marriages, including *ex parte* interim injunctions. It states that any child marriage solemnized in contravention of an injunction will be void and whoever disobeys such injunction shall be punished with imprisonment.

(f)   The Act lays emphasis on the prohibition of child marriages by providing for the appointment of Child Marriage Prohibition Officers (CMPO) by the state governments and gives powers to these officers to prevent such marriages.

The PCMA depends heavily on determining the age of the petitioners at the time of marriage. We will discuss the issue of age in general in a following section. However, it needs to be pointed out that the age question is complicated by a gamut of legislations that contradict and speak differently to each other. The inconsistent nature of personal laws confuses the legal age for marriage. Under the Hindu Marriage Act 1955, even though the law mentions that a girl should be 18 years and a boy 21 years before they are married, the question of age is absent in the several conditions laid down that make a marriage void. Thus, such marriages are not void under the Hindu Marriage Act, though punishable by PCMA. According to Muslim Personal Law (Shariat) 1937, puberty, presumed at 15 years, is considered the minimum age for marriage. In the Christian Marriage Act 1872, marriage of minors is not considered invalid as long as consent of the minor's guardian has been obtained. It is only under the Special Marriage Act 1954, that all marriages are declared void when either of the parties to the marriage has not attained the requisite age. Inconsistencies between the appropriate age for marriage between the personal laws and the PCMA have caused complications and led to varied judgements from courts. This impedes the implementation of PCMA.

TO LOVE OR NOT TO LOVE?

PCMA does not consider 'child' marriages void but voidable at the discretion of the contracting parties. It is only in circumstances detailed in Section 12 that child marriages are void. Thus, child marriages are still not illegal. While conducting our field survey we came across two types of marriages: marriages of self-choice (mostly elopements) and arranged marriages. In marriages of self-choice, it is highly unlikely that one of the parties will ask for annulment. Even in cases where one party or both regret the decision of an early marriage, they do not wish to annul their marriage on attaining adulthood. Some of our respondents, who have married by elopement at a young age (below the legal minimum) have later regretted the decision, not because they are unhappy at the marriage itself but because of opportunities lost in adolescence. The possibility of annulment of a marriage after it has taken place according to rites and customs is still not easily acceptable in rural society. If one or the other party is unhappy in the marriage, desertion and informal divorces are more common. We have found no case of a couple seeking annulment of a marriage on grounds of PCMA. In most cases, such regrets take the form of aspirations for the next generation; they would not like their children to get married early. They all agree that early marriage means responsibilities that one is not ready to take.

In case of arranged marriages where the elders take the decision, the girl may or may not be given a choice. Even if she exercises consent on her choice of partner, it must be sanctioned by the elders. In such cases, the very decision of marriage is a mix of parental initiative and social expectations. In such cases, the revocation of the marriage is even more difficult. Few child brides attain autonomy immediately upon adulthood. Their ability to challenge a child marriage or seek its annulment depends on the support of the natal family. The same elders, who had instituted the child marriage, may prevent their choice of exercising the provisions of the PCMA to annul the marriage.

In our survey in six rural districts of West Bengal we have found that the general attitude towards marriage both by the young and the old is that of a lifelong bond. Ghosh (2011) writes that the breakdown of a marriage in rural Bengal is regarded as a bad omen. When Kasturi Roy of Jalpaiguri was asked whether she was happy in her marriage she said, '*Nije biye korechi khusi hote hobe*' (I got married of my own accord; I have to be happy). When the interviewer asked her if she was having any difficulties she said, 'If one gets married once, can there be a second marriage? We are women!'[3] For some of our respondents, the question of whether she was happy in her marriage was incomprehensible. When Rabeya Bibi of Birbhum was asked whether she was happy in her marriage, she did not understand the question. She first replied, 'I do not understand what you mean.' The interviewer reframed her question and asked whether she liked the person chosen by her parents. Rabeya Bibi confirmed whether the interviewer was actually asking her about her choice in the marriage and finally answered, 'Yes, whatever parents choose must be to my liking.'

In the two cases cited above Kasturi exercised her agency to enter a marriage whereas Rabeya did not, she accepted the partner chosen for her by her parents. However, in both these instances, the women see no possibility of agency in determining exit from a marriage and marriage is seen as irrevocable. Nevertheless, men and women do revoke marriages, men much more than women. In the case of men, this often takes the form of returning the wife to her natal home without any formal processes of annulment or divorce. These are options not easily available to women, though in our field work we have found a total of 5 cases where wives have initiated divorce, mostly in response to domestic violence. The gendered expectations from women in marriages are so entrenched and deeply internalized that for Kasturi Roy it is axiomatic that once married she cannot marry again.

In marriage, whether by parental arrangement or by choice, consent is largely meaningless. By convention, lack of consent is associated more with arranged marriages, since the decision of the marriage as well as the choice of the partner is exercised by elders in the family. By contrast, in marriages by elopement, the parties do exercise some choice with respect to their partners. However, these too are circumscribed by the social context of the couple. Parental decision-making in marriage directly reflects the class, caste, religious and linguistic group endogamy practised in India. Amidst rising individual thought and expression, marriage has become a ground where the younger generations fight for their right of sexual agency and the older generation justifies early marriage as a way to avert the socially constructed idea of dishonour that comes with elopement. Scholars have already pointed out that the contrast of love and arranged marriage is overdrawn. In the rural context today, elopements leading to marriage are often institutionalization of adolescent sexual desires in a context where there is no possibility of sexual agency outside of marriage. The couple are forced to get married as it is only in marriage that they can fulfil their sexual desires. We see that it is after such marriages that the young have regretted a decision, which had seemed right at the time of elopement. They accept that society equals love to marriage and regards marriage as the only site for legitimate sexual intercourse. In such an equation, law and legal age of marriage play minor roles.

In our field research, respondents have reported increasing incidence of elopements. Aparna Bandyopadhyay (2011) defines elopement as 'the voluntary flight of heterosexual lovers away from their respective homes for purpose of marriage or cohabitation'. Elopements are looked down upon since such marriages challenge the kinship structure of the family. It places individual agency in direct opposition to family/community interests. In the context of present day Bengal, however, there is much greater acceptance of voluntary flight than in previous generations. Families on both sides are grudgingly accepting self-choice marriages. There are, of course, cases where the eloped couple are shunned by their families and have to live on their own but often they are accepted in the groom's family home. Thus, elopements are getting folded into the 'normal' marriage system of rural society.

In order to understand this phenomenon, we need to take a quick look at the context. Marriage, which is a decision that affects virtually all aspects of an individual's entire life from the time of occurrence, is traditionally determined by the choices of elders in the family. However, in the last few decades there has been a significant rise in the cultural portrayal of elopements. Popular culture is dominated by imagery related to love marriage, eloping couples and exercise of individual choice. This dichotomy between the traditional social structure and the popular cultural imagery has encouraged young people to take matters of love and marriage into their own hands. It is interesting to note that irrespective of the mode of marriage, that is, arranged or eloped, we found that, there was no significant difference in the daily lives of married men and women. There is virtually no difference in gender roles in marriage, whether by parental or self-choice. Thus the exercise of choice of partners seems like one single act of rebellion after which most aspects of life revert to the socially accepted idea of normal.

What needs to be addressed in this context is the necessity of the institution of marriage in the lives of young people. The questions asked by the young persons who are involved with the act of elopement centre around their need to get married in order to address their sexual desires. Most of them do not question the need for a lifelong and binding institution like marriage. The normalization of the idea that marriage is the only institution within which sexuality can be addressed leads the young to take the elopement decision. One must also keep in mind that sexuality is a taboo topic in India. It is neither spoken of nor is it open to inter-generational discussion, especially in rural areas. With a lack of safe spaces to address or express sexuality as an adolescent, young people are often forced to turn to the only available option, which is early marriage. This problem persists in both Hindu and Muslim communities. In both these communities (which constitute 96 percent of our total collected cases) sexuality expressed outside the institution of marriage is not just looked down upon but even criminalized. If young people are caught in a pre-marital/non-marital sexual act, honour killings may follow. There is no socially acceptable option for young people other than early marriage.

Thus, the legal ban on early marriage does not address the root of the entire problem. One more important consideration in this context is the value put on virginity in the context of marriage. In rural society, there is still great premium placed on female chastity and virginity. The protection of a girl's virginity is her own responsibility as well as that of her natal family. The loss of virginity is supposed to be followed by marriage. Otherwise, drastic consequences may follow, such as slut-shaming to honour killing. However, popular culture often portrays the pursuit of a woman and the winning of her heart/submission to a man's desires, as the ultimate goal of young men in love. This sharp differentiation between how men and women are supposed to approach love creates a lot of tension in the minds of young people. They believe, moreover, that marrying according their own choice is a good alternative to living the life that one's parents choose for them. Arranged marriages do not carry the same promise of passion that is fulfilled by a love marriage/elopement. The creation of such easy binaries prevents young people from challenging the institution of marriage. In both arranged marriages and elopements, passion, desire and sexuality seek fulfilment in marriage. There is no possibility of sexual fulfillment outside of marriage. This results in women being given only an illusion of (self-)choice.

In our research, one of the most common reasons that parents of underage brides and grooms have given for early marriage is the fear of elopement and dishonour to the family. Many parents say that the rise of media, communication and mobile phones is allowing young people to choose for themselves against the wishes of their elders. There are cases, where the parents try not to marry off their children early, since they are aware of PCMA, but the children themselves choose to elope and get married. For example, we have the case of Jayanti Roy, whose mother could not stop her underage daughter from getting married. Sumona Das, the mother of another underage bride, had strong opinions against early marriage but could not stop her daughter running away. She was well aware of the law that prohibits early marriage but she found herself helpless when her daughter chose to get married on her own. She said to us, 'You might be discussing this law in public but the problem is that even though the parents are well aware of the setbacks of early marriage and are unwilling to give children in marriage, the children themselves are taking these decisions into their own hands and are going through with them. If I had given her in marriage, would I have done so this early? Of course not.' It is interesting to note that there was discouragement at school as well. The girl stopped going to school after marriage for fear of being chastised by her strict teacher.

In India, adolescent sexuality is hardly ever discussed outside the parameters of marriage. While the law has criminalized 'child' marriage, it is perhaps too blunt an instrument for the consideration of adolescent sexuality. Earlier, marriage was a way to harness the sexuality of young people and their labour. The law addresses 'child marriage' from within a developmentalist framework, without any consideration for social imperatives of adolescent sexuality. We next discuss two forms of sexual/cohabitation practices we found in the course of our field research, which are at opposite end of the spectrum of choice.

In our survey, we found the practice of *shanga* among adivasis in Purulia and Birbhum. Available evidence from the late nineteenth and early twentieth centuries shows that this term was used to describe a range of second or secondary marriages. In some communities, it was used to describe widow remarriages. At present, shanga involves couples eloping with or without social approval and living together for a period of time (up to one year in some cases) before the marriage is solemnized. This practice has wide social acceptance. It leaves the young people with an option to move out of the cohabitation situation if they feel it is not working. As opposed to the binding nature of marriage, this form of cohabitation allows space for sexual agency to young people.

Nibarun Chandra Murmu and his shanga partner are not married yet. They are staying together for the last few months and will marry after one year. If the wife becomes pregnant they will wait until the child is born since if he marries the pregnant partner he might inadvertently end up marrying the child in her womb as well. Bhabani Soren was in shanga with her husband for about a year before getting married. Their parents did not support the decision at first but eventually accepted it. While we were told by many of our respondents that this is a commonly accepted practice, it is interesting to note that it is widespread only among the ST population in some parts of Purulia and Birbhum. We did not encounter the practice or the term in the other five districts.

In sharp contrast to the culture of tolerance represented in the shanga, we also found two cases of non-consenting brides, who were forced to get married against their own wishes. In both cases, the marriages were passed off as elopements because even the family did not have any say in the matter. Members of the village community to whom we spoke described the marriage as an elopement, even though the girl was actually forced into it.

The first case is of Chumki Hembrom of Purulia. The man, who is now her husband, asked her to go to Mumbai with him for work. Seeing a lucrative opportunity, she agreed. However, after six months of cohabitation she returned home. The family refused to share details regarding the reasons behind this decision. After her return, she was forced to marry him, since she had already lived with him and in the eyes of society not marrying him would bring dishonour to the family. This is a case where a young girl's exercise of agency led her into a relationship in which she subsequently found herself trapped.

What this tells us is that while young girls have some scope to enter relationships of their choice, they have less agency to exit them. The second and the more striking case is of Nushrat Khatun from Murshidabad. In both these cases, the consent and agency of the young girl was compromised.

When Nushrat was 15 years old, she was kidnapped on her way back from school by a man who used to stalk her at school every day. He came on a bike, saw her outside her house and picked her up. He raped her that night and returned her to her father saying that the deed had been done and the only honourable way to deal with the situation was to arrange a marriage. The unwilling father had no choice but to relent. He even had to pay ₹50,000 as dowry. All was well for the first few months while the boy's father still lived. After his death, the husband got into bad terms with his own brother and started taking out his anger on the wife. One day Nushrat's brother-in-law helped her escape. The girl returned to her father's home. The husband came around in a few days and took her back. The domestic violence continued. Soon after the birth of her daughter, the situation became dire and she was forced to leave his home and return to her parents, where we interviewed her. She is currently fighting for divorce and is trying to get back the ₹50,000 that was given at the time of marriage as her dowry.

One very important point to note is the role of the school in the story of child marriage. PCMA allows for a friend or relative or well-wisher to lodge a complaint against an early marriage. For eloping couples the school becomes a space to be avoided at all costs. The transformation of a space from one of safety to one that challenges personal autonomy is extremely significant. There could be more (and innovative) thinking about what roles schools can play in elopements. The school serves as a space where awareness regarding early marriage is created among students and teachers often argue that the existence of married students in their rolls act as a bad influence. The closing of school doors to child brides merely reconfirms the ill-effects of child marriage. Rather, schools should make provisions for young girls who want to continue their education after marriage.

Even in the case of dowry, despite exercising individual choice, brides and their families are not spared the burden of dowry. Sunanda Das, a 16-year-old eloped bride from Birbhum, tells us, 'We are paying our dowry in instalments. Conventionally dowry is paid only in marriages where the amount is fixed keeping in mind the social standing of both families in a meeting prior to the wedding. Respondents in our Focus Group Discussions (FGDs) said that in some cases, very rarely though, parents prefer their children to elope since that saves on the costs related to marriage. However, sometimes, even in elopements, parents are forced to pay dowry. As in Sunanda's case, the elopement placed the bride in a more vulnerable position, since she had transgressed the norms of society. The groom's family was not willing to forego dowry.

The question of sexual consent in law complicates these social equations. According to Section 375 of the IPC (and the Criminal Amendment Act of 2013), the very act of sexual intercourse with a girl below the age of 18 years is defined as 'rape' and the woman's consent in such cases is irrelevant. Therefore, a girl below the age of 18 years cannot, even by her own consent, enter a sexual relationship without rendering her partner, the man, liable for rape. According to the recent highly celebrated SC judgment, sexual intercourse with one's wife below 18 years of age is to be considered as rape. This is a top-down approach and does not take into account social realities. This judgment may seem beneficial to women but it denies sexual autonomy to the young by criminalizing all forms of sexual activity. Moreover, this judgment does not really align with the PCMA. Since child marriages are not void by definition, does this mean that the young can get married but have to refrain from any form of sexual activity till the girl turns 18 years of age? At one level, the law continues to extend tolerance for child marriages. The young are caught up in the muddle of various complex and contradictory laws, which can be a potent weapon in the hands of parents/guardians who wish to control or proscribe adolescent sexuality. There are curious contradictions of love, sex and marriage within these two Acts. It places the adolescent girl between the ages of 15 to 18 in a curious limbo; she can be married but must refrain from sex.

AGE IS JUST A NUMBER

Indian legislation on child marriages with a focus on age has a colonial history. The very definition of 'child' in law is based upon digital age. PCMA is not outside this framework; it relies heavily on the determination of digital age for it to be effective (see Chapter 2). Much has been written about the reconstruction of time in modernity. The introduction of linear time in industrial capitalism in contrast with the cyclical agricultural time determined by the rhythm of seasons has been discussed in the context of Europe as well as in societies where economic development was late and uneven. In the Indian context, the slow rate of urbanization has meant that rural peasant societies have not been fully integrated into systems of linear chronologies. The delay in universalization of birth/death registration has contributed further to the survival of pre-industrial notions of time. In this context, digital age is often a supposition rather than a 'fact' and sits uneasily with legal age; the enforcement of laws relating to children has repeatedly faced this difficulty.

We found during our field work that most respondents do not give much importance to digital age. There is rather a notion of a 'stage' in life. There are children, the young, middle-aged and the old. Asked specifically about age in years, most conversations were inexact: *'Oi koto ar hobe'* (oh, how much will it be?), *'andaj moto ekta likhe daona'* (write something from your estimation). Field workers had to calculate the age of the respondent from events in their lives such as school-leaving, marriage, childbirth and/or family or public events. Anima Byadh from Jalpaiguri, when asked about her present age, said, 'I have turned around 18, I think.' One of her relatives said she was older, since she had been married for six years and her child was already 5 years. To this Anima said, 'Then it must be so.' Kalpana Hembrom from Birbhum has no voter's card or any proof of her age. Finally, the interviewer asked her to give an estimated age.

In their survey, UNICEF (2013) found the extent of child marriages is difficult to gauge, especially in rural areas, in the absence of birth and marriage registrations. NFHS 2005–06 shows that birth registration (for under 5 years) in West Bengal is 75.8 percent and in rural areas 73.02 percent. In our field work, we found that even if the respondents had a birth certificate, most of them were fradulent. Prabal Pal, who works in the Namkhana Registration Office in South 24-Parganas, explained that parents simply change their minor daughter's date of birth to legalize the marriage. More recently, in Meerut, a girl of not more than eleven years was being married off by her parents, by faking her aadhaar card wherein her age was stated to be nearly eighteen. Respondents gave an age when asked, but this did not match with their age in the documents. This is probably why Koyel Roy of Jalpaiguri said, 'It is difficult to say our original age'. Her daughter-in-law gave a prompt reply when asked, saying that she was 20 years, but a few minutes later, spoke of herself as 21 years.

Thus, digital age does not determine the sense of self among our poor, rural respondents in the same way as among the middle classes in urban societies. Rather, age is a social perception. If a woman has got recently married, she is young but not a child. If a woman has married off her daughter, she is middle-aged. From these, a supposition of age in years is inferred. Biman Maitro of Jalpaiguri attributes this to lack of education. They cannot make the calculations, many think. When we tried to probe further for an exact age rather than an age-range, most people tried to fish out documentary proof. This is because we understood that exact age is not really required in their everyday lives or their personal affairs. Thus, even those who have an exact age documented are unable to remember their age.

Focus Group Discussion (FGD) participants were asked about the importance of age, some participants claimed that they need their exact age only in official matters, such as NREGA enrolment, or for work in SHG groups, or when visiting a doctor. It was surprising that no one spoke of the need to mention age during marriage registration. This is, of course, because very few marriages are registered or if they are, they are signed on the basis of a supposed age rather than an exact 'legal' age supported by documentary proof. Thus, 90 percent of our respondents' marriages are not registered. Muslim marriages are usually registered, according to their personal law. In the case of Hindus, who have registered early marriage, do so by falsifying their age. Srabonti Das confessed that her father got her marriage registered even though she was not 18 years at that time. She mentioned that this falsification was expensive. The loopholes in administration often nullify intentions of law. Thus, the usual rhetoric of 'awareness' does not quite support our field experience. Most respondents, nearly all, were aware of PCMA and its provisions. There is not only the usual disregard for a law which does not match social practice, but active attempts to circumvent its provisions by using the corrupt machineries of state.

In rural society, the whole question of an exact age at marriage is something of a puzzle. It is obvious when a girl becomes marriageable, and the logic of this is driven by bodily changes of puberty. The age in years follows the logic of the body rather than in the reverse. No one feels the need to keep track of actual age. Clearly, this follows the general social connection made between marriage and reproductive sexuality. Thus, social and parental perceptions determine the appropriate age of marriage of daughters. Participants in our study emphasized factors like puberty, sexual maturity, dropping out of school due to disinterest, physical and mental maturity of individuals, family contexts, economic independence, especially of boys, maturity of girls in terms of readiness to handle familial responsibilities, anything but age as appropriate time for marriage.

If we look at the Table 4.1 we see that most girls in all six districts are getting married between the ages of 16–17 years followed by the age-range of 14–15 years. The numbers for marriages under 14 years is almost negligible, indicating that early (or adolescent) rather than child marriage is more in vogue. The average age for puberty among girls in our survey is 13 years. Once a girl attains puberty she is considered ready for marriage, which is why girls are getting married from 14 years on, whether by themselves or as arranged by parents. Along with the attainment for puberty, dropping out from school plays an important role in the determination of a marriageable age for girls. According to the survey, the maximum level of educational attainment is till Class 10, with only 10.7 percent of girls enrolling in higher secondary education and 2.4 percent of girls in college. This is perhaps because girls receive free and compulsory education under Sarva Shiksha Abhijan till Class 8. In most cases, girls spend a maximum of another two years in school after which they drop out. Once a post-pubertal girl drops out of school, parents fear to keep her at home in case she becomes a target for sexual predators (TISS 2015).[4] One of our respondents

TABLE 4.1: Age at Marriage of 275 Respondents from Six Districts (rural)

Age groups	Underage Marriages						Total
	South 24-Parganas	Birbhum	Jalpaiguri	Purba Medinipur	Murshi-dabad	Purulia	
Below 14 years	2	0	3	1	8	2	16
14–15 years	16	7	9	15	14	11	72
16–17 years	26	10	40	54	12	4	146
18 years and above	1	7	14	3	8	8	41
Total	45	24	66	73	42	25	275

Data collected from field survey.

said, 'Keeping a daughter is a nuisance'. She got her daughter married before the legal age because she was beautiful and a number of suitors would queue before their home every day.

Thus, age in actual figures does not determine marriageability. It is other factors that influence the marriage decision. The legal age as prescribed by the PCMA has as yet no social resonance. Moreover, the PCMA requires the petitioners to file for annulment within two years of attaining adulthood; the same problems attend the question of attaining legal adulthood. If actual age in years is vague or fuzzy, the entitlement to file a petition for annulment is also difficult to establish. The proof of age is one of the greatest difficulties in the Indian court room. You can neither prove you were a child when you were married, nor that you are now an adult of not more than 20 years (or 23 years if you are a man) seeking annulment. It becomes difficult to determine whether a marriage is underage or within the legal age. For if one says that she got married at 17+or 18 years, the marriage is on the borderline of illegality. Since the whole success and applicability of the PCMA rests on the determination of one's age, the success of the Act depends on a much larger question, the universalization of the Registration of Birth and Death Act 1969. The question of compulsory marriage registration remains as fuzzy as the determination of age.

PERSISTENCE OF CHILD MARRIAGE: RESPONSES FROM THE FIELD

In the previous sections we discussed the limitations of PCMA. We will now explore the responses to PCMA from our fieldwork and try to understand the subjective reasons why even those who are aware of the provisions of PCMA take marriage decisions contrary to the law. Most respondents or other members of the household knew about the existence of PCMA; it was evident from their responses to our questions. Many were afraid that the truth would get them arrested.

We had to convince them that the interview would be used purely for academic purposes and that we would not report their case. Sumona Das's mother from South 24-Parganas kept saying, 'Both mother and daughter will be put in jail.' While conducting our survey in Jalpaiguri, particularly in Churabhandar, an arrest was made for a child marriage, this had alerted all the villagers in the area, so when we went to conduct our interview most of our respondents were very cautious. They all gave the age of marriage as 18 years for girls and 21 years for boys; quite clearly this was not always the truth.

We have tried to understand the reasons for underage marriages even when respondents and their parents knew that it was 'prohibited'. We have tried to group these responses into three for the sake of convenience. It must be noted that the three different responses are not exclusive but overlapping and one does not mean that the others are not applicable in any particular case.

The first could be described as a pragmatic reason, what we call, 'a good groom at the wrong time'. The premise is that the ultimate destination for a daughter is to get married. The compulsion of marriage, the dowry system and poverty combine in a vicious logic to prompt poor parents of daughters to flout law and contravene policy to give their daughters in marriage before 18 years, sometimes considerably before that age.

Konkona Mondol feels. 'Since I have had a daughter, I will have to get her married, now or a year later or two years later'. One of our respondents at the FGD in South 24-Parganas said, 'If I die without getting my daughter married? Who will look after her? If I do not get her married I will feel I have not done my duty, only if I can get her married will I be at peace.' It is a parental obligation to get one's daughter married. The logic of parental decision-making is that a good groom in hand is the best time for marriage. Rima Das was married at the age of 17 because the groom was very good. A 'good' groom for poor parents is one with some earnings and with low dowry demand. In Rima's case, a good groom who demanded a dowry of only rupees one lakh was not to be missed. Chandrima Parua from South 24-Parganas has three daughters; the eldest was married at the age of 14 and another one at 17; the third daughter, who is currently doing her higher secondary, has not been married off yet as she is in a relationship with a boy. The parents have accepted the boy because he is a good groom, as he is studying for an M.Sc and has good job prospects. Konkona (South 24-Parganas) said: 'If a good proposal comes one needs to get married. Girls are married based on the premise that a good proposal may not come later.' Parents prefer their daughters to be married to a good groom if one comes their way rather than allow them to pursue their studies or, for that matter, a job. Kusum and Jamini spoke of two unmarried girls aged 25 and 30 in their neighbourhood, who were currently working. The neighbours were pressurizing the parents to marry off their daughters to avoid gossip. Marriage, therefore, is not merely a matter of personal choice or preference but is considered to be a sacrament, a sacred duty of parents, and a social necessity to control women's sexuality. Parents face enormous social pressure to get their daughters married soon after puberty, whatever the legal age. A common term for daughters in North India is '*parayadhan*', wealth for/of others; in Bengal, they are not '*ghore rakhar jinish*' (to be kept in the house). Thus, as soon as a good proposal comes their way, parents prefer to get their daughters married. They fear that if they let go of one opportunity, another one may not come soon and they will be branded as careless parents or their daughter may dishonour them by sexual profligacy.

The second set of reasons is economic. As an institution, marriage involves economic transactions of various sorts, including monetary gifts such as dowry. Parents view the daughter as an economic burden that is to be transferred to the marital family. The marital family, however, asks for dowry to bear this burden. For families that are struggling with poverty, marriage decisions are influenced by dowry considerations. Even when there is no exorbitant dowry demand, it is expected that the girl is not sent empty-handed to her marital home. Nabanita Rana wants to get her daughter married; now currently in the second year of graduation. Her daughter wants to continue her studies but Nabanita fears that she might have to spend a lot of money if marriage is deferred. She tries to reason with her daughter by saying that since she is young and she can work hard and repay the loans that she will have to take for the dowry and wedding expenses. As she grows older, it will be more difficult for her.

The labour wives put into the maintenance of the family and the home is unpaid. In Bengal there is a famous phrase, *gharer lakshmi*, which translates into 'the wealth of the home'. A woman is considered to be the wealth of her household due to the unpaid labour she puts into her household. Yet, this is in relation only to a married woman and her marital home. There is not the same approach to the labour of a girl child in her natal home.[5] As a result, parents do not value the education of a girl child; they are taken out from school when the family faces an economic crisis. Moreover, since girls are reared to be wives and mothers, parents prefer that daughters excel in household chores, which will earn them legitimacy and appreciation in their marital family. Therefore, it is an easy decision to take daughters out of school in order to be married.

The third set of reasons are to do with control over sexuality. As already mentioned, a daughter's sexuality is the primary locus of a family's honour (Chakravarti 2005). Parents are responsible for protecting the daughter's virginity and chastity. The attitude towards sexuality is generally negative, but it is especially so with regard to adolescent sexuality. Parents engage in strict surveillance of their daughters (TISS report 2015). This creates the ground for pre-emptive child marriages. Out of fear that their daughters will elope and taint 'family honour', parents sometimes get their daughters married the moment they see them getting friendly with any boy. Sharmishta Byapari from Jalpaiguri has a daughter, who is currently studying; when asked whether she would get her daughter married even if she gets a job she replied:

> If my daughter stays good then I may keep her but if she listens to others keeping her will not be possible.... There is a likelihood that she may get friendly with boys. I may be dishonoured. No parents want to be dishonoured, it's better to get her married and be safe than face the possibility of being dishonoured. This is what happens in the house of the poor, is it not?

Parents thus invoke the ideal of 'honour' to condition women into appropriate behaviour, or shame their inappropriate behaviour.

In a research conducted by TISS (2015), it was pointed out that marriage was often seen as a punishment and a means of disciplining 'bad' girls, who had engaged in relationships with boys. In our field survey too, we came across parents telling us that their got their daughters married as she was doing a lot of *badmashi* (mischief). When Shatadru Haldar was asked why he had married off his elder daughter who was just studying in Class 9, he replied: 'I married my elder daughter as she was getting mischievous . . . girls in school are getting so mischievous nowadays. They gossip here and there, then they are calling this one up or that one . . . got her married before I could be dishonoured. Once dishonoured, you are talked about which I do not like.' In both cases parents feared that their social standing would be lowered by daughters running away. Parents therefore have no regard for the PCMA in such situations, they are more cautious of their family honour.

Increasingly, however, parents take a pragmatic view of 'love' if despite their surveillance, love happens. Once a daughter has eloped, they accept the match, either after the fact of the marriage or by organizing a social function. In many cases, weddings that followed elopements included all the features of arranged marriages including dowry payments. However, parents are always nervous about the possibility of elopement. They prefer to keep marriage decisions in their own hands; thus, the logic of early marriage is often pre-emptive. Parents want to marry off a daughter before she falls in love and desires to exercise control over her own marriage decision. This argument appeals to the rural community. Thus, overall, despite awareness of the legal prohibition, child marriage is widely condoned.

It is often said that in India marriage involves the whole family. Feminist scholars have argued that this is a euphemism for denial of consent in marriage to women. Our research shows that in rural society it is still common for parents to take all crucial decisions regarding marriage of daughters (and also sons) and any attempt by the young to try to exercise choice in partners and/or wedding rituals and ceremonies is frowned upon. However, there is change. Most respondents have reported an increase in 'love marriages' and elopements and there is greater acceptance of such marriages by parents. For some parents, this is a reluctant acceptance. In rural society, by and large, there is simultaneously condemnation and a pragmatic acceptance. Three varieties of responses may be noted: first, parents accept an elopement as a fait accompli and arrange what is called a 'social marriage', that is, with all relevant rituals and ceremonies, including often dowry; second, poor parents (of daughters) accept elopements as a means of avoiding the high costs of marriage/wedding or accept marriage as the most honourable solution to an elopement, even if they are unhappy and reluctant; and third, parents, who do not accept an elopement marriage.

Table 4.2 sets out the responses we received regarding the mode of marriage. In a few cases, we did not receive adequate detail about the mode of marriage to classify accurately. We have left out these responses. In all the interviews marriages sanctioned by parents, arranged by middlemen or

TABLE 4.2: Modes of Marriage among 323 Respondents in 7 Districts

	South 24-Parganas	Birbhum	Jalpaiguri	Purba Medinipur	Murshidabad	Purulia	Kolkata	Total
Love	3	6	24	18	2	4	26	83
Eloped	9	3	0	10	0	6	0	28
Arranged	31	21	40	30	33	17	36	208
Kidnapped	0	0	0	0	1	0	0	1
Matrimonial websites	0	0	0	0	0	0	3	3
Total	43	30	64	58	36	27	65	323

through know sources is seen as *bhalo bhabe biye kora* (marriage by proper means). This is 'Arranged Marriage'. The contrast is marriage by elopement which displeases the parents, causing them to be a topic of discussion. Parents, fearing that their 'honour' has been compromised, may sever ties with the couple, but this is becoming increasingly rare. In most cases, there is resignation and acceptance of such marriages. In many cases, the parents arrange a social marriage for the couple. This we have classified as 'Love Marriage'. In South 24-Parganas, Supriya Das eloped and married at the age of 15. Her mother said: 'She ran away . . . yet as parents we brought her home and performed a proper ceremony since she has already got married and there was nothing more to be done.'

It is interesting that such an attitude towards elopement in our field study is in stark contrast to the attitudes towards elopement in the places like Haryana and Delhi. Chowdhry (2011) found in rural Haryana that marriage without consent of parents even if within the community is not accepted as marriage but is considered *badmashi*. Parents usually have nothing to do with it. Since such marriages are not considered to be a valid marriage, parents try to separate the couple. According to Chakravarti (2005), there are a series of steps that lead to the criminalization of such marriages in North India. In such criminalization of elopements, the state stands as the overarching patriarch.

We have not found such criminalizing and delegitimizing of marriages in our survey areas. Even when parents have not accepted an elopement marriage, the state is not involved. None of the 28 elopement cases (Table 4.2) were reported to the police. Parents accepted the couple; indeed, in one case, parents tried to prevent the marriage from breaking down. Shikha Mondal got married by her own choice to a local youth of whom her parents did not approve. However, since she had already got married the parents accepted it. After a few months, Shikha's husband and in-laws started to torture her; sometimes it was so serious that she needed medical care and she was sent to her natal home to recover. Each time her parents nursed her and sent her back to her marital home, her parents even offered her in-laws money to pacify them but to no avail. After three such incidents, she finally left him. Thus, even though the parents may have been displeased at their daughter's choice of partner, once married, they did not revoke it or advise the daughter to abandon the marriage. At times, parents expect their daughters to remain in a self-chosen marriage even if they wish to exit. Though parents have a strong notion of 'honour', this does not necessarily involve violence. Though there is tension between the couple and their parents, it does not take the form of violence. The notion of 'honour' is invoked before the daughter elopes, but once she does, parents along with the society accept the marriage.

STATE INTERVENTIONS: KANYASHREE PRAKALPA

Government schemes to address the issue of child marriages have mostly been indirect. Keeping girls in school is seen as a measure to curb child marriages. It is also argued that education will make girls economically independent. However, economic independence can only be achieved when there are adequate opportunities for girls to be employed. In rural areas, lack of proper schools or absence of protection for girls when they go out of the home for education or employment are often used as an excuse to get them married off early.[6] To address these issues and to incentivize parents of girls to defer marriage, there have been a number of schemes floated in different states of India. However, there were no such governmental efforts in West Bengal until Mamata Banerjee introduced the Kanyashree Prakalpa.[7]

When this study was conducted Kanyashree Prakalpa was extending economic support to girls between the ages of 13–19 and studying between the classes of 8–12 as this was when most girls dropped out. The scheme was available to families with an annual income of ₹1.2 lakhs. The scholarship was given at two tiers. In K1, a sum of ₹750 was given annually to unmarried girls enrolled in any government-recognized educational or vocational institution between ages 13–18 and in K2, an annual sum of ₹25,000 was given to girls who were part of an educational or vocational institution and not been married below 18 years.[8]

In the six districts that we surveyed most of the households knew about the Kanyashree Prakalpa, though inadequately, which resulted in very few receiving benefits from the scheme. In South 24-Parganas only 5 household out of 42 availed Kanyashree benefits, In Birbhum only 5 household out of 30, In Jalpaiguri 5 out of 67 households and Purba Medinipur only 4 out of 65 households availed Kanyashree benefits. These were recipients of benefits according to the K1 of the scheme. Though at the time of the study, the website of Kanyashree Prakalpa claimed that the annual sum in K1 was ₹750, all the recipients of the survey received only ₹500. The increased sum was not received even though the decision to increase the annual sum of ₹500 to ₹750 was decided to be given from the 2015–16. We have found from our field that many are still not clear about the K2 benefits. In the case of Lipika Roy from Jalpaiguri, who got her daughter married before the legal age, she was not aware that her daughter was no longer eligible to receive the sum of ₹25,000. Most knew that if they fill a form in Class 7 they will get an annual income, but that if they refrained from marriage before 18 years a sum of ₹25,000 could be received was not understood by many.

There is also considerable unhappiness about the amount of money offered by Kanyashree. One respondent said that the amount was paltry and did not cover her daughters' education expenses. Many fill the form for the benefits but are too impatient to wait for the money. Suranjana Byadh had filled the form but could not avail its benefits as she got married in the meantime. In some cases, many have stated that they did not receive the money even after waiting for a year, while some have not been able to apply for the scheme because the forms were not available in the schools. Even in cases where the money was received, it got used for purposes other than for the education of the girl child. Biman Maitro from Jalpaiguri has five daughters, out of whom three have been married off and the other two are studying and are receiving Kanyashree benefits. The money received by one is being saved and a gold chain has been made with the other daughter's money. At our FGD in the South 24-Parganas, participants said that the money from Kanyashree Prakalpa was too low to be important. One participant said, 'For the sake of ₹25,000, one does not give up a marriage proposal where the groom earns ₹45,000!'

Table 4.3 shows, comparing the education of mothers and daughters, that while levels of education are increasing, they remain low. Most daughters have not been able to pursue their education beyond Classes 9–10. In South 24-Parganas we see while none of the mothers could, 14 daughters have been able to study beyond Class 8. But only one daughter has been able to pursue graduation. In the case of Birbhum, only 6 daughters have been able to study beyond Class 8 in relation to none of the mothers. However, only 8 daughters are studying between Classes 11–12 in relation to none of the mothers. None are pursuing graduation. In Jalpaiguri, 21 daughters have been able to study beyond Class 8 but only 3 daughters have been able to pursue their graduation, which is a great improvement in a generation but still a modest achievement. The results are similar in Purba Medinipur.

As has been mentioned earlier, most girls are getting married between the ages of 16–17 years, this age range being before they can claim K2 benefits from the Kanyashree scheme. Claiming K2 benefits with authentic documents

TABLE 4.3: Education

Daughter's Education

	0 – Illiterate	Class 1 – 5	Class 6 – 8	Class 9 – 10	Class 11 – 12	Graduation and above	Others	Literate but not specified	Not specified
South 24 Parganas	9	10	12	10	0	0	0	2	0
Birbhum	4	8	5	5	2	0	0	6	0
Jalpaiguri	14	16	11	13	6	0	0	4	3
Purba Medinipur	6	14	22	13	1	1	0	6	2
Kolkata	16	13	13	7	3	0	0	4	1
Murshidabad	7	6	17	4	3	0	2	4	0
Purulia	10	6	7	4	3	0	0	2	2
Total	**66**	**73**	**87**	**56**	**18**	**1**	**2**	**28**	**8**

Mother's Education

	0 – Illiterate	Class 1 – 5	Class 6 – 8	Class 9 – 10	Class 11 – 12	Graduation and above	Others	Literate but not specified	Not specified
South 24 Parganas	17	14	4	0	0	0	0	7	2
Birbhum	10	1	12	0	0	0	0	8	0
Jalpaiguri	36	15	5	3	0	0	0	8	0
Purba Medinipur	19	14	21	2	0	1	0	6	8
Kolkata	30	2	6	0	0	0	0	14	5
Murshidabad	19	2	11	2	0	0	2	7	4
Purulia	26	2	4	2	0	0	0	0	4
Total	**157**	**50**	**63**	**9**	**0**	**1**	**2**	**50**	**19**

means that the girl has been married after attaining the age of 18 years. Indeed, we did not see much change in the ages of marriage for mothers or daughters. Looking at this data, we cannot say that Kanyashree Prakalpa has had a major impact. A later study conducted by Sen and Dutta (2018), based on a survey of 1050 households from six blocks in three districts of West Bengal, Howrah, Murshidabad and Cooch Behar, found that though many girls were using the money received from K2 for marriage, a majority were using it to fund their higher education. The study found that though the programme appears to have succeeded, a substantial proportion of girls discontinue their education, thus not coming under the aegis of Kanyashree. Women are limited to very few badly paid jobs and possess limited opportunities for migration. In the absence of any employment opportunities, parents visualize a future for their daughters through marriage, rather than through education (Chowdhury 2018). The lack of such schemes for boys is also a reason for some parents to discontinue the education of their daughter. An equally qualified groom is not only difficult to find but also considered to be a greater expense, in terms of higher demands for dowry. To be successful, Kanyashree Prakalpa needs better linkage with jobs and economic opportunities, so that parents look beyond marriage for a secure future for their daughters.

CONCLUSION

The Prohibition of Child Marriage Act 2006 has come into force to tackle what is perceived to be a social problem. For the first time, the legislature has attempted to put some teeth into such social legislation. Even so, law-makers have been wary of forcing a radical discrepancy between law and custom. PCMA does not make child marriage illegal. Moreover, its efficacy depends on determination of age, both to prove the marriage and to establish competence for annulment. Age however is a matter of speculation in rural society. There is a radical misfit between the focus on digital age in law and the social perception of age and readiness for marriage. By this reckoning, most girls are married between the ages of 16–17 years, followed by 14–15 years, as 13 is the average age for attainment of puberty for girls. In social perception, a girl becomes ready for marriage as soon as puberty sets in.

We have argued that girls are married early, often by taking them out of schools, for a complex set of reasons that are economic and social. In dominant perception, a daughter's labour is dedicated to the marital household, thus her labouring life begins with marriage. In rural families, daughters and their bodies are repositories of 'honour'. Parents are anxious about adolescent sexuality and worried about possibilities of elopement, which brings shame to families. Add to these factors the lack of employment opportunities, landlessness and general poverty—parents are compelled to withdraw daughters from school and arrange early marriage.

Elopements appear to be on the rise. There is pragmatic acceptance of elopement marriage. We have come across no example of parents criminalizing the act of elopement and delegitimizing the marriage. Parents have not resorted to violence or sought state intervention to separate couples who have taken their own marriage decisions.

Kanyashree Prakalpa has been introduced by the state government to address the issue of underage marriages. This scheme was implemented in West Bengal from 2013. When we went to the field Kanyashree Prakalpa was yet to have any discernible impact. A small number of households received its benefits. The number of girls benefitting from K2 was negligible. Moreover, the people we spoke to were unimpressed by the meagre amounts of benefit under the scheme and were not willing to change marriage decisions for such small considerations.

Our study has shown that law is not a good instrument for change for such things as the marriage system. Especially given that such laws do not (or even cannot) tackle underlying problems such as a social consensus on universal and compulsory marriage. Moreover, the agency in child (or under-age) marriage is shifting from parents to the 'child'. If young people are eloping and taking their own marriage decisions at ages below the legal minimum, the case for a law prohibiting child marriage becomes considerably weaker. We have to try and understand why this phenomenon is on the rise and how policy rather than law can address the issue. One of the weakest links in the chain is the indetermination of age on which law so heavily relies.

NOTES

1   https://thelogicalindian.com/awareness/child-marriage-report/, accessed on 7 August 2018.

2   The survey and methodology is explained in the Introduction. To be noted that names of respondents have been changed. The two essays from the project have followed the same changes in name.

3   The quotes from respondents have been translated by the authors or by the supervisor of the project, Samita Sen. The original Bangla in each case is not given in this chapter.

4   https://coeay.tiss.edu/cmap/wp-content/uploads/2015/10/CMEM-REPORT.pdf, accessed on 5 March 2017.

5   This has been discussed in more detail in Chapter 6.

6   http://www.ohchr.org/Documents/Issues/Women/WRGS/ForcedMarriage/NGO/HAQCentreForChildRights1.pdf, accessed on 12 February 2017.

7   http://www.oneindia.com/india/wb-govt-launches-kanyashree-to-prevent-child-marriage-1316601.html, accessed on 12 February 2017.

8   http://www.ohchr.org/Documents/Issues/Women/WRGS/ForcedMarriage/NGO/HAQCentreForChildRights1.pdf, accessed on 12 February 2017.

REFERENCES

Bandyopadhyay, Aparna. 2011. 'Of Sin, Crime and Punishment: Elopements in Bengal 1929'. In *Intimate Others: Marriage and Sexualities in India,* Samita Sen, Ranjita Biswas and Nandita Dhawan, eds. Kolkata: Stree.

Chakravarti, Uma. 2005. 'From Fathers to Husbands: Of Love, Death and Marriage in North India'. In *'Honour': Crimes, Paradigms and Violence against Women*, Lynn Welchman and Sara Hossain, eds. London: Zed Books.

Chowdhry, Prem. 2011. *Political Economy of Production and Reproduction: Caste, Custom and Community in North India*. New Delhi: Oxford University Press.

Chowdhury, Ishita. 2018. 'State Intervention to Prevent Child Marriage: Kanyashree Prakalpa', *Economic and Political Weekly* (henceforth *EPW*), 53, 3 (20 Jan.).

Forbes, Geraldine. 1979. 'Women and Modernity: The Issue of Child Marriage in India', *Women's Studies International Quarterly* 2, 4: 407–19. doi: 10.1016/S0148-0685(79)90455-X.

Ghosh, Biswajit. 2011. 'Child Marriage, Society and the Law: A Study in a Rural Context in West Bengal, India', *International Journal of Law, Policy and the Family* 25, 2: 199–219. doi:10.1093/lawfam/ebr002.

Nirantar Trust. 2015. *Early and Child Marriage in India: A Landscape Analysis*. New Delhi: Drishti Printers.

Sarkar, T. 2001. *Hindu Wife, Hindu Nation: Community, Religion and Cultural Nationalism*. Ranikhet: Permanent Black.

Sen, Anindita, and Arijita Dutta. 2018. 'West Bengal's Successful Kanyashree Prakalpa Programme Needs More Push From State and Beneficiaries', *EPW*, 53, 17.

Sen, Samita. 2009. 'Religious Conversion, Infant Marriage and Polygamy: Regulating Marriage in India in the Late Nineteenth Century', *Journal of History* 26: 99–145.

TISS. 2015. *Child Marriage and Early Motherhood: Understandings from Lived Experiences of Young People*. Mumbai: India Printing Works.

UNICEF. 2013. *Communication Strategy on Kanyashree Prakalpa: Prevention of Early Marriage in West Bengal*. Kolkata: UNICEF.

5

Schooling, Work and Early Marriage: Girl Children in Contemporary Bengal

Deepita Chakravarty

A MONG THE FIFTEEN major states of India, under-age marriage of girls, as discussed in other chapters, is relatively more prevalent in West Bengal. I argue that more than poverty and illiteracy, the non-availability of new employment opportunities because of the poor performance of the economy of the state in general and the industrial sector in particular is mainly responsible for persistent child marriage in the state. The existing work opportunities for women (adults and girls) both in the rural and in the urban areas of the state are not in contradiction with the practices of early marriage and early motherhood. In this overall context of generation of no new work opportunities for women and thereby no incentive for parents to continue education of their daughters to higher levels, existing cultural practices persist. The chapter is based on secondary data in the main with occasional references to some primary evidence from a recent survey done by the author.

In India, marriage of girls below the age of 18 years is barred by law, though incidence of below 18 girls getting married is notably high in the country. However, most of the states that showed a high incidence of under-age (below 18 years) marriage of girls have experienced a notable decline over the last one decade or so (Chapter 3). West Bengal (WB), a state among the top ranking ones in the incidence of under-age marriage for decades, has also experienced a considerable decline in this regard. But in this state the fall is not as significant as it is in many others such as Rajasthan or even Uttar Pradesh. As a consequence, WB now stands at the top in the incidence of under-age marriage in India. It is important to note that in terms of per capita income, sex ratio, literacy rate and in many such development indicators WB is not among the poor performers (Kohli 2012). There is thus an obvious contradiction among the different performance records of this state. The objective here is to understand the reasons behind this contradiction or to put it more precisely, the persistence of the high incidence of under-age marriage of girls over the years in a state which is at least an average performer in many other respects.

The uneven pattern of the incidence of child marriage in different states is a combination of several factors and therefore it is difficult to pinpoint the exact reasons behind the incident in every case. But one of the factors explaining the significant decline in women's under-age marriage all over the country in the recent years is likely to be the result of state initiatives in many directions targeted at the development of girl children (Govt. of India 2015). These are large in number. States like Tamil Nadu, Haryana, Gujarat and some others started taking such initiatives as early as the beginning of the 1990s. Much later these policies started coming up in all states especially when the 2011 Census suggested a worrying decline in the child sex ratio. However, the first and the only policy targeted to the girl child in WB comes as late as 2014. There is no reason to think that the states which have introduced such policies earlier or pursued them more vigorously are particularly gender-sensitive in their approach. However, it is difficult to deny the positive impact of such populist policies in these states.

It is documented that in India prevalence of endemic poverty and illiteracy are among the major reasons behind the persistence of under-age marriage of girl children (Kannabiran et al. 2017). Existing literature also highlights that the increasing incidence of dowry even among the lower strata of Indian society and long term cultural traditions lead to child or adolescent marriages in West Bengal (Ghosh 2011). I focus instead on implications of a relatively less discussed question of availability of new work opportunities and the nature of work available to women and girls for the persistence of under-age marriage and motherhood in the state.

The non availability of new employment opportunities due to the poor performance of the economy of the state in general and the industrial activities in particular assumes especial significance in the context of a lack of women-oriented state initiatives in WB. In this overall context of generation of no new work opportunities for women and thereby no incentive for the parents to continue education of their daughters to higher levels, long-term cultural practices have tended to persist. It is important to note here that gender-related development record of WB is not particularly remarkable. Women's work participation rate has been historically low in this region. In spite of the fact that colonial Bengal was one of the main centres of a social reform movement which focused on the improvement of the status of women, the average age at marriage has not changed significantly throughout at least the last hundred years for a considerable section of girls in this part of South Asia (comprising Bangladesh and West Bengal). In 1929 after much debate the age of consent or the permissible age of cohabitation was fixed by law at the age of 14 years.[1] In 2016, a nationwide survey found that around 40 percent girls were still being married below the age of 18 in WB. A section of them have become mothers before they reached 18 years. A combined impact of expansion of women's work opportunities on the one hand, and targeted state initiative to prepare the girl child to avail of such opportunity in the future on the other, could have been successful in drastically eradicating under-age marriage. But the absence of both and the existence of long-term cultural bias against women together seem to have played havoc in this state.

The absence of labour-intensive industrial activities in this area failed to pull women out of home in large numbers as it has happened in Tamil Nadu (within India) and in Bangladesh, Thailand, Indonesia and others outside the country. In these countries, export-oriented industrialization resulted in increasing economic opportunities particularly for young women. New industrial work opportunities especially in the export sector are contingent upon some level of school education. Let us take the example of Bangladesh, historically akin to WB. Female workforce participation in Bangladesh which was even lower than WB in the early 1980s has shot up to around 40 percent in recent years. This was mainly the result of the extraordinary performance of garment manufacturing activities since the middle of the same decade. Female share in this new industrial employment grew from 39 percent in the mid-1990s to around 60 percent by 2000 in Bangladesh (Kabeer and Mahmud 2004). Amin et al. (1998) note that Bangladeshi society was traditionally characterized by early marriage and early motherhood. However, they have also noted a trend towards later age marriage from the 1980s. Incidentally this was the decade when garment industry took off and the demand for women's labour increased phenomenally in the country. Amin et al. have documented how factory employment creates strong incentives for delaying marriage in Bangladesh. But it needs to be mentioned here that in spite of the significant increase in employment opportunities of women in the garment manufacturing industry in Bangladesh and an increase in the age at marriage, the country is still among the top in the incidence of child marriage. Probably, economic opportunities for women are yet to expand enough in the country in order to eradicate deeply entrenched cultural practices.

The once industrially advanced West Bengal went into decline even before the colonial era ended. After the war, along with Independence, came major dislocations, such as partition, that severely affected trade links between the East and the West of the region. At independence, central government policies of freight equalization for coal and steel, and emphasis on import-substitution, dealt a further heavy blow to Bengal's industry. This was aggravated by the confrontationist strategy on the part of the state — followed since the beginning of the Congress rule and carried on by the Left Front government and now by the Trinamool Congress — which prevented it from lobbying pragmatically to obtain licenses and industrial investment. Further obstacles to industrial resurgence were the formation of radical trade union movements, backed by leftist intellectual support. Moreover, the central government policy of ceasing investment in the infrastructure sector in the mid-1960s adversely affected WB's engineering industry and precipitated large-scale unemployment in formal manufacturing in the state. No significant new investment came in that could have absorbed the rising work force as it has happened in the case of some other states, such as Tamil Nadu. Textile and then the garment manufacturing units along with other industrial activities started coming up even in the rural areas away from the large cities in Tamil Nadu over the last few decades after independence (Cawthorne 1995). The export-oriented garment industry to begin with and later the smaller spinning units started employing younger women in large numbers influenced by the received idea of exploiting relatively cheap labour of women (Standing 1989).[2] More focused education programmes began very early and made it possible to create an educated workforce, signifiantly among younger women.

Industrial stagnation, and the consequent downward trend in job opportunities during the late 1940s and early 1950s in Bengal, was accompanied by large scale immigration from bordering East Pakistan, now Bangladesh to WB till 1971, creating an unprecedented increase in the size of the labour force. Most workers naturally concentrated in and around Calcutta, which provided greater hope of a livelihood. The novel presence of women and children amongst this labour force was significant, as prior to the 1940s migrant labour to the city consisted mainly of single men from neighbouring states. Chakravarty and Chakravarty (2013) in this context showed how a predominantly male occupation of domestic service was transformed into a female occupation and also girl children's occupation in the state over the next 50 years or so. They have also documented how the growing absence of economic opportunities have led both elderly women as well as girl children to migrate from the rural areas to cities to work as domestic maids in city homes at times of distress. It is assumed that 'domestic service' does not require any kind of skill except learning to perform the tasks expected from a girl child in a poor Indian family. In any case, in India, domestic servants are not expected to have formal education. On the contrary, industrial factory work especially in the export sector requires at least some amount of schooling (Majumdar and Sarkar 2008: 220).

Prevalence of under-age marriage is more in the rural compared to the urban areas of WB. Consequently, the recent decline in the incidence of under-age marriage is also more pronounced in the villages. In order to understand the dimension of the problem of women's under-age marriage in the state, I have decided to look at WB in a comparative frame. In the next section, I analyse some relevant secondary data for WB in the context of the 15 major states of India. I refer to examples from different states. But given the specificities I do not venture to deconstruct the incidences of those states. The subsequent two sections discuss how unavailability of new work opportunities and the continuing engagement of women in traditional work help perpetuate the age-old cultural practices of under-age marriage.

1. INCIDENCE OF UNDER-AGE MARRIAGE IN WB IN A COMPARATIVE FRAME

We get comparable data for under-age-marriage from the National Family Health Survey (NFHS). NFHS collects information on the percentage of women in the age group of 20 to 24 years, during the time of the survey, married below the age of 18 years. Table 5.1 gives information on the incidence of under-age marriage in the 15 major states of India over the last two decades. From Table 5.1 it is clearly seen that the incidence of under-age marriage has come down significantly over the last two decades in all the 15 major states of India. During the closing years of the last century the incidence of under-age marriage of women was the highest in Bihar closely followed by Rajasthan, Madhya Pradesh, Uttar Pradesh and Andhra Pradesh. While all these states experienced some decline in the year 2005–06, they still remained among the highest performers. The incidence of under-age marriage in the next three states of Maharashtra, Karnataka and WB was quite similar to each other but much distant from the incidence of child marriage in the first set of states. In 2005–06 when every state showed a decline and that too quite notable in some cases, WB showed almost a 10 percent point increase and had moved up to the fifth position.

In 2015–16 the picture for WB is even more intriguing. I have already mentioned that in the latest year all states have experienced a decline in the under-age marriage of women in India. WB also has experienced a decline though not as significant as the other top ranking states. As a consequence, it is now at the first rank in the incidence of under-age marriage in India. According to the latest estimates a little more than 40 percent girls are married in WB below the age of 18 compared to 53 percent in 2005–06 (Table 5.1).

Deepita Chakravarty

TABLE 5.1: Incidence of Under-Age Marriage in 15 Major States of
India (in Percent) (Rural + Urban)

States	1998–99	2005–06	2015–16
AP	64.3 (4)	54.8 (4)	32.7 (3)
Bihar	71.9 (1)	60 (2)	39.1 (2)
Gujarat	40.7	38.7	24.9
Haryana	41.5	39.8	18.5
HP	10.7	12.3	8.6
Karnataka	46.3 (6)	41.2	23.2
Kerala	17	15.4	7.6
MP	64.7 (3)	53 (6)	30 (5)
Maharashtra	47.7 (5)	39.4	25.1 (6)
Orissa	37.6	37.2	21.3
Punjab	11.6	19.7	7.6
Rajasthan	68.3 (2)	65.2 (1)	35.4 (4)
TN	24.9	21.5	15.7
UP	64.3 (4)	58.6 (3)	21.2
West Bengal	45.9 (7)	53.3 (5)	40.7 (1)
India	50	47.4	26.8

Source: *National Family Health Survey*, Fact Sheets for different years.
Note: Numbers in the parenthesis refer to the relative rankings in different years. Latest available figures for each year have been considered.

TABLE 5.2: Incidence of Under-Age Marriage and Motherhood in
Rural and Urban WB in 2005-06 and 2015-16 (in percent)

	Areas	2005–06	2015–16
Under-age marriage	Rural	63.2	46.3
	Urban	32.2	27.7
Under-age motherhood	Rural	30.0	20.6
	Urban	11.3	12.4

Source: NFHS, Fact Sheets 2005–06; 2015–16.

The decline mainly was due to about 20 percent reduction in the incidence in the rural areas of the state as against a meagre 5 percent decline in the urban areas (see Table 5.2).

Of course, one of the major reasons behind the notable decline in the incidence of under-age marriage over all states may be the increase in the incidence of ten years of schooling

TABLE 5.3: Incidence of Under-Age Motherhood and Incidence of Ten Years of Schooling for Women in 15 Major States of India (in percent) (Rural + Urban)

States	Under-Age Motherhood		Incidence of Women Attaining 10 Years of Schooling or More	
	2005–06	2015–16	2005–06	2015–16
AP	18.1 (3)	11.8 (3)	NA	34.3
Bihar	25 (2)	12.2 (2)	13.2	22.8
Gujarat	12.7	6.5	23.5	33
HP	3.1	2.6	44.7	59,4
Haryana	12.1	5.9	29.6	45.8
Karnataka	17	7.8 (5)	27.8	45.5
Kerala	5.8	3.0	48.7	72.2
MP	13.6	7.3	14	23.2
Maharashtra	13.8	8.3 (4)	30.7	42
Orissa	14.5	7.6 (6)	15.6	26.7
Punjab	5.5	2.6	38.4	55.1
Rajasthan	16 (4)	6.3 (7)	11.7	25.1
TN	7.7	5	31.8	50.9
UP	14.3	3.8	18.3	32.9
WB	25.3 (1)	18.3 (1)	15.7	26.5
India	16	7.9	22.3	35.7

Source: NFHS, Fact Sheets 2005–06; 2015–16
Note: Numbers in the parenthesis refer to relative rankings of different states.

of girls over the last decade (Table 5.3). However, the large successes of some states, especially Rajasthan and Bihar, are difficult to explain only by the increase in the years of schooling. While there is not much difference in the gains in terms of achieving ten years of schooling between Rajasthan and WB, the difference in the decline in the incidence of under-age marriage is huge. It needs to be examined whether more targeted campaign by both the government, the NGOs and the like working in the state of Rajasthan is responsible for this achievement.

It is worth noting here that a recently conducted primary survey in four districts of WB by the author indicates the mean age at marriage is now around 15–16 years in the rural areas. Primary investigations also suggest that around 10 years earlier the mean age at marriage was generally lower. It has been noted that the adolescent brides have attended school till Standard 3 or so in the recent years. Secondary data show not only a 100 percent school enrolment for girls in WB but also a significant decline in the dropout rates at the secondary level. According to the NFHS (2015–16), in rural WB, around 20 percent girls undergo ten years of schooling. Anecdotal evidence suggests a likely positive role of the Kanyashree' scheme of the state government to encourage schooling of girl children in recent years. It has been found that parents are willing to invest in daughter's education as long as there is some direct support from the government.

In order to understand the broader consequences of under-age marriage, it is instructive to look at the incidence of under-age motherhood also. While marriage significantly changes the roles and responsibilities of a woman, motherhood forces her to be biologically more home-bound. Table 5.3 represents data on under-age motherhood. NFHS reports information on the percentages of women in the age group 15 to 19 years, who were either already mothers or pregnant at the time when the data were collected. Before commenting further on the trends emerging from Tables 5.1 and 5.3, some caution is needed. First, while there are some trends clearly emerging from these tables (as we will be discussing shortly) we need to remember that the samples considered for these data sets are extremely small in size and therefore suffer from the 'small sample problem'. Second, the age cohorts used to evaluate under-age marriage and under-age motherhood are different and therefore these two data sets are not strictly comparable. With this caution, let us take a look at the numbers reported in Table 5.3. The available data suggest a notable decline in the incidence of under-age motherhood as well. In the year 2005–06 WB stood first in under-age motherhood closely followed by Bihar. Then came AP and Rajasthan, respectively, with a gap of around 10 percentage points. In 2015–16, WB remained at the top followed by Bihar and AP. Rajasthan has come down to the eighth position.

It is noted that the decline in under-age motherhood has been experienced both in the rural as well as in the urban areas of all the first four states in 2015–16 except WB. A slight increase in the incidence of under-age motherhood can be detected in urban WB in the year 2015–16. Unless this is a sampling error emanating from a typical 'small sample', the trend is worrisome. It needs to be remembered that the incidence of under-age marriage has declined by only 5 percent in urban WB and still around 27 percent girls get married before they are 18 years in the cities and towns of the state. According to NFHS data, however, in the urban areas, more than 40 percent women acquire 10 years of schooling or more in 2015–16. The Kanyashree scheme of the state government might have played an important role in this regard as well. Unfortunately, this increase in the incidence of number of years of schooling could not influence the age at marriage and more so under-age motherhood much, especially in urban areas. However, as I have already mentioned, this policy was initiated only in 2013. Therefore, we need to wait a few more years to see whether Kanyashree will have any positive impact on the age at marriage.

Apart from education, the other important factor that is likely to have decisive influence on the incidence of under-age marriage is opportunities of work participation. In fact, participation in schooling, especially with no immediate assurance of remunerative jobs, has to be ensured through direct and indirect incentives, provided by the government, such as the midday meal schemes, some monetary help. Remunerative work opportunity, on the contrary, can, on its own, ensure participation and considerably delay marriage. In the next two sections I discuss the issues related to work.

2. WOMEN AND WORK IN THE VILLAGES

The incidence of women's paid work in rural India is relatively much higher than in the urban areas. While this is true for rural Bengal also, the state shows the second lowest incidence of female work for pay among the fifteen major states of India. Interstate variation in rural women's work in India to a large extent can be explained by the differences in agricultural work participation. WB is an exception. A predominantly rice cultivating state with relatively poor mechanization, WB has the lowest WPR for women in agriculture among the 15 major states of the country in the rural areas even in 2009–10 (Chakravarty and Chakravarty 2016).

It has been documented that in rural areas women generally are engaged in three types of work: wage work and self-employment outside the household, self-employment in cultivation and industries related to the household sector and various domestic work in and around the household. Because of cultural reasons, domestic work has not been considered as an economic activity by the major data generating systems of India. Unpaid domestic work is often intertwined with and inseparable from self-employment within the household. Women, all over India contribute to a large extent in pre- and post-harvest operations at home and not in the field. In addition poor peasant women also often assist their male relatives in the field. But women of upper echelons of the society usually will not do 'outdoor' work (Duvvuri 1989). While this explains the low WPR of women all over India, historians have argued that cultural bias against women's paid outside work is particularly strong in WB (Sarkar 1989; Sen 1999 among others). It is understandable that these different types of work are not considered to be in contradiction with the ideas of under-age marriage and also motherhood that make women more home bound.

There are very few detailed studies on the time allocation of women between various activities. However, it is generally acknowledged that the working day of a poor woman in India may be anywhere from 12 to 16 hours. On the basis of a detailed study on time allocation of rural women in Rajasthan and WB, Jain (1985) argued that while in Rajasthan women participate more significantly in visible work such as cutting grass and grazing cattle, women work predominantly at home in Bengal.

Historians on colonial Bengal have traced the exclusion of women from industrial work and from paid outside work in general in the 1920s and 1930s (Sarkar 1989; Sen 1999b). They have pointed out the growing social inhibition to women's work outside the home in Bengal in the closing years of the nineteenth century. The middle-class ideology of glorifying the housewife as against the working woman was quite influential even among the lower levels of Bengali society (Bandyopadhyay 1990). Devaki Jain (1985) observed this cultural inhibition still present in the 1970s. On the basis of a survey of some villages in WB, she observed that even poverty failed to push women to seek outside work to the extent it did in other parts of the country. Her findings indicate that while women in general spent three hours on an average in cooking in WB, in Rajasthan they spent only an hour or so.

We now turn to a comparative analysis of the incidence of rural women's work in WB over the period 2004–05 to 2011–12 in the context of 15 major states of India (Table 5.4). While most states have experienced a considerable decline in the incidence of women's work in rural areas over this period, WB is among the few that suggests an increase. One might be tempted to relate this increase in the incidence of WPR with the notable decline in the percentage of under-age marriage in rural areas. But a comparison of age-group wise work participation data for these two years suggests something interesting (Table 5.5). Except in the lowest age group of 5 to 9 years, a consistent decline can be delineated for all the age groups between 10 and 24 years for rural women in WB. This decline in the WPR is partly explained by the increase in the incidence of schooling especially for younger women. However, the decline in the incidence of work outside the home for the later age groups till 24 is something to worry about as this can have close relations with incidence of both under-age marriage and early motherhood. Table 5.5 also suggests a more or less consistent increase in the WPR of rural women in the later age groups and especially among the elderly over these two years of observation. The rural economy of the state is almost stagnant mainly in

TABLE 5.4: Women's Work Participation Rates in 15 Major States of India
(usual status, per thousand populations)

States	Rural		Urban	
	2004–05	2011–12	2004–05	2011–12
AP	483	445	224	170
Bihar	138	53	65	45
Gujarat	427	278	151	133
HP	506	524	241	212
Haryana	317	162	132	97
Karnataka	459	287	181	163
Kerala	256	221	200	191
MP	366	239	154	115
Maharashtra	474	388	190	166
Orissa	322	246	148	155
Punjab	322	234	133	166
Rajasthan	407	347	182	141
TN	461	378	241	201
UP	240	177	117	102
WB	178	189	155	174
India	327	248	166	147

Source: NSSO Report No. 554 and 515 (part 1).

terms of lack of generation of new opportunities outside agriculture over many decades now. Moreover, some recent modernization, particularly in threshing, has displaced a large number of human hands, including women. Stray instances apart, recent NSS data suggest that MGNREGA did not do well in the state in general. This increase in the incidence of WPR of older women is thus unlikely to be demand-driven and suggestive of a distress-driven outcome. However, it needs a differently focused study to comment conclusively on the nature of older women's work in the rural areas of the state in recent years.

Young women, both married and unmarried, hardly work in the fields as a result of a typical prejudice in rural Bengal. Anecdotal evidence suggests that women who do not work in the fields often engage in different kinds of home-based

TABLE 5.5: Age-Specific Workforce Participation Rates (usual status, per thousand populations) of Women in WB

Age group	Rural		Urban	
	2004–05	2011–12	2004–05	2011–12
5–9	01	05	20	00
10–14	55	40	67	27
15–19	174	158	160	108
20–24	218	213	256	172
25–29	309	320	222	301
30–34	362	348	234	262
35–39	369	332	235	273
40–44	293	377	257	318
45–49	309	274	159	266
50–54	270	272	180	220
55–59	130	216	172	245
60 and above	84	NA	37	NA
60–64	NA	160	NA	98
65 and above	NA	58	NA	42
All	178	189	155	174

Source: NSSO Report No. 554 and 515 (part 1).
Note: For 2004–05 data for the age group of 60–64 is not available. Therefore, WPRs for the age groups 60 and above for the two years are not strictly comparable.

manufacturing such as biri rolling, making bags out of leaves or old newspaper, and so on. Older women sometimes also engage in petty trade. With the help of relatively more educated younger women in the family, often a daughter-in-law, older women run small tea shops in the front portion of the house. Engaging in all these work doesn't intrinsically hinder the practice of early marriage or that of the early motherhood.

Recent field work by the author in Birbhum and Burdwan districts indicates that more recently, younger women particularly the unmarried ones are participating in a typical home-based embroidery work popularly known as kantha stitch. Over a decade or so a large number of boutiques of different sizes have come up in this region often with links in Kolkata. These boutiques through contractors organize the home-based stitching activities at an unusually low rate of remuneration compared to the price of the finished product they sell in the market. This particular work opportunity does not demand any level of necessary schooling. Thus girls do both: a bit of schooling as well as some work, the remuneration from which can be used as a source of dowry. Early marriage thus continues.

A contrast can be offered from Tamil Nadu (TN) in this regard. Over the last few decades, a large number of spinning and garment manufacturing firms have been setting up units in the outskirts of larger towns and cities in the state. Many of them are involved in exporting. Labour intensive by nature, these units employ young women in large numbers, especially from poor families from the interiors on a fixed contract basis (Chakravarty 2004; Solidaridad 2012; Lothar 2015). This particular scheme is known as 'Sumangali'.[3] The growing criticisms notwithstanding, this work opportunity is likely to have created an incentive for families not to marry off daughters when they are adolescent. The families send their young daughters after some years of schooling to work in these manufacturing units and to earn their own dowry for the marriage that is anyway inevitable. Let us remember the high incidence of work[4] and significantly low incidence of under-age marriage and motherhood of women in the state of TN over the years under consideration. Even in recent years, when the incidence of female work participation is notably decreasing in TN both in the rural and in the urban areas, female WPR for the age groups of 15 to 19 years (186) and 20 to 24 years (386) in rural areas of the state is perceptibly much higher than that of West Bengal (158 and 213 respectively) (NSS, 2011–12). Moreover, working in manufacturing units with machines requires some ability and discipline to understand and follow instructions. This in turn is highly contingent upon some schooling. The hundred percent school enrolment of girls and zero incidences of dropout rates till the middle level for girl children in TN are to be noted here. Incidentally, till 14 years hardly any girl children are reported to be working even in rural TN, according to the most recent NSS data. Examples can be drawn from other countries as well, such as South Korea or China or even Bangladesh.

In the industrial organization literature it has been discussed how a certain level of education becomes absolutely essential for acquiring on-the-job training in the manufacturing setup. Incidentally, while conducting a primary survey in an export promotion park near the city of Hyderabad I heard several times the management explaining the necessity of some education to work efficiently, especially in an export-oriented firm. However, apart from the purposes of better assimilation of training and discipline, schooling up to a certain standard turned out to be necessary for these export-oriented employers for another reason as well. I have found that employers often make it a point to ask for a certificate of passing the eighth standard as this certificate states the age of the entrant. They were insistent upon this to avoid the hazards of the stringent anti-child labour regulations of the importing countries (Chakravarty 2004). Similar findings are reported by Amin et al. in 1998 from Bangladesh garment manufacturing units. The information we get both from the Bangladesh garment manufacturing or from the Tamil Nadu textiles suggest that newer work opportunities supported by state-sponsored longer schooling did ensure a decline in the under-age marriage of girls in these places. But there is not enough evidence to show that these work opportunities for a few years before the women workers finally get married lead to any kind of skill formation that would help them obtain a better living in the later years. It has been documented time and again that during the fixed contract period of the 'Sumangali' system in Tamil Nadu, the young women employees hardly gain any skills that would enable them to get opportunities for better work in later years. The story is similar in Bangladeshi garment manufacturing units. The ultimate aim of joining such a scheme or work is to earn dowries to get married or to provide some support to the family in times of distress. As mentioned above, these export-oriented mills and factories all over the world prefer young unmarried women for various reasons and that too for a short period. So, the age at marriage as a result of such developments is likely to move up from say 16/17 to 21/22 or so.

Turning to WB, recent research highlights one more emerging avenue for girls in the rural areas of the state. It has been documented that, as a result of the continuous poor performance of the village economy, a significant quantum of migration is taking place from rural parts of WB to urban centres all over the country. Apart from single male migration, the family as a whole often migrates to cities in search of a living. What is less noticed is the single migration of girl children to cities to work as whole-time domestic maids in middle-class city homes to cope with distress or to earn the dowry (Chakravarty and Chakravarty 2016). These girls are brought back home to get married once they attain puberty. There is plenty of evidence to suggest this singular phenomenon in WB from secondary data till the middle of the 2000s. As the detailed tables from the latest Census are not yet available, it is difficult to say anything certain about this trend in more recent years from secondary sources. But there is no reason to think that the trend has changed substantially as primary surveys conducted both on the basis of small as well as large samples drawn mainly from villages and also from the cities do not show the contrary at all (Save the Children 2009; Sen and Sengupta 2016).

3. PREDOMINANCE OF DOMESTIC SERVICE IN URBAN WOMEN'S WORK

Turning to urban areas, we find an increase in the workforce participation of women in WB in comparison to many other states (Table 5.4). It is interesting to note that, while there is a consistent decline in WPR of urban women till the age group of 20 to 24 years, there is also a very consistent increase in the

WPR in all the age groups starting from 25 to 29 years (Table 5.5). The decline in WPR in the lower age groups is consistent with the increase in school enrolment and decrease in dropout rates as mentioned above. However, the decline in the age group of 5 to 14 years may be partly the result of under-reporting especially after the ban imposed on the use of child domestics in 2006 in WB.

Decline of WPR in the age group of 15 to 24 is actually quite worrisome given the fact that under-age marriage in the urban areas of the state has not declined much over the last ten years of 2005–06 to 2015–16. Moreover, under-age mother-hood has in fact increased in the urban areas during these ten years, as discussed earlier. At the same time, we find a sub-stantial percentage of women (40) have achieved ten years or more schooling in urban areas of the state. While the 5 percent decline in under-age marriage in the urban areas might have been caused by the increase in school attendance, the question is: does this education offer any better work opportunity to the young girls that might ensure a better future?

Chakravarty and Chakravarty 2016 give a comparison of women's work behaviour over two decades on the basis of broad industry classifications. They demonstrate that about 50 percent women are concentrated in the community services sector alone in urban areas of the state followed by manufac-turing and trade in 2009–10. Compared to women, male work participation is comparatively less concentrated and mainly in trade, manufacturing and transport. The concentration of female work force in the services sector is on the increase in recent years, primarily at the cost of manufacturing.[5] In fact, the decline in the female work participation in the manufac-turing sector was so severe in 2009–10 over 2004–05 that the considerable increase in services employment during the same period failed to arrest the overall decline in the female work force participation in urban areas in 2009–10. This decline, however, confirms a country-wide trend (Neff, Sen and Kling 2012).

Women's loss of industrial jobs in Bengal can, however, be historically traced. Banerjee (2006), Mukherjee (1995) showed how the avenues of women's work in this region shrank between 1881 and 1931 as a result of the introduction of the 'limited version' of modernization in industry. Traditional household industries and modern industries, such as jute, tea and coal-mining, were the main employers of women. With changes in production processes and the decline of traditional crafts, women lost their household jobs. New factory laws barred them from the coal mines. The jute industry, which had nearly 20 percent women among labour at the turn of the nineteenth century, started employing single male upcountry migrants at the cost of local women and men workers. It is interesting to note that during the same period, there was a growing social inhibition in Bengal towards women's work outside the home.

After independence, WB saw a continuous decline in the industrial activities till date for a number of reasons as discussed in the introduction. Consequently, hardly any new gainful employment has been generated in the formal manufacturing in the state. Moreover, frequent closure of factories and firms in this sector leaves a large number of mainly male workers out of jobs every day. Bagchi et al (2005) pointed out a notable decline in the manufacturing employment in the state as a whole. Apart from the decline in employment in the formal sector, they have shown that employment in informal manufacturing has also either remained stagnant or experienced a slight decline over the years. Given the nature of employment in the informal sector, the trend of employment is ambiguous. This is more so as Chakravarty and Bose (2011) have shown that the informal manufacturing is performing much better in the state even when output is considered.

The jobless and also better qualified workers from the formal sector manufacturing enter the burgeoning unorganized activities of the state. The majority of these workers are likely to be men as they have better possibilities of being skilled, at least notionally. These workers along with the new entrants in the labour force, mainly the better-educated young men, are likely to out-compete with older women in preferred jobs. This is happening in the context of no serious decline in the incidence of urban women's work followed by a substantial increase in recent years compared to the early 1990s. As a result of ever-increasing competition from male workers, as mentioned above, women are forced to enter those sectors which will be least preferred by men, the jobs that are more compatible with 'femininity' and 'domesticity'.

What are these activities? Table 5.6 summarizes urban women's major avenues of employment in WB.

On the basis of 1991 data, Chakravarty and Chakravarty (2008) showed a much higher concentration of urban women in domestic service among all work categories in WB with respect to 15 major states of India. In 1991, the percentage share of domestic service in urban women's work was around 20 in WB. In 2001 the percentage share of domestic service in urban women's work in WB has gone up to about 23 when it is only 10 percent in the country as a whole. Primary surveys conducted during the later years of the 2000s indicate that the high concentration of women in domestic service continues unabated. Some of these surveys are quite large in size. The persistently high concentration of women in the services sector during the recent years also indirectly supports this picture.

TABLE 5.6: Percentage Distribution of Women in Different Categories of Work in Urban WB in 2001

Categories of work	Percentages of women
Domestic work (ayah, cook, maids, gardener, driver etc.)	22.52
Bidi binding	8.17
Spinning and finishing of bed covers	6.89
Textile garments	5.63
Tailoring	3.11
Education and health related work	14.02

Source: Chakravarty and Chakravarty, 2016.

Researchers have shown that the importance of domestic service as a job avenue for poor urban women is increasing all over the country. Most of these women domestics migrate from the rural areas to urban centres in search of work (Unni and Raveendran 2007; Neetha 2004). Domestic service does not require any specific educational qualification and, therefore, schooling is not essential. This work is considered to be an extension of what 'women are born to do' and matches perfectly with high incidence of under-age marriage and increasing incidence of under-age motherhood in urban areas of the state even today (see Chapter 6 for related discussions).

The second highest concentration of urban women in WB is in the categories of health and education. Women who work in these sectors are likely to be the better paid middle-class professionals of different grades working as teachers, clerks, receptionists, call centre employees, nurses and also, to a limited extent, doctors. Apart from the newly emerging call centre jobs, all these professions are known as 'suitable' for women in urban India for a long time. A woman doctor is usually a gynaecologist! These women are also most likely to be the employers of paid domestics. Moreover, the women who work in these categories are from the relatively well-off sections of society and unlikely to be candidates for under-age marriage.

The other main categories of work that absorb urban women fall in the manufacturing sector. Most of these activities are performed at home and not in factories. These activities are often highly tedious and known to be suitable for women. Women's femininity characterized by 'nimble fingers and docility' helps them enter into these traditional manufacturing sectors of bidi-rolling, tailoring and to some extent textiles also. In all these cases, workers do not require much training. As a result, they are not on a trajectory to acquire some education followed by a somewhat later marriage. While there is a clear increase in the schooling of the poor girl children from city slums it is mostly to improve the marriage prospects (Chakravarty and Chakravarty 2016).

We close this discussion by mentioning an emerging area within domestic service that requires a certain amount of education and ensures a better wage. It is the service of ayahs. These ayahs are often trained in basic care-giving, especially of patients with chronic health problems and this requires some education. Anecdotal evidence says that the demand for such care services is on the rise in Calcutta and in other cities in recent years. The increase in demand for such services is likely to be for two reasons: first, the significant increase in the life expectancy of middle- and upper-income groups; and second, the increase in the work participation of women outside the home particularly from these classes.

To conclude, our analysis suggests a relatively high prevalence of under-age marriage in WB. We have argued that in the absence of new economic opportunities both in urban as well as in rural areas, schooling till a higher age has not become essential for women. The spheres of women's economic activities demarcated by cultural practices are well in conformity with early marriage and motherhood. The policy interventions focusing on girl children in recent years is likely to play some important role in pulling the age at marriage above 18 years. However, it is apprehended that the parents will wait exactly till girls turn 18, get the benefits, and then marry them off. This will surely meet the legal requirements but will hardly make the girl's life different. Our analysis also problematizes the question of new work opportunities that could, along with increasing school attendance, ensure relatively late marriage for women. It is likely that more than new work opportunities as such the nature of the work is important in determining the possibilities of skill formation and in turn getting better employment eventually. Studies have shown that export-oriented industrialization creates stereotypical jobs for women in the factories often leading to a slightly late marriage. The employment of young unmarried women in this sector, even if it confers on these women some agency temporarily, does not lead to the kind of social change we deem desirable. What happens when these women grow older and are possibly fired? Can contract-based short-term employment, which are typical of these above mentioned export-oriented industries, ensure a better future for a woman worker even if she is married, say, at twenty instead of seventeen? To answer such questions further study is badly needed.

NOTES

1   Historians such as Dagmar Engels (1999: 44–45) have pointed out that while the upper castes and classes generally supported the move to raise the age of consent to 14 years the lower and poorer castes and classes resisted it. On the basis of evidence from the Census she has shown that as a reaction to the Sarda Act of 1929 there was an increase of 200 percent in marriages of minor girls in the Bengal province between 1921 and 1931.

2   Lim (1990), in the context of East and Southeast Asia argues that export-oriented production exploits but also liberates women at the same time. In Bangladesh along the same lines Amin et al (1998) notes that although women work long hours and under inhospitable conditions of work often at low wages in the garment manufacturing units these opportunities are better than the alternatives they have.

3   Employing young unmarried women under a short-term of one to three-year contract as production workers in spinning mills and garment factories in Tamil Nadu is a well-known phenomenon now. Under this system girls often below the age of 18 are recruited by the textile firms for a fixed period of one to three years. During the period of employment they are supposed to live within the mill premises in a hostel provided by the management with a paltry sum of daily wages. They also get a lump sum amount of money at the end of the contract. None of the girls get a permanent position or even a second term with the firm they work. The system is widely known as 'Sumangali scheme'.

4   TN among some other Indian states is showing a very significant decline in the workforce participation of women according to the latest NSS data; the explanations of which are not yet very clear (see Neff et al. 2012).

5   The 2011–12 data suggest a significant improvement in the WPR in the manufacturing sector of the state. In the absence of any new

industrialization in the state one is curious to find out which sectors of manufacturing have generated so much employment for women in WB in the recent years.

REFERENCES

Amin, S., I. Daimond, R. Naved and M. Newby. 1998. 'Transition to Adulthood of Female Garment-Factory Workers in Bangladesh', *Studies in Family Planning* (Population Council) 29, 2: 185–200.

Bagchi, A. K., P. Das, S. Chattopadhyay. 2005. 'Growth and Structural Change in the Economy of Gujarat 1970–2000', *Economic and Political Weekly* (henceforth *EPW*) 40, 28: 3039–47.

Bandyopadhyay, S. 1990. 'Caste and Social Mobility'. In *Caste, Politics and the Raj:-Bengal 1872–1937*. Kolkata: K. P. Bagchi and Co.

Banerjee, N. 1985. *Women Workers in the Unorganized Sector: The Calcutta Experience*. Calcutta: Sangam Books.

———. 2006. 'Working Women in Colonial Bengal: Modernization and Marginalization'. In *Recasting Women: Essays in Colonial History,* K. Sangari and S. Vaid, eds. New Delhi: Zubaan: 274–76.

Cawthorne, P. M. 1995. 'Of Networks and Markets: the Rise of a South Indian Town, the Example of Tiruppur's Cotton Knitwear Industry', *World Development* 23: 43–56.

Chakravarty D., and I. Chakravarty, 2008. 'Girl Children in the Care Economy: Domestics in WB', *EPW* 43, 8: 93–100.

———. 2013. 'For Bed and Board Only: Women and Girl Children Domestics in Post-Partition Kolkata', *Modern Asian Studies* 47, 2: 581–611.

———. 2016. *Women, Labour and the Economy in India from Migrant Menservants to Uprooted Girl Children Maids*. London: Routledge.

Chakravarty, D., and I. Bose, 2011. 'Industry, Labour and the State: Emerging Relations in the Indian State of West Bengal', *Journal of South Asian Development* 6, 2: 169–94.

Chakravarty, D. 2004. 'Expansion of Markets and Women Workers: Case Study of Garment Manufacturing in India'. *EPW* 39, 45 (Nov): 4910–4916.

Duvvuri, N. 1989. 'Work Participation of Women in India: A Study with Special Reference to Female Agricultural Labourers, 1961- 1981'. In *Limited Options: Women Workers in India*, A.V. Jose, ed. India: ILO-ARTEP: 63–197.

Ghosh, B. 2011. 'Child Marriage, Society and the Law: A Study in a Rural Context in West Bengal, India', *International Journal of Law, Policy and the Family* 25, 2: 199–219.

Government of India. 2015. *Compendium on State Level Incentive Schemes for Care, Protection and Education of the Girl Child in India*. New Delhi: Ministry of Women and Child Development.

Jain, D. 1985. 'The Household Trap: Report on a Field Survey of Female Activity Patterns'. In. *Tyranny of the Household: Imaginative Essays on Women's Work,* Devaki Jain and Nirmala Banerjee, eds. New Delhi: Shakti Books.

Kabeer, N., and S. Mahmud, 2004. 'Rags, Riches and Women Workers: Export-Oriented Garment Manufacturing in Bangladesh'. In *Chains of Fortune: Linking Women Producers and Workers with Global Markets.* London: Commonwealth Secretaria: 133–164.

Kannabiran, K., S. K. Mishra, and S.S. Raju, 2017. 'Investigating the Causes for Low Female Age at Marriage: The Case of Telengana and Andhra Pradesh', *EPW* 52, 18: 57–65.

Kohli, A. 2012. *Poverty Amid Plenty in the New India.* Cambridge: Cambridge University Press.

Lothar, A. 2015. 'The "Sumangali Scheme" and the Need for an Integrative Ethic Management Overall the Supply-Chain', *The Business and Management Review* 5, 4.

Majumdar, D., and S. Sarkar, eds.2008. 'Dualism in Indian Manufacturing'. In *Globalization, Labour Markets and Inequality in India.* New Delhi: Routledge.

Mukherjee, M. 1995. 'Women's Work in Bengal, 1880–1930: A Historical Analysis'. In *From the Seams of History: Essays on Indian Women,* B. Ray, ed. New Delhi: Oxford University Press: 237–39.

Neetha, N. 2004. 'Making of Female Breadwinners: Migration and Social Networking of Women Domestics in Delhi', *EPW* 39, 17: 1681–88.

Neff, D., K. Sen, and V. Kling. 2012. 'Puzzling Decline in Rural Women's Labor Force participation in India: A Re-Examination', GIGA working papers, No. 196.

Sarkar, T. 1989. 'Politics and Women in Bengal'. In *Women in Colonial India: Essays on Survival, Work and the State,* J. Krishnamurty, ed. New Delhi: Oxford University Press.

Save the Children.2009. *Small Hands Big Work.* Kolkata: Save the Children.

Sen, S. 1999. *Women and Labour in Late Colonial India,* Cambridge: Cambridge University Press.

Sen, S., and N. Sengupta. 2016. *Domestic Days: Women, Work, and Politics in Contemporary Kolkata*. New Delhi: Oxford University Press.

Solidaridad-South and South East Asia. 2012. 'Research Report: Understanding the Characteristics of the Sumangali Scheme in Tamil Nadu Textile and Garment Industry and Supply Chain Linkages; Fair Labour Associations.

Standing, G. 1989. 'Global Feminization through Flexible Labor', *World Development* 17, 7: 1077–95.

Unni J., and G. Raveendran. 2007, 'Growth of Employment (1993–94 to 2004–05): Illusion of Inclusiveness?' EPW 42, 3.

6

Wives and Workers: Early Marriage in West Bengal

Samita Sen and Anindita Ghosh

THE POPULAR NOTION that Indian women do not work was challenged by feminist scholars in the 1980s. They pointed out that in fact women worked hard and long, but their labours were invisible because they themselves and most of their work were hidden in the home. New research drew attention to the figure of the bahu, the young bride, labouring from dawn to dusk, subject to near-absolute familial authority. Her 'domestic' work spanned cooking, cleaning and collecting water, but also field labour, home-based wage work, extended domestic work such as cattle-rearing and vegetable growing, subsistence work such as food processing, fuel gathering, childbirth, childcare and myriad emotional labour in the family (Sharma 1980; Chowdhry1994; Sen 1999).

There has been some, not enough, discussion about the marriage system that produces this maid-of-all work with infinitely elastic supply of labour. It has been noted that village exogamy and virilocality play a part, removing the young bride from her natal home and kin-network to be isolated in the marital household. It is also a system from which there is no exit, the irrevocability of marriage inviting comparison with forms of bondage. Without doubt, asymmetrical gender relations within marriage are the sine qua non of these harsh labour arrangements. Moreover, the universality of marriage in Indian society ensures that almost all women—at least of the middling to poor rural social stratum we are concerned with in this study—are drawn into a labour-net mobilized through wifehood. While bridal labour itself is near-universal, however, its nature and quantum varies by caste, class and region.

Popular media 'discovered' bride trafficking in the 1990s. It was found that young men in Haryana and western Uttar Pradesh had to 'buy' brides from other regions of the country in the east and south, which had better sex ratios, leading to a brisk trade in brides. This was not just village exogamy but women removed from their language and culture worlds to be married into distant lands. We were confronted with images of brides toiling in conditions of near-slavery, serial transactions in wives, the 'sale' of daughters, leading often to the doors of bazar brothels (Chowdhry 2005; Kaur 2012). Some of the oppressive aspects of women's household labour thus began to receive wide public attention. There could be no clearer illustration of feminist analyses that pointed to the entanglement of marriage and prostitution, bride-exchange and trafficking. Moreover, such practices appeared to signal the return of bride price after nearly a century of an accelerating dowry system and its steady incorporation of social groups from the margins (Sen 1999).[1] Given the regionally concentrated nature of this new bride-trafficking, however, its associated consequences could be dismissed as outliers. The normative marriage system continued to be understood as constituted by dowry and domesticity: fathers having to pay dowry to shift the economic burden of unproductive daughters to the marital household. Thus, the analytical and statistical purdah (Radha Devi 1981) on bridal labour acquired a few holes but retained its chief invisibilizing function.

In this chapter, we try to open a bigger window in this purdah, by exploring the variety of labour performed by wives among the rural population of West Bengal. In most discussions on the bridal labour regime, the worker is usually 'young': young enough to be capable of hard labour; and young enough to accept imposition of family authority. The question of how young does not usually feature in these discussions, perhaps because the context of child marriage has been an implicit given. We will explore the links between the bridal labour regime and child marriage. Deepita Chakravarty (Chapter 5) has argued that the lack of employment opportunities has kept the age at marriage low in West Bengal through a comparison with other states of India. She has shown that where there have arisen market opportunities for wage labour for young and unmarried women, families have deferred marriage.[2] She also argues a counter factual: that the pattern of women's work in West Bengal is not at odds with cultural norms of early marriage. We take this last argument further, arguing that there is an economic rationale in rural West Bengal for early marriage of women. This follows from the convergence of an economic squeeze on the household, which demands even greater quantum and intensity of unpaid labour from women, and an ideology of domesticity, which imparts near infinite elasticity and invisibility to the labour of wives and mothers.

The crux of the argument lies in marriage being a key rite of passage into the adult world of reproductive labour, which includes, apart from sexuality and childbearing, domestic labour that is critical for rural households. This is not to say that unmarried girls do not work; in the first section, this chapter will compare the involvement of girls/women in labour before and after marriage. It will show, however, that from the perception of our respondents, the imperative for early marriage for women lies in the performance of domesticity, which is not only the chief and most significant expression of femininity, but also a capacious category within which ever-expanding labouring needs of the household may be fitted. There are social sanctions against unmarried girls being involved in public labour, while married women are able more fully to participate in the range and diversity of rural economic activity. Thus, the natal home is not the site of the disciplinary regime that commands women's work; parents are generally indulgent and unwilling (or even unable) to extract hard physical or manual labour. The site of women's work is the marital household, which is fashioned by a combination of early marriage, village exogamy, virilocality, patriarchy and, significantly, generational structures of female authority. In West Bengal, marital authority is enhanced by a relatively large age gap between husband and wife: typically 4 to 10 years. This is an acknowledged means of maintaining power over wives. The imperative to maintain this age difference exerts a downward pressure on the age of brides. Moreover, wives have to negotiate not only with husbands but also other family members; popular commonsense regarding the significant role of the mother-in-law is not misplaced. The generational division of labour among women in natal and marital households is very marked, so is the experience of transition from one to the other by the new bride. The combination of gender and generation in the household's division of labour is coded in the marriage system and should be seen as part of the productive and reproductive labour arrangement of rural India, which is discussed in the second section of this chapter. While these divisions are not inflexible, there is a general trend for young married women to remain close to home and to be limited to home-based work. For kinds of work that require mobility outside the home and into more public spaces involving more interaction with non-kin men, men first but failing men, older women take responsibility. These patterns show some but not a great deal of variation by economic position, caste and community.[3] They are flexible nevertheless, according to the needs of the household and even young brides will work for wages if required. A strongly held perception that domestic work is not work enables considerable flexibility in women's work patterns, as we shall see in section three 'Domesticity and Domestic Work'. The ideology of domesticity cloaks the quantum and value of women's labour, invisibilizes their economic contribution, promotes the myth that women 'do not work' and thereby helps to maintain the gender asymmetry of power in the marriage system.

The context of change and continuity in rural women's work is a two-decade long agrarian crisis in India, which has taken a specific form in West Bengal, where small-holding agriculture predominates. Peasant households have suffered chronic indebtedness as a result of falling prices and rising input costs, which has led to expropriation, especially of land. There is thus much greater numbers of people looking for opportunities of wage labour. Meanwhile, the drastic reduction in the state's spending on rural development has led to loss of employment and reduced purchasing power in rural society. Moreover, concurrent trends of de-industrialization have meant no new employment generated in the economy (Patnaik 2005; Rawal 2008). There is declining income and surplus labour, leading to a growing dependence on unpaid and subsistence work.[4]

Thus, women's economic profile has been growing, even in West Bengal, despite historical and overall low rate of women's workforce participation. There is in West Bengal, as has been controversially argued for the country, a 'feminization of agriculture'.[5] In the closing decade of the twentieth century, from 1991 to 2001, more women were counted as working in agriculture than previously. When rural households are desperate, they deploy women's labour even in sharp divergence from custom. Thus, while female workers in own cultivation increased marginally, at a time when wages were stagnant, women agricultural wage workers increased by almost a million. Our survey has managed to capture the increase in women in agricultural wage labour in comparison to own cultivation. In the first decade of this century, there was a 32.8 percent increase in the share of women agricultural workers in total agricultural workers of West Bengal: a 21.7 percent increase in women cultivators (among total cultivators) and a 26.8 percent increase in agricultural labourers (among total agricultural labourers) (Sengupta 2012). In the same period, women in household industry increased by nearly three times (from about 0.4 million to about 1.2 million) (Chakraborty and Chakraborty 2010). A steep increase in male migration has enhanced and diversified women's involvement in the rural economy.

WANTED, A YOUNG BRIDE: TO WORK AT HOME

If opportunities for wage labour for young unmarried women lead to deferment of marriage, economic circumstances that augment the significance of unpaid and household-bound component of women's labour may, by inverse logic, support the early harnessing of women in marriage and, thus, in their primary labouring roles. In West Bengal, the marriage system remains the institutional framework for the domestic deployment of women's labour; the greater the requirement for such labour, more the imperative for early marriage. Marriage is the mode of recruitment of the labouring bride! Contrary to popular characterizations, thus, our research indicates a *demand* for the labour of wives, of which some of our respondents gave us very categorical statements. We recount three by women of different ages, districts and communities. Saleha Bibi (Muslim) (61 years) of Birbhum, when asked by the interviewer how she would choose her daughters-in-law, replied that she wanted a hardy girl able to do the housework. Haimabati Bhar (SC) (42 years), from South 24-Parganas, said about her son's prospective bride that she will come into a poor household and will have to work. Chameli Soren (ST) (19 years), also from Birbhum, has a very young son. Looking ahead, however, she ruminates on what kind of a woman she wants as a bride for her son: 'someone who can work'.

The labour of very young woman are required on multiple counts, such as to undertake heavy domestic work, to free older women for work outside the home and to contribute to the household's agrarian and non-agrarian activities. This can sometimes draw in young daughters. There are many examples of unmarried girls, who are withdrawn from school to do housework or expected to do housework over and above study. They are required to substitute the labour of the mother, forced to go out to earn wages or engaged in home-based work for wages. Gayetri Adak, for example, gave us a sad story of deprivation. She is now 24 years old. Her siblings were quite well educated. Her elder sister lived with an aunt, fell in love with and married a schoolteacher and, therefore, got an opportunity to study. She is now studying in an M.A. programme. The younger sister finished school and joined a nurse-training course. Gayetri, the middle daughter, was able to pass only Class 8. She stopped studying when her father fell ill and required nursing at home. Her mother had to go out to work. Gayetri dropped out of school to help her mother. A few of our respondents spoke about having to handle a heavy burden of housework before marriage and a much smaller number of other kinds of work they did as young girls before marriage.

Some parents are too poor to be able to protect girls from the grind of housework or even wage work. Generally, however, the taboo against unmarried girls working for wages outside the home holds. We did find girls working on the family's land before marriage but they were very few. Shampa Mal, for instance, was married at 17. She dropped out of school at the age of 10 to do domestic work and field labour on the family farm. Clearly, one acceptable family strategy in the face of dire poverty is to deploy the labour of the girl child in a variety of work. It is, of course, significant that the girl rather than the boy works, at domestic work or, by extension, on the family's land or, by a different form of extension, at paid domestic work.[6] In fact, West Bengal has the highest rate of girl children recorded as working in the country (Chakravarty and Chakravarty 2016). It is noteworthy that the one occupation common for young unmarried girls, at ages as low as even

5 years, is live-in domestic work (Sen and Sengupta 2016). This particular wage-earning occupation does not transgress the taboo against public appearance and labour.

So far, this is a known and familiar story. What we found surprising was the protection and indulgence many parents extend to their daughters before marriage. Most parents try to avoid sending young unmarried girls outside the home for work. Our respondents expressed this as affection and/ or protection, parents not wishing to subject young girls to harsh physical labour or male gaze/attack in public spaces, or in terms of social transgression. Equally, of course, parents acquiesce with (or even actively promote) customs that require early induction of their daughters into womanhood, wifehood and motherhood. Nevertheless, in most cases, relationships between parents and daughter are replete with care and affect. In many cases, mothers, especially, seek to compensate for the future they know is in script for their daughters. Jashoda Mondol has to go out to work, so her second daughter does all the housework. She has not given her in marriage yet, because she feels the daughter is not ready. The in-laws will not care for her, feed her well or let her sleep longer. Some mothers do not wish their daughters to help in the house before marriage because they will have to do such work for the rest of their lives. Madhabi Biswas told her daughter Sati, 'I say you don't have to do any work, you study in school'. This was to no avail because Sati married of her own choice, the marriage failed and she had to migrate to the city to enter live-in domestic work. Many parents want their daughters to study rather than enter into an early marriage but are apprehensive they may elope, not only bringing scandal to the family but also ruining their own future happiness. Laila Bibi (now 21 years) had an easy childhood but she eloped and married at 16 years, had a child soon after, suffers from a number of gynaecological problems. She has to work very hard in her marital household, without any help. Tabassum (now 20) and Debi (now 21) were given in arranged marriages at the young ages of 15 and 16 respectively.

Both came from loving homes, where they did not have to do any work. Both have to carry heavy burdens of domestic work after marriage. For many of our respondents, marriage marked the journey from natal to marital household as well as from a childhood under parental care to adult labour under the control of male and female elders of the conjugal family. The fact that most young brides have their first child in the first year of their marriage means that marriage and adulthood is associated with the triad of sexuality, reproduction and labour.

In the nineteenth century, proto-nationalist publicists spoke of marriage as a *samskara* and compulsory for both men and women. For women, marriage is the key rite of passage to adulthood; it marks the transition from girlhood to womanhood. It marks their induction into the adult world of sex and procreation, including all the labours of reproduction. A number of anthropological studies have shown that in the case of women, age and life-stage determine the pattern of work and role in the family's decision-making. As the need for sexual control lessens with age, women's participation in family activities becomes more diverse. For the poor, this can also mean more involvement in public labour. There are two major stages in this transition: first, the attainment of their own wifehood and motherhood; and second, acquiring power of the deployment of other young women, daughters, and, much more importantly, daughters-in-law. As mothers-in-law and grandmothers, they command power and respect. Thus, women's negotiating strength builds over time, with age and by marriage relationships (Dasgupta 1995; Dyson and Moore 1983; Vatuk 1987).

If marriage marks the passage to adulthood, 'child' or 'infant marriage' is surely a contradiction in terms. In recent years, there has been some attempt to unpack the complex cultural codes by differentiating digital age and biological age. This has added further to the conundrum of naming child marriage. There is no indigenous term for child marriage; marriage is connected to puberty and, therefore, child (or early) almost by definition. As mentioned in the introduction, in the nineteenth century, social reformers invented the term *balyavivaha* to begin a process of naming what would become the key gender problem of the century. However, by tradition and practice, a child becomes an adult at marriage, so what is child marriage? Let us put this in another way: The child will become an adult upon marriage; thus, all marriage is child marriage.

Equally, the 'child' ceases to be a child at marriage. This would mean, if girls are married at 7 or 8 years, and become women upon marriage, that childhood is of very short duration. These cultural codes are at odds with the notion of an absolute digital age (now at 18 years) marking entry into adulthood and capacity for marriage. The traditional marriage system, however, also carried relative notions of age. Even a few decades ago, there was virtually no lower threshold on the age of marriage, but all (especially infant) brides did not attain adulthood upon marriage. More than a century ago, this issue had surfaced in the age of consent debate. At what (digital) age was a bride an adult, that is, capable of a sexually active marriage? One way to address this question within received tradition was the two-stage marriage: An unconsummated marriage in infancy followed by a second ritual at puberty, the 'real marriage' in sexual terms. In present-day West Bengal, the two-stage marriage is all but forgotten. After repeated questioning, we got a few responses from very few women who had themselves experienced a second marriage (two women above 60 years) and few more, who remembered a mother or mother-in-law or even a grandmother having a *phulbiye* or a *khoibiye* (the formal term for which is *garbhadan*).[7] The bride's journey to the marital home was immediately after the second marriage and marked the triple association of adulthood with sexuality, reproduction and labour.

The centrality of biological age in marriage customs has facilitated the gradual rise of marriage to puberty, eliminating the two-stage marriage. The spreading awareness of the values of school education, now increasingly promoted by state policy, may also explain growing hesitation to marry off children prior to puberty. As noted in the introduction, child marriage is declining across regions and social groups. In the six districts of West Bengal we visited, what may be termed real child marriage (pre-pubertal marriage or in digital terms, below 14 years) is becoming very rare. It is not yet obsolete; we have found a few cases of marriage at 12 or 13 years, but the usual age range is 15 to 18 years. This is legally child marriage, but observers have been arguing for it to be termed 'early' rather than child marriage.

Earlier, young girls were confined to the house after puberty until marriage, a custom that itself impelled marriage as soon as possible after puberty. This was common in rural and urban communities half a century ago and has been slow to change. Rabeya Bibi (married at 17 now 41) says that she reached puberty at the age of 15 and she had to stop going out of the home. For many young girls, puberty also meant the cessation of schooling. In recent years, this particular taboo is on the wane. Generally, parents do not hold back girls from school at the onset of puberty. Nevertheless, such habits can contribute, along with lack of sanitary facilities, unsafe roads and fear of boys and girls mixing in schools, to girls dropping out soon after puberty.[8] If a girl does not go to school, her mother protects her from labour at home, social custom does not allow her to go out to work, or very much at all, what is she to do? The unmarried adolescent girl is perhaps the new problem without a name in Bengal's countryside.

These factors together converge towards the marriage of girls soon after puberty. There is no longer the practice of the two-stage marriage required in pre-pubertal marriages. We found that almost all marriages are marked by immediate transition: a shift to the marital home, regular sexual activity and induction into domestic labour. We found a few cases where marriages failed because the bride wished to continue to study. The proscription against young brides going to school is on many counts, but the most important is the neglect of domestic duties. The most striking is the story of Manashi Jana. Her parents are not poor and she was given in an arranged marriage with all the accompaniments of gifts and jewellery, when studying in Class 9. Her mother-in-law and others in her marital family beat her for her insistence on attending school. She returned to her natal home and at the time of the interview, she had been back for two years. Among all our respondents, only one under-age bride was encouraged to continue to study. Tusi Guria had studied up to Class 10 and wanted to appear for the Madhyamik, when she was suddenly married off without her consent. Her mother-in-law was quite willing that she should continue, but after marriage and childbirth, Tusi was too shy to go to school again. Tusi's case is clearly exceptional. For adolescent women, education is leisure or at least a privilege available only in the natal home. Its denial to young brides, even in relatively better-off households, is in tune with the pressure to induct women into labour as early as possible, especially domestic labour. Thus, early marriage makes sense to its participants. Young men enter the labour market; young women enter marriages. In its function to harness the labour of young women when they achieve the capacity for hard labour, early marriage is economically rational.

Usually, it is as wives rather than daughters that women experience hard physical labour. In households with young sons, parents, usually mothers, express a need for a young bride to undertake domestic work. Almost never is 'young' expressed in digital age, though in the imagination of most prospective mothers-in-law, the bride is an adolescent girl. Some parents wish for a young woman in the house after a daughter's marriage. Families without young daughters justify bringing home a child bride for an adolescent son. Sabitri Ojha is 17 years old and just married; her mother-in-law told us that she had arranged the marriage because she needed someone to help with the housework. She has two sons and no daughter. Minati Kala is 20 years old now; she was married at 17 and had her first child the next year. Asked about her early marriage, she said that everybody had agreed on the marriage, what could she say? 'I was bound to say "yes" then.' Her mother-in-law commented that she insisted that her son be married when she discovered that she had contracted tuberculosis. It became a matter of grave urgency to have someone in the house who could take care of the cooking and other housework. Shyamali Sheet (21 years) told us the story of her own marriage at a young age. Her mother-in-law is differently-abled and unable to cope with the household's work. Shyamali was 'brought in' to do household chores. Amina Bibi (now 20 years) was married at the age of 14. Her husband's mother died; he married quickly so that he could 'get hot rice on his plate'.

Chandana Haldar gave us the most elaborate (and entertaining) perspective of a needy mother-in-law. She is blind in one eye. Her father gave her a lot of land at marriage in compensation. They live off the land but also sell land when they need large sums. Her daughter was married when she was in Class 11 to a much older man, an electrical engineer. The marriage was on condition that there was no dowry demand. The elder son used to work in Puri, where he met a woman he liked but Chandana did not approve because she was low caste. Later, he 'met' someone on the phone and married her. There was no dowry; he got a few gifts at marriage. Usually a mother with one daughter and two sons looks forward to a handsome profit in dowry. Chandana, however, has no great opinion of dowry, because it makes the bride arrogant. Moreover, she wanted dark girls for her sons, willing to work and adapt to a poor family: 'A beautiful bride will become a VIP! She will cook one day and not the other. I do not need a VIP.' When her younger son came to know a girl through the mobile phone, Chandana spoke to her and found her to be everything she wanted. She came from a very poor family but from East Bengal, like them. Chandana encouraged the girl to elope. The girl came to Howrah with a friend; Chandana took her elder son to give puja at Dakshineshwar, picked up the girl and brought her home.

The girl's family is poor; they were not able to organize the wedding. I had given my daughter in marriage; I needed a woman in the family. We have a shop selling food; there were a lot of problems. I felt we needed someone to do the work. I asked her whether she wanted to come. The girl said that she was ready. She came with her friend without telling her parents....

How do we describe this marriage? Is it a love marriage? There is certainly an element of self-choice: boy 'met' girl on the mobile phone! This is a common enough story across the country today. However, the frank labour calculation on part of the groom's mother, who is the cupid in the love story, explains the logic of early marriage.

There is a mix of irritation and amusement among Bengali middle classes about a ritual routine at ceremonial weddings. The groom's mother usually does not attend the wedding. In earlier times, when the groom's family had to travel to the bride's (possibly distant) village for the wedding, only male relatives accompanied him and were termed *borjatri*, literally groom travellers or those who travel with the groom. When the groom left his own home for the journey to the bride's home, the mother performed an elaborate ritual blessing (*baran*) and the groom said to her, by dictum of *lokachara* or popular custom, 'Mother, I am going to fetch a *dasi* [literally, slave woman or a maid servant] for you.' This particular custom, if taken literally, resonates strongly with the approach to marriage that we found and underscores the labour dynamics of early marriage.[9]

PRECEPT AND PRACTICE: GENERATIONAL DIVISION OF FEMALE LABOUR

Brides are in demand in rural West Bengal for *gharer kaj* (domestic work), an appellation that covers a wide range of activity. There is first, the usual domestic work (cooking, cleaning and care). There is what is sometimes termed 'extended' domestic work, that is, work around the home, which may include income-earning activities but is usually producing commodities for household consumption (kitchen gardening, livestock rearing, collecting and foraging). Third, there is household-based productive work, which could mean participation in the household's economic activity, such as caste-based artisan work or minding the shop from time to time, and includes field and related labour on the family farm. Only formal wage-work outside the home is excluded from gharer kaj and considered to be earning activity: *chakri* (usually salaried employment) or *rojgar* (earning) or *majuri* (daily wage labour). For the rural poor, majuri is the most common earning activity and there is some variety, the most important being agricultural labour. Of increasing significance is work under the NREGA scheme.[10] Women also do a variety of work with SHGs and they have been included in categories two, three or four as and when relevant rather than treated as a separate category.

Normatively speaking, there are clear-cut divisions of labour along lines of gender and generations, overlapping with familial relationships, that organize these four categories of work. The reality, especially at times of economic hardship, is far messier. In this section, we try to navigate the complicated interplay between prescriptions and practice that shapes the multifarious patterns of women's work in rural Bengal today. On the one hand, there are established gender and generational work roles; on the other, there is greater variety and intensity in labour demands made on women. Given the social restrictions on the mobility and visibility of unmarried girls, it is young married women who are better able to respond to these demands of flexibility. Thus, female generational substitution in the household is more effective between mothers-in-law and young brides than between mothers and daughters.[11]

Let us first look at what existing literature has to say about women's involvement in these different categories of work. Sen and Sen (1985) have offered some insights from NSS data.

It should be borne in mind that their analysis (and the data) are now more than 20 years old. However, we quote their findings because some of these resonate with ours. It appears that rural families seek to stabilize income by a diversification along gender lines: women work on the family farm, while men work for wages outside the home, especially as agricultural labourers. Some scholars have argued that women in South Asia prefer household-based work because of ideologies of seclusion/segregation and/or to accommodate work and family. Others argue, however, that such preference is also a response to discrimination in the market. Since women earn lower wages for all kinds of work, their decision to work in the family farm, while men go out to work for wages, is a rational one, which maximizes household returns (Desai and Jain 1994). In this sense, women's work in the family farm is not just 'domestic' or an extension of the domestic.

Table 6.1 needs two explanations. First, we have taken the primary occupation, where women have reported several occupations. Thus, all women do domestic work but those who have said they do only domestic work are in column 1. The numbers reported in column 2 are low because many women, who work on the family farm or some other household activity, also work for wages, which they report as more important. These numbers are in column 3. We could not avoid the

TABLE 6.1: Distribution of Types of Work by Age Group Reported by 264 Women Respondents in Six Districts of West Bengal

	Age Group	1. Only Domestic Work	2. Work in Family Farm and Other Household Activity	3. Wage Work	4. Total
1	5–14	1	0	1	2
2	15–29	87	19	29	135
3	30–44	24	12	46	82
4	45–59	11	4	25	40
5	60+	3	0	2	5
6	Total	126	35	103	264

overlap between column 2 and 3 even though it has meant some under-representation in column 2. Second, the category extended domestic work is overlapping with other work (no respondent reported this as primary work) and, therefore, not included in this table.

There is broadly a gender division of labour, with women in home-based work or household-based work or labour on the family farm and men in wage work outside the home, including on others' lands. However, as other researchers have reported, there is increasingly more women involved in field work. The real import of Table 6.1 is that there is generational substitution among women. If we take rows 2–4, which is where married women of working age are concentrated, we see that the young bride is entrusted with the domestic work or even the extended domestic work, including at times the household economic activity (such as labour on the family farm), freeing older women, usually the mother-in-law, to undertake wage labour. Thus, there is remarkable divergence when it comes to wage work between the first group and the two others. In the age group 15–29, about 21.4 percent women report wage work as their chief occupation, for the age groups 30–44 and 45–59, this is 56 percent and 62.5 percent respectively. Clearly, the participation of women in wage work rises with age and then falls after 60 years. Expectedly, the proportion reporting only domestic work in these two age groups is lower at 29 percent and 27.5 percent, while 64 percent in the age group 15–29 report themselves to be only in domestic work. One look at the total figures row affirms the arguments about the overwhelming significance of domesticity in constructions of gender: nearly 48 percent of the total women respondents do 'only domestic work'. We will see in the next section that this is highly effective ideology at work, since 'only domestic work' can and does cover a huge range of economic activities.

To understand the link of this generational substitution with early marriage, we have to focus attention on the age group 15–29, since under-age brides are within this group.

TABLE 6.2: Distribution of Types of Work by Marital Status Reported
by 264 Women Respondents in Six Districts of West Bengal

Marital Status	Only Domestic Work	Work in Family Farm and Other Household Activity	Wage Work	Total
Unmarried	2	0	1	3
Married	117	35	96	249
Widow	3	0	2	4
Separated/Divorced	4	0	4	8
Total	126	35	103	264

There is a clear preference for married rather than unmarried women for most kinds of work. When older women need to go out of the house to work, they prefer the daughter-in-law rather than the daughter to be the substitute worker in the home, in home-based work or in the family farm. Let us take a quick look at work participation according to marital status in Table 6.2. If we add the categories other than married as 'single' women, we have 15 women of whom 9 (60 percent) do only domestic work, while 7 (47 percent) are engaged in wage work. None is working on the family farm. Let us add to this the findings of Sen and Sen from NSS data that in the never married sub-group in the 15–29 age group, the incidence of women doing only domestic work is much lower. We have an interesting profile of the economic activities of the 15–29 age group which seems defined more by their marital status and familial roles than merely by age. With the caveat that the numbers are small, the fact that none of the single women report working on the family farm or a household activity is a remarkable affirmation of scholarship that has emphasized the significance of marriage in women's access to family-household resources. Those single young women who do not do 'only domestic work' usually undertake paid domestic work (Chakravarty and Chakravarty 2016). This squares the logic of early marriage: it is young brides and recent mothers, who concentrate on domestic, extended domestic or household-based work.

According to Table 6.1, the proportion of women who work on the family farm is more or less similar in age groups, 15–29 and 30–44 at 14 percent and 14.6 percent but is significantly lower for the 45–59 age group at 10 percent. We looked closely at the responses we received regarding women's participation in fieldwork on own land, set out by age, religion and caste in Table 6.3. Of our total respondents, 16.3 percent are landless and a little less than 10 percent reported more than 5 bighas of land. The great majority, at 43 percent, have less than a bigha and those with 1–4 bighas of land are 23 percent. Of the 264 rural respondents, 45 have no land and 22 have only homesteads, no cultivable land. Thus, out of 197 households, who have some land, 74 women report that they have some role in own cultivation. This table includes all women who do some work on the family farm, not only those who report this as their main occupation. As a proportion of the total respondents, women undertaking own cultivation is 28 percent; however, as a proportion of those who have cultivable land, this is 37 percent.

The numbers given in Table 6.3 have not been disaggregated by district. However, in Murshidabad, there is a lower propensity for women to work in the field. Out of 43 respondent households, there are 12 without cultivable land (8 with only homestead land). If we consider the number of women in own cultivation without Murshidabad, the proportion works out to 42 percent. The number of women from Murshidabad who reported own cultivation is only 4 out of 31 (who have cultivable land). This works out to be 12 percent. In distribution by age, this is 24 percent in the 15–29 age group, 29 percent in the age group 30–44 and 40 percent in the age group 45–59. There is an increasing propensity with age to work in the family farm. This bears out the statements made by respondents that mothers-in-law will work on the field while daughters-in-law will work at home-bound occupations.

TABLE 6.3: Family Farming by Age, Religion and Caste for 264 Respondents
in Six Districts of West Bengal

Age Group	Total Female	Hindu				Muslim	Total
		General	SC	ST	OBC		
5–14	2	0	0	1	0	0	1
15–29	135	8	10	11	0	4	33
30–44	82	3	12	4	5	0	24
45–59	40	4	5	4	0	3	16
60+	5	0	0	0	0	0	0
	264	15	27	20	5	7	74

A close reading of the interviews suggests, however, that there are quite different statements of 'norms'. There is a clear pattern of preference but there is also considerable divergence, determined by economic necessity in a time of crisis. We heard clear articulations of norms from respondents such as Sabita Soren (ST), who said that a new bride will not work on other people's land but may work on the family's own land. Dolly Ankure (SC) (married at 13, now 18) said that a young bride will not go out to work, either in their own field or others' fields or even for NREGA. Older women spoke of different norms, even when engaged in a wide range of activities. Mou Patra (42 years) (SC) works on the family farm; she also works under NREGA; participates in cooking mid-day meal in their local school through an SHG; however, she will not work as agricultural labour as her husband does. Maya Tarafdar (40 years) (converted Christian) has two bighas of land and does most of the field labour such as the sowing, cutting, harvesting and de-husking of the paddy but will not work as wage labour. These women working on their family farm confirm that the labour demands are very heavy indeed. The workload of women in families with more land can sometimes be more than that of landless women (I. Sen 1983 and Cain et al, 1979).

However, as secondary data are showing, for the last two decades, it is in agricultural labour, rather than own cultivation, that women's employment has been increasing

(Chakraborty and Chakraborty 2010). Our findings resonate with these general observations. Even though some of our respondents have restated norms that young women will not undertake wage-work, especially outside the home, in fact, 'domestic work' itself is a capacious category and can include wage-work within it. Moreover, many young married women too have to undertake general or agricultural labour from time to time.

Table 6.1 illustrates that in land-poor communities, wage work is of great significance and most married women cannot restrict themselves to work on the family farm. Simran Bibi (45 years, married at 14) does all sorts of work. The women in her family work on their family farm, since they cannot afford hired labour. They have nearly two bighas of land. Even though Muslim women in her area do not usually work outside the home, in pressing circumstances Simran has worked in others' fields too. We met much younger women, who began working as agricultural labourer or in general labour soon after an early marriage. For instance, Amina Bibi, married at 14, now 20, takes agricultural work when she can find it throughout the year. It is not so remarkable that Jaba Dandapath works in NREGA and as agricultural labourer, since she is 45 years old now, but her daughter, recently married, also works as agricultural labour. Chameli Soren, who wished for a working daughter-in-law, is only 19 years old, married for three years, with a two-year-old son. She has to take labouring jobs in addition to her domestic work.

Given the heterogeneity of work, a straightforward gender or generational division of labour does not always obtain. In several districts, however, we found that men are more rigid about work choices. In lean seasons or during a crisis, it is women who will undertake whatever work is available however poor the returns. This is why women's labour is critical to households, especially in times of crisis. Families command an extraordinary degree of flexibility in the nature and the extent of women's labour. Take the case of Madhu Mandal (21 years). Her husband is unemployed. They have a little patch of land and they both work on it but this is not enough for the sustenance of the family. The husband supplements family income with agricultural wage labour. At the time of the survey (July), he was 'unemployed' because there was no work available. However, Madhu took jobs as general labour and plucking in tea plantations, enabling the household to tide over the crisis.

Intersecting relations of class, caste and community complicate gender and generational division of labour. The maintenance of non-earning non-working women, the substitution of their labour by hired labour, has always been a marker of upper class and higher status. Given that there are few affluent families among our respondents, we have not found much example of this. Yet, caste and class do shape the gender and generational patterns of a household's response to chronic poverty or short-term shocks. Class and caste dynamics of the ideology of domesticity influence, even determine, performance and valuation of women's work. It has been widely noted that in South Asia, one aspect of the purdah system is the link between status and women's visible work. In Samita Sen's earlier work, she has shown that colonial modernity deepened caste and class differentiation in women's work (S. Sen 1999). There are two noticeable tendencies. First, is the phenomenon of withdrawal of women from visible and public labour. Thus, better-off families do not allow younger women to work outside the home; or with improving household conditions, families may withdraw women from wage work into extended or pure domesticity. Thus, the analysis of NSS data showed that family income increases with size of landholding but women's economic activity declines (Sen and Sen 1985; Desai and Jain 1994).

Most women in upper-caste households prefer not to work outside the home. Among the 282 respondents, we have found only nine brahmin families and some of these are very poor. Let us take the case of an inter-caste marriage such as that of Suchitra Bera (SC). She was 17 when she married into a brahmin family. She was in employment as a domestic worker and after marriage gave up work. Three years ago, Surupa Chakrabarty (SC), aged 16, married into a brahmin family. She does not have to do any work, she said, because they employ a domestic worker. The exception is Shibani Panda. She is 35 years old. Her husband is a migrant worker, absent for most of the year. Shibani does most of the work on their own field.

Rumki Das is at the other end of the caste scale. They are an SC family and her daughter has been married into an SC family, but she is an adherent of seclusion and domesticity. She is not very well and her husband does not like her to go out, so she cooks but does not 'work'. She will not allow her hypothetical daughter-in-law (she has a young son) to go out to work though she will have to do all the housework. She spoke rather proudly of her daughter, who was married at 16. The groom's family is quite 'rich', she said, and women do not go out; she cannot go out of the house; she is not even given any pocket money for personal expenses. Rumki may not have been able to afford such a marriage for her daughter. The father-in-law had waived dowry because he met and liked the girl.

There is a different attitude to educated employment. Rina Acharya (brahmin) is 17 years old and married very recently. Her parents were very poor, so she helped by taking tuitions. In her marital family, the women do not do fieldwork. Even though they are very poor, they hire labour both for fieldwork and for cattle grazing. However, her parents-in-law are not averse to her taking on tuition. Very late in the interview, it transpired that the whole family is engaged in cashew peeling, including the young bride. The family saves this money for special expenses. Even in better-off families, there is a positive attitude to better quality work opportunity. Malaya Maiti (SC) (now 24; married at 16) is married into a well-off family; they have land and several ponds. A large part of this was her husband's mother's inheritance, which makes her quite a powerful presence in the family. Malaya does not have to work but she has passed Madhyamik and is now in an IT training course. Asked if she will be allowed to work, her mother-in-law said, 'If she gets a job, they will decide what is good for their future. We will not live forever.' The exceptions made to established rules, the varieties of responses by caste, community, economic circumstances of the family and the nature of jobs, shows a situation of flux. There are norms but these are stretched according to need and if advantages are perceived. Overall, flexibility has increased the value of female 'domestic' labour and the significance of its recruitment system, that is, marriage.

DOMESTICITY AND DOMESTIC WORK

In the first section 'Wanted, a Young Bride: To Work at Home', we introduced Shyamali Sheet, who had been married young, because her disabled mother-in-law was unable to manage the domestic work. The second part of Shyamali's story is equally important because it gives us great insight into the elasticity of gharer kaj. When families bring in young women as brides, very few are as frank as Chandana about their labour calculation. In fact, the opposite is mostly true. There is a general denial of even the fact of labour, cloaked by marriage and the ideology of domesticity. The unpaid labour of wives and mothers (including their labour *as* wives and mothers) is easily invisibilized, folded into domesticity. Thereby marriage is rendered 'culture', devoid of economic content.

In addition to cooking, cleaning and childcare, Shyamali helps her husband and in-laws peel cashew skin. The head of the family receives the raw material as well as the whole of the wages, even though women do most of the work. Shyamali's contribution to her marital family's economic activity has become an extension of her household work. When questioned further, she said that this work is in the nature of help she gives her family during leisure hours. Yet, she peels 5–6 kg cashews per day and knows that this fetches ₹7 per kg. In this district, nail-making is organized on similar lines and women do this as a part of housework. Thus, women who participate in home-based wage work do not identify their own work, their individual wages or the returns of their labour. They participate in familial and social undervaluation of their work by subsuming it within domesticity. Papri Bibi (20 years) is somewhat unusual, since she is a Hindu (SC) married into a Muslim family, but she explained to us her notion of 'work': NREGA and housework should not be seen as work because the first is intermittent and in the second there is no earning. The same, she said, applied to own cultivation. Even though they consume the rice from their own land, 'this is not an earning'. Very few women in our survey asserted the economic value of their household labour. Even when it was evident that households relied critically on the labour of women, perhaps for this very reason, their labour was folded so insistently and often with ease into domesticity.

Feminist scholars have attempted to open up the category of 'domestic work' to underline the significance of women's unpaid work. From the 1970s, they have challenged the 'statistical purdah', which made women's work invisible in economic theory and measurement (Jain, Singh and Chand 1979). Yet, domestic work continues to be perceived as a part of women's assigned gender roles and shorn of economic significance. In Jalpaiguri, we met Purna Sarkar, a young widow of 19 years. She was married at the age of 13 years and had her first child at the age of 14 years. Now she has two young children. She was not able to give us basic information such as her caste or her identity papers, the family's landholding or income. We understood that she was kept at the margins because she was viewed as a dependent. Yet, she worked in the family farm, and in the family's jute business, helping with cultivation and trading. She participated wholly in the economic activity of the family but did not perceive her role as economic; she considered all her work to be a part of her domestic duties.[12]

Our respondents in Murshidabad were mostly Muslim women, and they did not describe their labour on the family farm as work. Many women contributed towards processing jute. They did not participate in the cultivation but did almost everything else. Out of 43, only eight women self-identified as workers, since they had separate and visible earnings. Of these, four were engaged in home-based biri rolling, two in tailoring and two in the family's jute business. Rashida Bibi at first said that she does nothing but housework. Much later in the interview, she said:

> I work all day. I cut vegetables... I take the food to the labourers in the field. I bring the utensils back home. I have to pay the labourers.... I don't work in the field, but I dry the jute. When the jute is sown, we don't go to the field, but I know the work and can do it.

Farzana Bibi said something very similar. She too said that she did not work in the field but when the men brought the paddy home, she boiled it, dried it and de-husked it. 'Whatever farmers do, I do', she said. It was not only Muslim women who gave us the rote response to questions about work. In South 24-Parganas, Chandra Giri told us that she was a housewife and does only housework. She was 17 years old and had been married for a year. It was much later in the interview that she mentioned that she worked on the family farm. She did not consider her work in the family as 'work' but a part of her domestic duties.

Fultushi Murmu (Purulia) is an ST, belonging to a community known historically for high workforce participation rate of women. Her husband is a first year undergraduate student and he teaches at a school. Fultushi works on their land of 8–10 bighas to produce the paddy that is the mainstay for the year. In addition, she makes leaf-plates at home. According to her husband, these plates are for use at home and not for selling. The field worker noted, however, that metal utensils are used at home. Caterers use leaf plates at large-scale social events. In the area, this is a common piece-rated home-based work organized through middlemen, which serves markets across the state. It is highly likely that Fultushi had a cash contribution to the monthly income of ₹6,000–7,000 that the family reported. Yet, she does not 'work'. These stories tell us that an expansive domesticity subsumes all kinds of work done at home. From our interviews, we find the invisibilization of different kinds of work, from artisan work, cash crop cultivation to piece-rated wage work.

What about the conventional understanding of gharer kaaj? As already mentioned, while the norms are being stretched in all directions, there is still a strong articulation of a social order with rules about gender and generational division of labour. In this worldview, young wives and mothers are responsible for core domestic work, cooking, cleaning, childcare. The literature on women's work emphasizes that domestic work is 'residual' work, that is, first, all women do domestic work, and second, those who do no other work report domestic work as their chief activity. Thus, the numbers of those who do only domestic work increase during lean agricultural seasons. However, the most important variable is age and marital status. It is young brides and young mothers, as argued in the previous section, who tend to report 'only domestic work' as their primary occupation. Table 6.1 shows that 28.2 percent of women in the age group 30–59 are engaged in 'only domestic work', this percentage is 64 for the age group 15–29. If we look at the breakup of those engaged in 'only domestic work', moreover, we find that 69 percent fall in the age group 15–29.

As mentioned earlier, most young brides have their first child in the first year of their marriage. Thus, the young bride is also the mother of one or more young children, who require attention and supervision. Thus, domesticity centred on childcare is an important consideration in the division of labour among women in the household. In the literature on women's work, the deleterious effect of maternal absence and children's exposure to alternative care has received some attention (Basu and Basu 1991; Khan, Tamag and Patel 1990). This can become an argument against women undertaking wage labour outside the home or in favour of their opting for traditional and home-based work. Young wives and mothers of young children tend to undertake 'only domestic work' along with extended domestic work. Investigating the 87 women of the 15–29 age group who have reported 'only domestic work' as their occupation, we see that 54 have children below the age of 10 years. Only four in the age group 30–44 and none in the other age groups have children of that age. Of the four, three are in only domestic work and one does wage work. In the 15–29 age groups, however, women with children below 10 years also work on the family farm (11) and wage work (23). This means that what mothers of young children do if the need is urgent is to work outside the home. We find corroboration of this from women who have said that they have been working from the age of 10, especially at domestic work, because their mothers had to go out to work. Thus, the age-related distribution of work may not be only a question of age but also the woman's situation in the reproductive cycle.

Desai and Jain (1994) argue that domestic responsibilities in poor households are so heavy that even stay-at-home mothers have little time for quality childcare. The literature shows only very slight decrease/increase in the time women spend on children whether they work or not. The major factor is the time devoted to housework. There appears to be very little difference between housewives and women working on family farm with regard to children's health and well-being. This is highly suggestive. The presence of young children determines a work arrangement that does not actually allow much childcare. The demands of domestic work can be so onerous that children suffer considerable benign neglect.

There is a tendency to overlook the drudgery involved in routine domestic work, especially in the rural context. For at least half a century, feminists in other parts of the world have questioned the notion that home technologies alleviate women's burden of housework. In rural households in West Bengal, the absence of technology results in a heavy physical burden on women. Even routine domestic work such as cooking and cleaning are highly labour-intensive and physically demanding. There has been a great deal written about procurement of fuel and water. This is not to say that field labour is less physically demanding, but housework is a relentless cycle of fuzzy time.

Our respondents said almost in one voice that domestic work is not work. They did this for their household. It is 'labour of love' or a valued aspect of femininity. It has to be done and is done unquestioningly. There is nothing said about the exactions and tribulations of domestic work. It is as though it is nothing at all, evacuated of all content, including its manual and emotional demands. The common answer to our insistent questions: 'It is nothing'; 'We do nothing, only cooking and housework'. We noted with great surprise the invisibility of housework in speech. Perhaps, speech is superfluous. Since all women do this work, they know what is entailed and do not feel the need for (or do not have the words for) description or discussion.

The exacting nature of housework in the rural setting may explain in part why older women prefer to relegate housework to young brides and opt for wage labour. There are also ideological factors at play and immobilizing young women in the home is a form of sexual control. In many families, we were told, young women are kept at home. Disha Sikdar was married at about 21, two years ago. The age is more than ordinarily confused in her case. Her mother-in-law interrupted the interview to say that she did not want Disha to pursue her education because the area was not good and she would not allow her to go out of the house. She herself was engaged in a range of earning activities: she worked in a nursery under the NREGA scheme, worked as an agricultural labourer and did home-based biri-rolling. In the little patch of land they have of their own, she grows flowers, makes flower garlands and sells them. They do not admit to Disha helping her with any of this work, though some of it is home-based. According to them, Disha only looks after the child; she does not even do much of the housework.

For many women, the transition from domestic work to wage-earning work was made because of the failure of their marriages. Shikha Mondol (domestic worker), Shampa Mal (domestic worker), Sarbari Sarkar (training to be a nurse), Bindu Bala (food processing) and Mrinmayee Mondol (making incense sticks) suffered a diminution of their status and well-being when failed marriages forced them to go out to work. Many such young women also have young children. In some cases, their mothers look after the children or they have to manage on their own. Similarly, as women grow older and the sons start working, even poor women may be able to give up working and return to a desired domesticity. Purabi Mondol is 45 years old and used to carry a very heavy workload. She is happy that her sons have enabled her to withdraw from all work other than cattle grazing.

The attitude of older women to domestic work is reveal-ing of its ubiquity and its oppressive nature. According to NSS data, women above 60 participate less in all kinds of work except unpaid domestic work, in which their presence is dis-proportionately high (Sen and Sen 1985). We have only five respondents of this age, so we cannot support the point with numbers. Of the five, three women do only domestic work and two are still engaged in wage work. However, we saw a lot more women above 60 years in the course of our fieldwork. There is some involvement of older women in housework, even though this may be restricted to some tasks if there are younger women in the family-household. There are two points to be made in this connection. First, domestic work is manual and strenuous and older women pass this on to younger women, when they can. Somaya Bibi (70 years) is lucky that her daughters-in-law do the housework: 'Now I am old. Can I work anymore? Now the daughters-in-law do the work, I eat. If they go away, I have to clean the house, wash the utensils, and do the cooking.'

Second, many older women cannot escape the drudgery of domestic work, even at quite an old age. Rasika Besra was married at the age of eleven, before puberty. She has been engaged in domestic work since then. She is now about 65 years old. She is still doing some of the domestic work. She shows us a hill at a distance from which she collects firewood. Jubeda Bibi (70 years) told us:

> Now I have to do all the cooking and all the work. The daughter-in-law has come; she will do the housework with me. What is the work of women? Cooking and serving food, doing the housework.

Kaberi Dolui (65 years) still works in others' lands for wages, does fishery in her own pond over and above domestic work: 'We are illiterate! What work can we do? This housework, making fuel balls, catching fish, cooking for the home, grazing the cows, yes, we don't have jobs, we don't do any work.' Thus, domestic work defined sometimes in narrow terms, sometimes in the most elastic terms, is the great continuity — across class and social status as has been noted by scholars from many parts of the globe — but it is also a continuity in an individual's lifespan, across age and life stage.

The compulsions of domesticity and domestic work, itself a product of shrinking economic opportunities, create the demand for the workers produced by early marriage: young brides who will take over from a mother-in-law, either tired or unable to cope or required to step out of the house to earn wages for the family. Equally, families give away their daughters because there is no incentive to defer their marriage. The only form of employment for young unmarried girls that has some traction in the state is paid domestic work, which is now drawing in married women as well.

CONCLUSION

Addressing the question of child marriage through the perspective of women's work brings to the fore the contradiction in the very naming of the phenomenon. It is not a coincidence that the Bangla word for childhood was explicitly male until Taslima Nasrin invented a word for girlhood, *meyebela*, at the close of the twentieth century.[13] Such a word had not been required earlier because of the universality of early marriage. There was no social requirement to 'construct' a girlhood since it was so short a stage in life. At present, the age of marriage of girls is concentrated at the age of puberty, immediately before or after. The dual need to induct women into productive and reproductive labour as well as to control their sexuality impels marriage as close to puberty as possible. Traditionally, marriage was the social institution, which combined sexual and labour control and this continues to be the case in West Bengal today.

The non-recognition of the labour content of wifehood allows the marital household to make a double gain. The argument for dowry is that the marital family requires compensation for the acquisition of 'unproductive' brides, but brides are required in addition to toil unremittingly.

In rural West Bengal (and South Asia in general), the household continues to be a key determinant in labour arrangements, for men too but overwhelmingly so for women. The crisis in agriculture and the general lack of employment opportunities keep women trapped in domesticity. It is still important to families to believe that their women do not work or work only within the home and at unpaid housework. The coordinates domestic femininity continue to subsume the economic activities women undertake within the household, often collectively, such as artisanal activity or piece-rated production. They are working on the family farm more than they used to and even more women are agricultural workers than workers in their own land. Yet, families continue to try and keep younger women close to home while older women go 'out to work'.

Women's work matters more than ever before. The households we visited cannot survive without the myriad range of
labour women perform. In the case of women, marriage is the
induction into the adult world of labour and sexuality and for
poor families this transition cannot be deferred to the legal age
of 18 years. For bride givers, sexuality is a primary concern,
for bride takers labour is an equally important calculation. In
this context, it should be pointed out that the glass half empty
is also half full. While labouring compulsions may have kept
the age at marriage below the legal minimum and propelled
West Bengal at the top of the child marriage league table in the
country, it has also meant a steady increase in the age of marriage. There is very little 'child' marriage properly so-called,
below the age of 14–15 years. What we see is a pervasive practice of adolescent or early marriage, with parents giving in
marriage but also girls in their early teens marrying by self-
choice at the teeth of parental opposition. The young participate in the urgency to enter the adult world of labour, sex and
reproduction. The social role and position of adolescent girls
need to be at the centre of our policy agenda if adult marriage
defined by the digital age of 18 years is our goal.

NOTES

1   There have been many decades of feminist emphasis on dowry,
    which casts very different light on the economic value of the labour
    of wives. In this chapter we have not included much information on
    dowry, even though it is so closely connected to the question of the
    value of married women's labour. Our research shows that in poor
    rural communities in West Bengal, dowry is not really as much of
    a menace as it is often portrayed. These findings of the project are
    slated for future publication.
2   There is quite a significant body of literature addressing the question
    of whether and how women gain advantage from various kinds of
    work (Vatuk 1987; Wilson-Moore 1989; Greenhalgh 1991; Vlassoff
    1994; Kabeer 1997). One aspect of this question is whether it raises
    the age of marriage and whether rise in age of marriage under these

circumstances changes their quality of life. I am not addressing this literature in any great detail, since some of it has been discussed in Chapter 5.

3   We are using the category 'class' in this chapter somewhat loosely. Our respondents are, almost entirely, from the lower end of rural society; while there is variation by economic position this does not qualify as class difference. There is a general literature regarding variation of women's work by class on which we draw but we do not deploy the category class with any precision or rigour in this chapter.

4   These issues have also been discussed in Chapter 5 and are not being repeated here.

5   There is a considerable body of literature on this, for a recent analysis of data as well as summary of the debate see Pattnaik and Lahiri-Dutt (2017); also see Sinha (2005).

6   There may be a difference among communities in this regard and this has to be explored further. There are indications that in Muslim families young men go to work and daughters get a chance to study.

7   For more on *Garbhadan*, see Tanika Sarkar (2001). Several respondents have reported that they were married between 7–12 years but even they have not had *phulbiye* or *khoibiye*. Two have said their mothers or mothers-in-law had *phulbiye*. Given that such a few respondents reported the ceremonial second marriage, one presumes it is all but forgotten. This requires much more exploration. In the case of Muslims, there is a *chauthi*. This is probably on the fourth day of marriage and more akin to *ashtamangala* or *dwiragamana*.

8   We found that another contributing factor to children, especially girl children, dropping out of school was violence, both in the school but also in the journey to and from the school.

9   It should be noted that there are other interpretations possible: The son may be reassuring the mother that the young bride will be subservient to her, not threatening her pre-eminence in the family.

10 I have slightly modified this categorization, roughly following the NSS. For more details, see Gita Sen and Chiranjib Sen (1985).

11 This pattern is seen in regions other than Bengal (Chowdhry 1994).

12 There were several other respondents in this district, who participated in jute cultivation or processing but said they did not work. The case of Jalpaiguri requires separate attention. If West Bengal's

economy is in crisis, this is more acute in the case of north Bengal. There are a number of reasons for this, but the crisis in the tea industry has an important role to play. In a recent study of three villages in Jalpaiguri district, an alarming decline in female agricultural wage labour has been noted. It is argued that de-agrarianization in combination with the revived patriarchal 'good woman' ideology led to the crises of female wage labour. Women in poor landless and marginal farms are faced with various obstacles in becoming self-employed entrepreneurs, which is being offered as the solution (Schenk-Sandbergen 2018).

13   Taslima Nasrin, *Meyebela: My Bengali Girlhood*, was published in 1998. This autobiographical book was banned in Bangladesh because it may hurt the existing social system and religious sentiments. She said in the book that she could not go out and run in the fields, since she was supposed to stay home to learn how to cook and clean. Women in Bengali society, she said, have been taught for centuries that they are slaves of men.

REFERENCES

Banerjee, Nirmala, ed., 1990. *Indian Women in a Changing Industrial Scenario.* Indo-Dutch Studies on Development Alternatives, 5. New Delhi: Sage.

Basu, Alaka Malwade, and Kaushik Basu. 1991. 'Women's Economic Roles and Child Survival: The Case of India', *Health Transition Review* 1: 83–103.

Cain, Mead, Syeda Rokeya Khanam and Shamsun Nahar. 1979. 'Class, Patriarchy and Women's Work in Bangladesh', *Population and Development Review 5*, 3: 405–38.

Chakraborty, Indrani, and Achin Chakraborty. 2010. 'Female Work Participation and Gender Differential in Earnings in West Bengal', *Journal of Quantitative Economics* 8, 2, (July).

Chakravarty, Deepita, and Ishita Chakravarty. 2016. *Women, Labour and the Economy in India: From Migrant Menservants to Uprooted Girl Children Maids.* New York: Routledge.

Chowdhry, Prem. 1994. *The Veiled Women: Shifting Gender Equations in Rural Haryana 1880–1990.* New Delhi: Oxford University Press.

———. 2005. 'Crisis of Masculinity in Haryana: the Unmarried, the Unemployed and the Aged', *Economic and Political Weekly* (henceforth *EPW*) (3 Dec. 2005).

Dasgupta, Monica. 1995. 'Life Course Perspectives on Women's Autonomy and Health Outcomes', *American Anthropologist* 9: 481–91.

Desai, Sonalde, and Devaki Jain. 1994. 'Maternal Employment and Changes in Family Dynamics: The Social Context of Women's World in Rural South India', *Population and Development Review* The Population Council, 20, 1 (March): 115–36.

Dyson, Tim, and Mick Moore. 1983. 'On Kinship Structure, Female Autonomy, and Demographic Behavior in India', *Population and Development Review 9*, 1: 35–60.

Greenhalgh, Susan. 1991. 'Women in the Informal Enterprise: Empowerment or Exploitation?' *The Population Council*, Research Division Working Paper No. 33. New York.

Jain, Devaki, Nalini Singh and Malini Chand. 1979. 'Women's Work: Methodological Issues'. In *Women and Development: Perspectives from South and Southeast Asia*, Rounaq Jahan and Hanna Papanek, eds. Dhaka: Bangladesh Institute of Law and International Affairs: 128–70.

Kabeer, Naila. 1997. 'Women, Wages and Intra-Household Power Relations in Urban Bangladesh', *Development and Change* 28, 2 (April): 261–302.

Kapadia, Karin. 1995. 'The Profitability of Bonded Labour: The Gem-Cutting Industry in Rural South India', *Journal of Peasant's Studies* 22, 3: 466–83.

———. 1998. 'Mediating the Meaning of Market Opportunities: Gender, Caste and Class in Rural South India', *EPW* 32, 52: 3329–35.

Kaur, Ravinder. 2012. 'Marriage and Migration: Citizenship and Marital Experience in Cross-Border Marriages between Uttar Pradesh, West Bengal and Bangladesh', *EPW* 47, 43.

Khan, M. E., A. K. Tamang and Bella C. Patel. 1990. 'Work Patterns of Women and Its Impact on Health and Nutrition — Some Observations from the Urban Poor', *Journal of Family Welfare* 36, 1–22.

Patnaik, U. 2005. 'Theorizing Food Security and Poverty in the Era of Economic Reforms', Public Lecture in the Series 'Freedom from Hunger', *India International Centre*, Delhi (12 April).

Pattnaik, Itishree, and Kuntala Lahiri-Dutt. 2017. 'Tracking Women in Agriculture through Recent Census Data in India', GIDR, Working Paper No 242, http://gidr.ac.in/pdf/wp-242-4407.pdf, accessed on 1 August 2018.

Radha Devi, D. 1981. 'Women Workers in Kerala: A Census Analysis'. In *Dynamics of Population and Family Welfare,* K. Srinivasan and S. Mukherjee, eds. Mumbai: Himalaya Publishing House: 269–98.

Rawal, Vikas. 2008. 'Ownership Holdings of Land in Rural India: Putting the Record Straight', *EPW* 43, 10.

Sahai, Suman. 2007. 'Are Genetically Engineered Crops the Answer to India's Agrarian Crisis?', https://genecampaign.org/wp-content/uploads/2014/07/THE_AGRARIAN_CRISIS_IN_INDIA.pdf, accessed on 1 August 2018 at 2.30 pm.

Sarkar, Tanika. 2001. *Hindu Wife, Hindu Nation: Community, Religion and Cultural Nationalism.* New Delhi: Permanent Black.

Schenk-Sandbergen, Loes. 2018. 'De-Feminisation of Agricultural Wage Labour in Jalpaiguri, West Bengal', *EPW* 53, 25 (23 June).

Sen, Gita, and Chiranjib Sen. 1985. 'Women's Domestic Work and Economic Activity: Results from National Sample Survey', *EPW* (RWS) 20, 17: 49–56.

Sen, Illina. 1983. 'Class and Gender in Work Time Allocation', *EPW* 23, 33: 1702–06.

Sen, Samita. 1999. *Women and Labour in Late Colonial India: The Bengal Jute Industry.* Cambridge: Cambridge University Press.

Sen, Samita, and Nilanjana Sengupta. 2016. *Domestic Days: Women, Work, and Politics in Contemporary Kolkata.* New Delhi: Oxford University Press.

Sengupta, Anindita. 2012. 'Status of Women Agricultural Workers in West Bengal during the Post-Reform Period', *Social Work Chronicle* 1, 1 (May): 55–88.

Sharma, Ursula. 1980. *Women, Work and Poverty in North-West India.* London: Tavistock.

Sinha, Suchorita. 2005. 'Female Work Participation Rates in Rural West Bengal: A Village Level Analysis', *The Indian Journal of Labour Economics* 48, 3: 563–77.

Vatuk, Sylvia. 1987. 'Authority, Power and Autonomy in the Life Cycle of the North Indian Woman'. In *Dimensions of Social Life: Essays in Honor of David G. Mandelbaum,* P. Hockings, ed. Berlin: de Gruyter: 23–44.

Vlassoff, C., 1994. 'From Rags to Riches: The Impact of Rural Development on Women's Status in an Indian Village', *World Development* 22: 707–19.

Wilson-Moore, Margot. 1989. 'Women's Work in Homestead Gardens: Subsistence, Patriarchy and Status in North-West Bangladesh', *Urban Anthropology* 18: 281–97.

7

Linking Child Marriage and Prostitution:
The Last Girl

Tinku Khanna and Juanita Kakoty

ARTI WAS MARRIED at a young age to a boy from the Sapera community who ignored her and spent his earnings on a mobile phone, which he used to stay in touch with other women. Arti was immensely pained by this but she could not change his philandering ways. When Arti conceived, he asked her to go for an abortion, saying he could not bear the expenses of a wife and a child. Finally, one day, he disappeared forever. Arti later learnt that he had started living with another woman in some other part of the town. A few years ago, Arti remarried, again to someone her mother chose for her. She said she could not choose a man herself because no one wanted to get married to a woman who has been married before. So finally her mother arranged a marriage with a man, who demanded ₹1.5 lakh as dowry. Her mother took this amount on loan from a moneylender. The amount has now doubled to ₹3 lakh since Arti has not been able to repay the money to the moneylender. She has no source of income and her new husband is jobless. He earns a little and that too sporadically by playing the drum during the wedding season.

Arti spent most of her childhood in poverty. She and her family still use wood to cook food. She told us how, when she was young, she used to go with other girls of her community to the nearby woods to collect firewood. Often, the men there harassed them, sometimes even tried to molest them. She said a few girls were sexually molested. Arti is from the Sapera community in Najafgarh, in the outskirts of Delhi.

The name of the caste or community, 'sapera', is taken from 'saap' or snake. The traditional occupation of this community was catching snakes and extracting venom. They had considerable knowledge of traditional medicine and some of them were entertainers, putting up shows with snakes. They are one of a number of semi-nomadic communities found in several parts of North and eastern India. They have close connections with the Nath, who also engage in various occupations relating to snakes. These communities are also experts in extracting venom from snakes, which allows an extension of traditional caste-based work. There are many divisions within this group, reflecting the diverse origins of the community in different parts of the country. They have Scheduled Caste status in some states, such as Haryana, but are usually counted among the lower castes in most regions of the country. Given that there is not much scope for their traditional occupations in urban areas, migrants seek the usual low-paid and unskilled jobs at the lower rungs of the labour market. The lack of jobs and earnings of the men lead to greater pressure on women to provide for sustenance of the household. In such cases, there is a clear convergence of caste and class; low-caste status reinforces, cyclically, urban poverty.

Among other castes of similar status, we find institutionalized exploitation of women. It has been noted quite widely now that some castes had been forced into inter-generational prostitution as a regular livelihood. Take the case of Geeta who was 12 when she was trafficked into prostitution by the man who pimped for her sisters. Following her sister's death, the man 'married' her and later put her into prostitution. For three years, her trafficker took her from one brothel to another. When she was rescued by Apne Aap Women Worldwide, the man produced a 'marriage certificate' before the Court and he was awarded custody. Geeta did not object as she thought this was the only way she could provide for her family. She had always known that in her community, the 'girl' of the house has to be prostituted to save her family. Geeta died leaving a child in the clutches of her pimp. She died after fifteen years of being raped multiple times by thousands of customers.

Geeta had been born in a small low-caste Nat settlement in Forbesganj, Bihar, which had just been hit by the Kosi floods. The literal meaning of *nat* is dancer. These were traditionally communities of entertainers and jugglers. They are spread in many parts of North India, but have a large presence in Bihar. They are lower in caste status than the Nath or Sapera. They are treated as outcastes in many parts of the country and have Scheduled Caste status. There is also a parallel Muslim Nat community, a complexity which we do not need to pursue here. It should be noted that the association between Nat and prostitution was 'produced' by colonialism by the imposition of the Criminal Tribes Act (CTA) XXVII of 1871.

Subir Rana, whose doctoral dissertation focuses on this community, writes that this community (or caste) has been listed among the seven *antyajanya*, or lowest of the low in the caste hierarchy. In the Mughal period, they enjoyed a position of eminence as trainers in music, dance and acrobatic performances. In fact, Nat was a porous community and a term for an occupation rather than a bounded caste group. The imposition of CTA made it difficult for them to continue with the wandering trade. Deprived of their traditional occupations and stigmatized as 'criminals', the women were forced into prostitution. Caught in a cycle of extreme poverty, sex trade became inter-generational, 'inherited' and the 'traditional' caste occupation. Today, the Nat in Forbesganj and nearby areas like Araria, Dharamganj and Jogbani are associated with the sex trade, pimping, human trafficking and smuggling

(Rana 2015). Among similar groups are the Perna and the Bazigar. Some scholars suggest that they are all sub-groups of the Dom caste, classified as 'aboriginal' or 'semi-aboriginal' by colonial anthropologists. Women of these castes too have been forced into prostitution in some regions, even though in others they are a settled community and mostly agricultural labourers.

Hoor Bai is a prostitution survivor from the Perna community in Najafgarh, settled on the outskirts of Delhi. On 16 August 2017, she was attacked by her daughter's father-in-law and mother-in-law. She was beaten, her clothes were ripped, and her thin-as-reed seven-month pregnant daughter received blows on her protruding belly. The whole of Perna *basti* (slum) tenement in Dharampura witnessed these abuses, since they had gathered outside her house. But no one called the police.

Sometime later, Hoor Bai called up the Apne Aap Women Worldwide office. She just said, *Help me, I am being attacked.* Apne Aap activists dialled 100 and requested the police to go to her house immediately. It took exactly an hour for the Apne Aap activists to reach Dharampura from their office at Anand Niketan. Outside Hoor Bai's house, there was a big crowd but no sign of the police. When the police was contacted again, they said they had gone to help the victim but were sent away by the crowd with the word that it was a matter of the *biradari* (community) and that the *biradari* would settle it. The police said that this is how it always is at the Perna basti in Dharampura.

When Hoor Bai saw the Apne Aap activists, she was greatly relieved and her daughter's in-laws withdrew from the scene. The activists asked Hoor Bai to come with them and file an FIR at the police station. The gathered crowd, however, would not let her leave. They blocked her way and used all means to deter her from taking this step. They used threat, plea, emotional blackmail and what not. Someone even said that her daughter's father-in-law would be nominated as the pradhan (chief) of the caste panchayat[1] later in the year and so she should be cautious about complaining against him to the police.

As mentioned above, Hoor Bai is from the Perna community, some of whom are now in inter-generational prostitution. She was rescued from prostitution some years before the incident. She built a small two-room house for herself, where she lived without any extended family members, quite unlike the rest of the households in the basti. In August 2016, she had won a significant case at the panchayat with Apne Aap's help. Two of her daughters were married and two were in a private residential school in Najafgarh, with the support of Apne Aap. One of the married daughters, Megha, came home in August 2016 crying that her husband and in-laws were forcing her into prostitution. Hoor Bai supported Megha and told her in-laws that she should not be forced into prostitution against her wishes. This caused quite a furore in the neighbourhood. A panchayat was called by Megha's in-laws. After a grueling six to seven hour session, the panchayat finally gave the verdict in favour of Hoor Bai and Megha. This decision was influenced by the presence of Apne Aap members, and Hoor Bai's long association with Apne Aap.

Since then, Megha has been repeatedly asked by her in-laws to either enter into prostitution or pay them ₹2.5 lakh that they had spent on her wedding. She was harassed about this and she often escaped to her mother. That day, when the incident took place, her husband took off with the little money she had saved over the months with her mother's support. Apparently, he went to enroll himself in an *akhara* (a place where boys train in body-building and wrestling) with that money so he could kick his alcohol addiction. He did not think it appropriate to consult her before taking the money. Later, when the husband's father spoke to Apne Aap activists, trying to persuade them against filing a police case, he sought to argue that this was a husband's entitlement. His son, Megha's husband, had the right to use his wife's money for improving himself.

Hoor Bai was a child bride and inducted into prostitution at the age of 15, after the birth of her first child. She has faced tremendous criticism from her community for trying to help her daughters avoid entering prostitution. Megha became a mother at 14 years and is now pregnant with her second child. Her in-laws argue that they have a problem feeding her and her child since she does not earn.

These three cases narrated above have all been drawn from our field experiences at Apne Aap. In all three cases, we see a convergence of caste and class: of problems of low caste status and poverty reinforcing each other. In all three cases, we see a stark face of gender inequality, including violence and discrimination against women and girls. The 'criminal tribes' of colonial India are now called DNT (denotified tribe), thereby bearing the history of notification as criminal. The other two tribes we have discussed are of cognate status, all untouchables or near-untouchables. As Rana has pointed out in the case of the Nats, the history of CTA has cast a long shadow over some of the marginal castes and communities of India. CTA stigmatized entire communities and imposed severe restrictions on their movements. Many of these groups were confined in settlements and were subjected to mandatory attendance regimes as part of a system of surveillance. After Independence, it took the Government of India more than five years to repeal CTA. Some DNTs celebrate 31 August 1952 as their independence day (Agrawal 2016).

They do not all 'celebrate' 'freedom'. For many of these highly exploited people, 'denotification' has not translated into social and economic improvement. This is certainly even more applicable to women. We do not have very accurate estimates of the total strength of the DNT population but by some estimates, they constitute almost 10 percent of the total population (Agrawal 2018).[2] Many of them have a remembered history of adopting prostitution as a caste/inherited occupation. There has been considerable debate on this issue in recent years. In their report, the Renke Commission has challenged the popular perception that there is a 'tradition' of prostitution among the DNT. The fact that some members of a community may practice a trade should not lead to such hasty conclusions. Agrawal suggests, however, that it is useful to confront the reality that among some segments of the DNT, recourse to prostitution has become accepted and even formalized (ibid.).

It is important to note, however, that such practices have taken hold as a result of social marginalization and extreme poverty, especially in new urban locations. Scholars have pointed out that the criminalizing of the men of these communities enables a range of physical and sexual harassment of the women (Berland 1987; Hayden 1987; Sarthak 2016). Yet, men of these communities also use the women as resource. 'A manifestation of this kind of truce between men of marginal groups and men of dominant groups vis-à-vis their women's sexual availability', she argues, is seen in the prevalence of paid sexual liaisons between women of denotified communities and men from dominant castes and communities. This has serious implications in terms of the survival strategies that have been adopted by many DNTs (Agrawal 2018).

In these communities, women generally divested of decision-making in such important arenas of their own life, as when to marry and whom to marry, are forced into earning for their families by various forms of prostitution, especially after marriage. Challenging the romantic notion that women from such communities enjoy unique freedoms in comparison to their upper-caste counterparts, scholars have shown that these communities have strong patriarchal controls. The practice of prostitution denotes more rather than less control over women, since their sexuality is harnessed for the profit of the marital family. Indeed, such controls go together with child marriage and bride price customs (Renke 2008; Agrawal 2008).

The women of DNT find it very difficult to resist family and community pressure. Geeta, socialized into accepting such responsibility for the family, acquiesced into the decision which killed her when still young. A woman from a similar background, such as Megha, was able to resist the pressures of their 'traditional' occupation with the support of her mother and an external agency such as Apne Aap. Even so, her resistance was not received well in her marital family or in their wider community. The abrupt and violent initiation into prostitution is considered an inevitable part of women's life cycle.

In the three cases, we have a mix of young and middle-aged women. All the women were married young and forced into these decisions when they were young. Thus, apart from caste and class, their age too placed them at the receiving end of an influential power structure in South Asian societies. The young, especially young women, have very little space to assert their wishes or take their own decisions.

The girl defined by various axes of powerlessness is for us, in Apne Aap Women Worldwide,[3] the 'Antyajaa' or the 'Last Girl'.[4] The Last Girl is the most vulnerable of all human beings that we know. She is a poor, female, a low-caste teenager. Her intersecting inequalities of class, caste, age, and gender cut off her access to food, clothing, shelter, education and even social or legal protection. She is the most vulnerable to all kinds of exploitation; and this also makes her more vulnerable to trafficking.

The figure of the girl connects problems of trafficking with that of early marriage. The preponderance of young girls in trafficking nets reflect two opposite but intertwined social insti-tutions: first, there is a clandestine market for young women created by the sex trade, which operates on the basis of forced labour/slavery; and, second, there is a predominance of early and child marriage, which is the prime mode of circulation of girls. In most cases, society applies a rigid moral division between these two: prostitution and marriage. However, in the cases that we have just discussed, we see in fact that even this supposed moral distinction is contextual: by caste and class. Indeed, feminists have pointed out that the two cannot be sep-arated and in the world of the DNT, this intertwining is more apparent than at other levels of society. It is thus important for us to keep in mind how difficult it is to draw a line between marriage and trafficking. From our experiences of working with prostituted women and survivors of prostitution, we have seen that an overwhelming majority of children are trafficked in the name of marriage, followed by child labour, and in most of the cases, marriage and prostitution overlap.

India has the highest number of child brides in the world. It is estimated that 47 percent girls in India are married before their 18th birthday (Aziz 2017). The rates of child marriage vary between states and are as high as 69 percent and 65 percent in Bihar and Rajasthan (United Nations 2017). In Bihar, proportions of married girls below 18 years (4.4 percent) and married boys below 21 years (5.3 percent) are higher than those at the national level (2.8 percent and 3.1 percent) (Census of India 2001: 4). Among the larger castes, Bhuiyas have registered the highest proportion of married girls and boys below the legal age followed by Pasi, Musahar and others of similar status (ibid.). In Rajasthan, the proportion of married girls below 18 years (5.3 percent) and boys below 21 years (5.9 percent) is considerably higher than those at the national level (2.8 percent and 3.1 percent). Among the major castes, Khatik, Bairwa, Balai, Thori, and Chamar have higher proportions of married boys and girls below the stipulated age for each than those recorded by all Scheduled Castes (SCs) of the state (Census of India 2001).

Our field experiences reveal that vulnerabilities arising out of the intersecting inequalities of caste, class, race, age, sex, gender and geography, create the conditions of child marriage, trafficking, sexual abuse, violation of rights and prostitution. Hence, the state should aim at reducing these vulnerabilities by investing in creating opportunities for the Last Girls so that they can be empowered. In other words, the state needs to invest in education, safe space, livelihood linkages, bank savings, for the Last Girls. There has been much discussion on each of these issues. There have been scholars and activists bemoaning the lack of state resources committed to health, education and social welfare. Here we argue a need to bring together these concerns for the figure of the marginal girl child, defined by subordinations of caste and class. If we scrutinize the state's fiscal policies, we will see how little the state aims towards eliminating (or even reducing) vulnerabilities of the marginalized. The recent budgets have been very disappointing in this regard.

In 2018, the budgetary allocation for Sarva Shiksha Abhiyan was reduced by 33.54 percent as compared to the allocation in 2013–14. It was ₹13,192.87 crores in 2013–14; the new government slashed it to ₹7,050 crores in 2017–18 and then raised it to ₹7,839 crores in 2018–19, which is still ₹5,353.87 crores less than the allocation in the 2013–14 budget. The allocation from the total gender budget expenditure on Sarva Shiksha Abhiyan in 2013–14 was around 13.58 percent while the same for the 2018 budget is just close to 5.78 cent (CBG 2018). Allocation for the Mid-Day Meal scheme has been drastically reduced too. The earlier government had kept it at ₹5,550.30 crores in 2013–14, which the new government brought down to ₹3,000 crores in 2017–18 and nominally raised to ₹3,150 crores in 2018–19. The percentage allocation on mid-day meals from the total gender budget expenditure in the year 2013–14 was 5.16 percent while the same for 2018 is just 2.58 percent (CBG 2018). We have seen how mid-day meals have brought children to school, even if for the sake of one nutritious meal in a day. This slash is a big disappointment.

The allocation for the Integrated Programme for Rehabilitation of Beggars has declined since 2013–14, which was around ₹1.20 crores, to around just ₹0.15 crores in 2018 (CBG 2018). This is going to be a jolt to DNTs across the country, who live by begging, rag-picking, and related occupations.

Let us take a quick look at the budgetary allocation of two flagship schemes of the government, which were aimed at incentivizing women (or their families) to delay marriage to after 18 years. That is to say, the focus in these schemes is on making it worthwhile for families to defer the marriage of girls rather than to seek to prevent or punish early marriage. The SABLA scheme is meant to place a check on child marriage by incentivizing girl children to enrol in formal education. It seeks also to prevent early dropouts. The total allocation to this scheme for the year 2018 is ₹500 crores, which is far less than the allocation under 2013–14 budget, which was ₹750 crores. The percentage allocation has drastically dropped from close to 0.8 percent in 2013 to 0.4 percent in 2018 (Union Budget, 2013–14 and 2017–18).

The current government has introduced a national scholarship scheme for SC students of Classes 11 and 12 to decrease the dropout rates in schools. Called the Pre-Matric Scholarship for SCs, this scheme has been allotted ₹37.5 crores. However, this scheme is inclusive of additional allowance for students with disabilities studying in private un-aided recognized schools.

In the budget presented on 1 February 2017, the share for education has fallen from 2.40 percent to 2.34 percent, and it remains an under-resourced area given the national and international commitments and the goal of spending 6 percent of the GDP on children's education (HAQ 2017). Funds have been slashed by ₹40,000 crores for SCs and ₹18,000 crores for Scheduled Tribes;[5] and there has been an increase in funds by only ₹1,305 crores for the National Education Mission, which includes the Sarva Shiksha Abhiyan, the Rashtriya Madhayamik Shiksha Abhiyan (RMSA) along with teacher training and adult education. This small increase is not very heartening since India failed to meet the Millennium Development Goal of achieving universal primary education by 2015.[6] Also, in the budget presented on 1 February 2017, Pre-Matric scholarships for SCs (as above) have been reduced by 91 percent (HAQ 2017) and there has been a nominal increase of ₹300 crores in mid-day meals, which is totally insufficient to combat malnutrition among the millions of school-going children for whom mid-day meal has been a major attraction. All this does not project a positive picture since around 63 lakh children between 6–17 years are working for more than 180 days in a year in the country.[7]

The education of the girl child is related to the question of child labour. There are over 82 lakh child labourers (aged between 5–14 years) in India. It is in rural India that we still see a great deal of child labour. The union budget notes that 80 percent of working children live in India's villages and most of them work in agriculture. Some of them also work in household industries and are employed in home-based businesses. Children between 14–17 years engaged in hazardous work account for 62.8 percent of India's child labour workforce. Another 10 percent work unpaid in family enterprises. Over half of working adolescents do not study. This number is higher for adolescents doing dangerous work.[8] We see how forces of deprivation bear down upon our children.

While cuts in social sector spending are increasing vulnerability, changes in law and policy are making things worse rather than better. These changes include the legalization of child labour in hazardous industries, audio-visual entertainment, and family-based enterprises through loopholes in the new Child Labour Act passed in September 2017. Such changes are in direct contravention of India's constitutional and international legal obligations, such as the UN Convention on the Rights of the Child, Convention to Eliminate Discrimination against Women, UN Protocol to End Trafficking in Persons, and ILO's C138-Minimum Age Convention, 1973, and C182-Worst Forms of Child Labour, 1999. This is likely to adversely impact India's ranking in the achievement of the Sustainable Development Goals, especially clause 5.2, which enjoins elimination of all forms of violence against all women and girls in public and private spheres, including trafficking and sexual and other types of exploitation.

According to the UNODC Global Report on Trafficking in Persons 2016, trafficking for sexual exploitation and for forced labour are the most prominently detected forms (UNODC 2016); and according to the latest data available for the

2012–2014 period, which is in line with previous years, about 54 percent of the 53,700 detected victims have been trafficked for sexual exploitation (UNODC 2016: 28).

According to data from National Crime Records Bureau (NCRB), the number of registered human trafficking cases in India increased by 38.3 percent over five years (2009–13) and the conviction rate for such cases declined by 45 percent in this period. The data further reveal that in 2013, maximum crimes (65.5 percent) were registered under the Immoral Traffic Prevention Act 1956 whereas Procuring of Minor Girls (Sec 366-A) accounted for 31.1 percent of such crimes. The crime trends present an extremely worrying picture. We see that the cases under Sec 366-A have surged dramatically, by 416 percent, during 2009–2013, which means that minor girls are becoming increasingly vulnerable (Human Trafficking 2015: 4).

Thus, India has seen significant changes in laws, budgets and policies in the last few years, which have posed increasing threats to the most marginalized women and girls of our country. Hence, the Last Girls among communities such as Perna, Sapera and Singhi face greater vulnerability on many fronts, including the increasing threat of trafficking. Our field experiences show that vulnerabilities are created due to the intersecting inequalities of caste, class, sex, gender, age and geography. Within these intersections, there are cycles of marginalization and destitution for the Last Girl (the most marginalized of the marginalized), which in turn puts her in a complex web of violence that subjects her to abuse, trafficking for labour or sexual exploitation, violation of her rights. In most cases, these oppressions begin with child marriage.

In conclusion, we would like to highlight that among the most marginalized sections of our society, where the practice of child marriage is rife, there is also on-going linkage with prostitution and child labour. This link is often established by trafficking, though in some communities, such a link may be established even within existing structures of family and without overt forms of trafficking. For many DNT, dalit and

other backward communities, child marriage is in a contin-
uum of practices of sexual exploitation, beginning with the
family and shading into commercial sex trades. The patterns
of marginalization converge: the lack of access to education,
government jobs, livelihood, financial and emotional support
all come together to create a deeply oppressive environment.
The few women who seek nevertheless to define different
futures for themselves rarely find any support from either the
community or the state. Not only the lack of opportunities,
but active discouragement and withdrawal of state support
keep them trapped in the vicious circle of marginalization
and destitution, where women are all the more vulnerable to
exploitation because of the gendered dynamics of patriarchy.
There is almost an impossibility of imagination of any alternative way of living. If we are to address the girls in these
communities and return to them their childhood with all its
promise, we have to recognize the urgent need to invest more
in creating opportunities and choices for the Last Girl in these
communities.

NOTES

1   A council mostly made up of male members of the caste community.
As in case of other communities, among the DNTs too, the panchayats
are dominated by men.

2   Agrawal suggests there may be 666 'kabilas' (tribes) who can be
classified as nomadic and denotified communities. According to
the Renke Commission Report (2008) there are about 150 denotified
tribes and about 500 nomadic groups in the country. These estimates
have been complicated by various degrees of integration of these
tribes and groups.

3   Apne Aap Women Worldwide is a 15-year-old Indian non-
government organization founded by 22 women in prostitution
from Kamatipura in Mumbai and Emmy award winning journalist
Ruchira Gupta with a vision to create a world in which no woman is
bought or sold and a mission to end sex-trafficking by dismantling
the prostitution system. It is currently working in 11 sites, including
brothels, both urban and home-based brothels, and caste-ghettoes
in Delhi, Bihar and West Bengal.

4   This notion was conceived by Ruchira Gupta, the Founder of Apne
     Aap Women Worldwide.
5   Scroll.in, 22 Feb 2017, accessed at https://scroll.
     in/article/829882/
     with-its-nominal-hikes-and-many-cuts-education-activists-say-the-
     budget-is-a-let-down-again on 14 November 2017.
6   *The Wire*, 2 February 2017, accessed at https://thewire.in/104976/
     budget-education-2017/ on 14 November 2017.
7   Ibid.
8   Save the Children, 'Statistics of Child Labour in India State Wise',
     4 May 2016, accessed at https://www.savethechildren.in/articles/
     statistics-of-child-labour-in-india-state-wise on 2 July 2018.

REFERENCES

Agrawal, Anuja. 2008. *Chaste Wives and Prostitute Sisters: Patriarchy and Prostitution among the Bedias of India*. Delhi: Routledge.
———. 2016. 'Criminal Neglect', *Himal* (13 Jan.).
———. 2018. 'Gender Questions at the Margins: The Case of Nomadic and Denotified Communities', *Antyajaa*, 2018, 3, 2: 147–62. https://doi.org/10.1177/2455632718794756 (accessed on 25 July 2020).
Aziz, Saba. 2017. 'Indian Court Rules Sex with Minor Wife Is Rape', Aljazeera, 11 October 2017, accessed at https://www.aljazeera.com/news/2017/10/indian-court-rules-sex-minor-wife-rape-171011072605983.html on 2 July 2018.
Berland, Joseph C. 1987. 'Kanjar Social Organization'. In *The Other Nomads: Peripatetic Minorities in Cross-Cultural Perspective* Aparna Rao, ed. Cologne: Bohlau Verlag: 247–65.
Census of India. 2001. *Bihar, Data Highlights: The Scheduled Castes*. Accessed at http://censusindia.gov.in/Tables_Published/SCST/dh_sc_bihar.pdf and *Rajasthan Data Highlights: The Scheduled Castes, Census of India 2001*, accessed at http://www.censusindia.gov.in/Tables_Published/SCST/dh_sc_rajasthan.pdf on 2 July 2018.
CBG (Centre for Budget and Governance Accountability). 2018. 'Of Hits and Misses: An Analysis of Union Budget 2018–19', February 2018, accessed at http://www.cbgaindia.org/wp-content/uploads/2018/02/Of-Hits-and-Misses-An-Analysis-of-Union-Budget-2018-19-2.pdf on 2 July 2018.
HAQ Centre for Child Rights. 2017. 'Union Budget: A Window of Opportunity for Our Children? Budget for Children 2017–18', accessed at http://haqcrc.org/wp-content/uploads/2017/02/budget-for-children-quick-budget-analysis-2017-18.pdf on 14 Nov 2017

Hayden, Robert M. 1987. 'Conflicts and Relations of Power between Peripatetics and Villagers in South Asia'. In *The Other Nomads: Peripatetic Minorities in Cross-Cultural Perspective*, Aparna Rao, ed. Cologne: Bohlau Verlag: 267–89.

Human Trafficking. 2015. Compiled by Fr. Paul G Documentation Centre (Jan.– Dec. 2015).

Rana, Subir. 2015. 'For Whom the Wedding Bells Do Not Chime', *The Study, Newsletter*, 71, 8.

Renke, Balkrishna. 2008. *Report of National Commission for Denotified, Nomadic and Semi-Nomadic Tribes*, vols.1, 2. New Delhi: Ministry of Social Justice and Empowerment, Government of India.

Sarthak. 2016. 'Socio-Economic Status of Women of Denotified and Nomadic Communities in Delhi', National Commission for Women, New Delhi.

United Nations. 2017. Child Marriages in India, 2THEPOINT, 11 August 2017, accessed at https://www.2thepoint.in/child-marriages-in-india/ on 2 July 2018.

UNODC. 2016. 'Global Report on Trafficking in Persons 2016', UN Publications, Sales No. E.16.IV.6, ISBN: 978-92-1-130339-1, e-ISBN: 978-92-1-058408-1. Available at https://www.unodc.org/documents/data-and-analysis/glotip/2016_Global_Report_on_Trafficking_in_Persons.pdf, accessed on 14 November 2017.

8

Preventing Child Marriage in West Bengal: The Experience of Barddhaman District

Biswajit Ghosh

CHILD MARRIAGE IN WEST BENGAL

Child marriage is prevalent in all Indian states in varying degrees. For a long time, we were concerned about its acuteness in certain northern and central Indian states like Rajasthan, Madhya Pradesh, Bihar, Uttar Pradesh, Jharkhand and Haryana. Surprisingly, even in West Bengal, which witnessed a social reform movement since the early nineteenth century, the practice is rampant. According to the 2001 Census, 37.16 percent of the minor girls in the state have got married in between 1996–2001, while the corresponding figure for the country is 32.10 percent (UNICEF 2009: 4). The state had the seventh highest percentage of under-age marriages among all states in 2001. Surveys carried out subsequently have noted a rising trend of child marriage in the state. Thus, the National Family Health Survey-3, carried out in 29 states during 2005–06 (IIPS 2007), found that West Bengal, along with five other states, has experienced a rise in marriages of women under 18 years. The percentage of child marriage in West Bengal has increased from 45.9 percent during 1998–99 (NFHS-2) to 53.3 percent in 2005–06 (NFHS-3). The DLHS (District Level Household and Facility Survey-3) (IIPS 2008), conducted during 2007–08, has equally observed a rising trend, as 54.7 percent of currently married women aged 20–24 in Bengal are found to have married before 18 (Ghosh 2011a: 51). Our Malda experience in 2009 also pointed to the fact that marriage by the age of 15 or 16 was a normal 'rule' in many parts of rural Bengal (Ghosh 2010).[1] Though child marriage is seen even in developed and urbanized cities like Kolkata, in certain districts like Murshidabad, Malda, South Dinajpur, North and South 24-Parganas, Bankura, Birbhum, Purulia, Cooch Behar and Medinipur, the practice is rampant (Ghosh and Kar 2010). Census 2011 has also revealed that nearly 42 percent of girls in the state get married before reaching the legal age. Interestingly, Census 2011 data reveal that a sizeable number of boys (867,091 or 28.47 percent) were married before the legal age of 21. Despite the passing of the Prohibition of Child Marriage Act 2006 (PCMA), there was no drastic change in the number of early marriages solemnized in many parts of the country (Ghosh 2011c).

In 2012–13, the DLHS-4 survey, has, however, noted a decline in the percentage of child marriage in West Bengal from 54.7 percent in 2007–08 to 32.1 percent in 2012–13 (36.3 percent in rural areas, and 21.3 percent in urban areas). Yet, its position in the country remained quite high. The issue of child marriage and related gender crimes like trafficking in women and children therefore became a matter of intense scrutiny in intellectual and political circles in the state since the early years of the current century. The issue also became an agenda of political tussle driving the Government of West Bengal in 2005 to conduct field-based surveys on these issues. The Women and Child Development and Social Welfare Department of the government in association with UNICEF then involved professional experts from three postgraduate departments[2] from the state universities to conduct such a survey. Subsequently, in 2009, UNICEF joined the Malda District Administration to initiate another round of qualitative study under my direction (Ghosh 2010) to make the district a model in preventing child marriage.

The Malda study in particular has allowed us to take note of the critical role of adolescent school girls in preventing early marriage (Ghosh 2011b). It was a watershed in the history of research on the issue of child marriage in West Bengal. This research has allowed us to note that adolescent girls (and not previously identified stakeholders such as NGOs, political parties, Panchayat members, health workers, government officials or community leaders) hold the key to any campaign against child marriage in rural Bengal. These girls strongly feel that the age-old practice should go and girls be allowed to study. The demand for education today has reached even marginalized sections of the younger generation and they consider school as places of worship. Interestingly, even the male students have expressed their support for actual prohibition of child marriage and strong police action against offenders. Needless to say, school teachers provide the impetus to students to act positively. Given the role and status of teachers in rural society, campaign through schools appears to us as a solid strategy, at least in the beginning, to develop a school-community network. The Malda experience has revealed that the role of peer group and the experience of schooling create the most enabling environment for the construction of alternate identities among adolescent girls well beyond the parameters of family cultures.

Researching on the issue of child marriage in West Bengal has gradually made it clear to us that we have to evolve alternative strategies and look for new role models to promote the value of the girl child and gender equality in rural Bengal as the most powerful stakeholders were not seriously interested in bringing in socio-cultural reforms or changing gender relations. The first few instances of adolescent girls acting as role models to oppose child marriage in several Malda villages have opened up the floodgates.

STATE INTERVENTION

Our suggestion to involve adolescent girls in the campaign against early marriage and create an environment for their sustained education till they reach marriageable age was taken seriously by the Mamata Banerjee government that came to power in 2011. The first state government scheme to address the issue was Kanyashree Prakalpa (KP) declared in 2013. The Sumangali Scheme started in 1989 in Tamil Nadu, introduced a 'marriage assistance system' for the unmarried girls for the first time in the country. But this controversial scheme was withdrawn later for promoting the practice of bonded labour. In 1994, a better scheme entitled Apni Beti Apni Dhan (ABAD) was introduced by the state of Haryana. Later schemes like Girl Child Protection Scheme (Andhra Pradesh), Ladli Lakshimi Yojana (Madhya Pradesh, Jharkhand and Goa), Balika Samridhhi Yojana (Gujarat), Bhagyalakshmi (Karnataka), Kanya Jagriti Jyoti Scheme (Punjab), Beti Hai Anmol (Haryana), Majhi Kanya Bhagyashree Scheme (Maharashtra), and Mukhya Mantri Kanya Vivah Yojana (Bihar) were initiated by respective governments to address the issue. In 2013, the Indian government also introduced a scheme called Beti Bachao Beti Padhao. These 'conditional cash transfer' schemes, argue Sen and Dutta (2018), try to motivate families to educate their girl child. But these schemes are not directly conditional upon the girl remaining unmarried till 18, though indirectly they do delay child marriage by promoting education. To Sen and Dutta, KP by comparison is a finer scheme.

> It starts at the age of 13, when the girls are at their most vulnerable age. It requires the girls, themselves, to apply for the scheme, and the awareness is spread through schools.

This, coupled with very high political will ensure that the awareness about this scheme is almost universal. The small annual stipend, at least partially, covers the cost of education, encourages the girls to continue their studies and gives them a sense of self-empowerment. As there is no requirement of successfully completing any level, girls, irrespective of their merit are encouraged to continue studies and defer their marriage. Also, the entire process, starting from filing the application to receiving the amount, is electronically managed and the girls receive the money in their own bank accounts (Sen and Dutta 2018: 4).

In the case of West Bengal, KP for the first time made a direct attack on the practice of child marriage, providing that unmarried minor girls hailing from poor and marginalized families would be given financial and educational incentives until they reach 18 years of age. Its major objective is to stall early marriage of girl children and promote their education by preventing drop out. There are two benefits under this scheme: *(i)* annual stipend (K1); and *(ii)* one-time grant (K2). For obtaining a one-time grant of ₹25,000, the girl aged between 18 to 19 years, hailing from a family with an annual income of not more than ₹120,000, must be registered in an academic institution and remain unmarried. The benefit of an annual stipend at the rate of ₹750 (₹1,000 since April 2018) begins at the age of 13 (Kanyashree 1) and the scheme is extended also to college (Kanyashree 2) and university (Kanyashree 3) (https://www.wbkanyashree.gov.in). It has been claimed that KP has benefited nearly 6,000,000 girl children in the state so far and the government has spent over ₹70,00 crores since 2013 (*Times of India*, 14 Aug 2019).

A lot of other benefits were later added to this scheme. In 2015–16, a new scheme called Sabooj Sathi was introduced to provide bicycles to all students from Classes 9 to 12, studying in government schools. It particularly helped the poor girls living at a distance to reach school on time. Kanyashree Plus is being designed to ensure stronger inclusion of out-of-school adolescent girls in the Kanyashree CCT component, and facilitation of transition of beneficiaries from secondary education into tertiary education so that they may graduate into sustainable livelihoods and employment. The government also started Sabujshree scheme in 2016 to empower mothers of newborn daughters by planting saplings of trees in the name of their daughters (and sons). These trees once grown will be useful to educate their daughters. Again, in 2018, Rupashree scheme was added to promote late marriage of poor girls. It provides a one-time financial grant of ₹25,000 for economically stressed families at the time of their adult daughters' marriages. On the whole, both Kanyashree and Rupashree collectively provide a grant of ₹ 50,000 to poor parents to arrange the marriage of their adult daughters. Obviously, the huge financial benefit to delay the marriage of minor girls and continue their study is seriously felt in rural society in West Bengal for the first time.

There have been other efforts to create synergy in action and thereby realize the goals and objectives of these schemes in recent times. Thus, for instance, Kanyashree Club and a fighting group called Kanyashree Yodhyas have been formed to expedite the fight against early marriage since 2016. The toll free Childline number (1098) has become a handy resource for these volunteers to report cases of child marriage. A self-defence course has been initiated for Kanyashree II members in 2017. There have been initiatives by the Block Administration to take the help of school teachers, and others like brahmin priest, imam, decorators, barbers, SHG members, civic volunteers, to collect information about child marriage. They have been requested to check the birth certificate of the prospective girl/boy before helping them in arranging the marriage. They have been warned of legal action for being involved in child marriages. Efforts have been made to create public opinion against early marriage through seminars, cultural programmes and rallies of school students. The Kanyashree portal also publicises success stories such as achievements in examination and prevention of marriage of its members. Innovative campaign materials like display of banner at temple premises, where marriages are solemnized privately, have buoyed the campaign against child marriage. In certain cases, parents are invited to the school and asked to sign a voluntary one-page undertaking (in Bengali) which says that 'I will not get my daughter married before she reaches the age of 18. She will not be a school dropout. I will educate her and after she attains the age of 18, I will arrange for her marriage.'

All these certainly have had a visible impact on the enrolment of girl students in school in West Bengal. Thus, Pratham (2019) finds that the proportion of unregistered girl students in the age group of 15 to 16 in rural Bengal is only 5 percent and this figure was 25 percent in 2006. Obviously, the dropout rate has come down strikingly and Kanyashree has a positive impact on the mindset of girl students. The scheme has received national and international recognitions including UNPSA (United Nations Public Service Award) in 2017 for its design and features of good governance. A survey by Sen and Dutta (2018) in the three districts of West Bengal has revealed that

> Both dropout and early marriage have fallen among the age group covered by KP . . . The decline in dropout rates was most pronounced in Howrah (38.63%) and the least in Murshidabad (12.95%). Similarly, the change in under-age marriage assumes the highest proportion in Murshidabad (41.06%) and the lowest in Cooch Behar (15.70%) (4–5).

Another interesting finding of this research is K2 grants are used by girls mostly for higher studies. There are several instances of Kanyashree volunteers acting as role models in preventing child marriage during the last few years and in most cases, teachers, block or district officials and local police have helped them. As a corollary, news items are regularly published in local newspapers about such prevention, including campaign initiatives by stakeholders. Notwithstanding such success, Sen and Dutta (2018) have noted that a substantial proportion of girls are withdrawing from schools and getting married before 18. It is also argued that KP does not stress on attendance and talks only about 'enrolment', which does not automatically ensure the former. It is possible for a K1 beneficiary to get married early as the financial benefit is not much. For Sen and Dutta, the most important reason for this 'high attrition rate' is the absence of any scheme promoting education among boys. It is worth noting here that the proportion of dropped-out boys is more than the girls in West Bengal. As a corollary, girl students outnumber boys in School Final (Madhyamik) stage by 220,000 (Das and Pal 2019). As boys regularly drop out and migrate to faraway places for jobs, parents fear to educate their daughters after a certain stage, since finding equally literate 'suitable grooms 'becomes more and more difficult. Mukherjee and Sekher (2017) as well as Khanna and Khan (2018) have therefore argued that early marriage of boys is equally a problem though we have not paid serious attention to this issue. According to NFHS-4 (IIPS 2017), 24 percent of boys in West Bengal aged 25 to 29 have married before 21. Sen and Dutta (2018) have argued that economic factors do not affect the probability of a woman marrying before 18 in this state, suggesting that poverty is definitely not responsible for this malaise.

Interestingly, in our Malda study, we too have noted down the importance of non-economic factors such as: (i) prevailing pressure of patriarchal values and institutions; (ii) concern for security of unmarried girl; (iii) the menace of higher dowry in delayed marriage; (iv) concern for a suitable bridegroom in remote and inaccessible areas; (v) threat of elopement by adolescents; (vi) lack of opportunities for women in rural Malda; (vii) large family size; (viii) lower age at marriage of boys; and (ix) trafficking of girls (Ghosh 2011d). We have found out that marriage is considered a private affair of the family and any outside intervention results in community backlash. Prevention of child marriage, therefore, appeared to us to be an uphill task that means challenging age-old institutions, practices and values having deep roots in Indian society. It is therefore not surprising that NHFS-4 data collected during 2015–16 do not show any radical decline in the percentage of early marriage in the state even though the figure has gone down from 53.3 percent in 2005–6 to 40.7 percent in 2015–16. Ironically, figures stated in Table 8.1 reveal that West Bengal now tops the list of states in the rate of child marriage. It is far ahead of states like Rajasthan that were known traditionally for this evil. Even states like Bihar, Jharkhand and Uttar Pradesh have done remarkably well in preventing early marriage. Bengal's rank was fourth in the country after Bihar, Jharkhand and Rajasthan when NFHS-3 was conducted in 2005–06.

TABLE 8.1: Percentage of Women Aged 20–24 Years Married below Age 18 Years, and Men Aged 25–29 Years Married below Age 21 Years, 2015–16 (NFHS-4)

States (rank as per rate for women)	Women			Men		
	Urban	Rural	Total	Urban	Rural	Total
India*	17.5	31.5	26.8	14.1	24.4	20.3
West Bengal	27.7	46.3	40.7	19.7	26.5	24.0
Bihar	26.9	40.9	39.1	27.2	42.6	40.0
Jharkhand	21.1	44.1	37.9	19.4	34.9	30.5
Rajasthan	20.3	40.5	35.4	16.4	44.7	35.7
A. Pradesh	26.3	35.5	32.7	13.5	28.3	23.5
Tripura	25.6	34.8	32.2	9.6	25.8	22.2
M. Pradesh	16.6	35.8	30.0	24.6	46.2	39.5
Telangana	15.7	35.0	25.7	14.5	32.3	23.9
Karnataka	17.9	27.0	23.2	08.5	12.5	10.9
Uttar Pradesh	11.3	24.9	21.1	16.9	34.1	28.7
Haryana	19.6	17.8	18.5	25.7	35.8	31.3
Meghalaya	7.8	19.3	16.5	8.5	22.4	19.6
Tamil Nadu	13.0	18.3	15.7	18.4	15.2	17.0
Sikkim	16.1	13.6	14.5	18.8	18.1	18.5
Uttarakhand	12.2	14.8	13.9	15.3	25.6	20.9

* The national average is given for comparative purpose only.

PREVENTING CHILD MARRIAGE IN BARDDHAMAN:
ANALYSIS OF NEWS ITEMS PUBLISHED IN TWO DAILIES

Barddhaman is considered one of the advanced districts of the state[3] because of its unique blend of agriculture and industry.[4] While the eastern part of this district (Purba Barddhaman) is known for intensive cultivation of paddy, wheat, potatoes and other crops and vegetables, the western part (Paschim Barddhaman) has contributed to industrial development. Its index values on three parameters namely, education, health and income, are higher than the state average. This is notwith-standing the fact that a majority of population in the district (54.48 percent) belongs to poorer and socially marginalized sections like Scheduled Castes (27.41 percent), and Scheduled Tribes (6.34 percent) and Muslims (20.73 percent) in 2011 (Ghosh 2019).

In order to understand the gravity of the situation and also to understand the way the campaign against early marriage is becoming intense and effective in rural Bengal, I have decided to collect news items published on such a themes in two popular Bengali newspapers: *Anandabazar Patrika* and *Ei Samay*. Even though such newspapers did publish news of such prevention or campaign from all parts of Bengal, for analysis in this chapter, I have concentrated on the news items published only from the district of Barddhaman (both Purba and Paschim). Interestingly, both these newspapers have a separate Barddhaman page where news items from these districts are published. This made my task very easy. I started my endeavour on 25 May 2017 and ended it on 17 August 2019. While enumerating these news items, I have found both the newspapers publishing the same news on the same or nearby days. For making an accurate estimate, I have used only one reporting of an event. I also did not use the names of the victims while summarizing the news for obvious reasons.

Methodologically, this documentary research has certain advantages as well as shortcomings. The major advantage is that it locates change in the mindset and approach of people as well as stakeholders over more than three years. Interestingly, such news was published mostly when district officials and police along with other stakeholders went on secret operations to prevent marriage of minors and invited media persons to cover the news. The authenticity of these reports is, therefore, clearly visible. But the major shortcoming of this approach is that I might have missed many incidences of protest or prevention not reported by the media. In fact, I have noticed that these newspapers have only sporadically reported cases on prevention of child marriage in the district pages as they normally prefer news on popular, 'hot' and bigger issue like say Durga Puja festival (September to November), acts of violence or Lok Sabha Election (March to June 2019). As a result, during certain periods, there is no reporting on this issue in these newspapers. For instance, in the months of September, October, November and December in 2017, in the months of April, September, October, and December in 2018, and in the months of March, April, May and June, no report on such prevention was published in these newspapers. Yet, from the stories published, it is possible to develop an understanding about the current process of prevention as any field-based approach would have provided only a limited view. In order to supplement the data that I could collect from the newspapers, I have also collected data from Kanyashree portal (https://www.wbkanyashree.gov.in).

Let me now provide a synoptic view of 54 news items published in these dailies chronologically by dates in between 25 May 2017 to 17 August 2019 (Table 8.2).

ANALYSIS OF NEWSPAPER REPORTS

The news items above report 124 cases of prevention of child marriages by the stakeholders. Among these, 64 marriages were prevented very quickly just within three months in 2017, 47 marriages were prevented in 2018 and 13 cases were prevented within six and half months in 2019. Within 84 days

TABLE 8.2: Newspaper Reports

Sl. No	Date, Source / News Detail
1	27-05-17, Anandabazar Patrika
	Kalna Administration had prevented an early marriage of a 13-year-old girl of Class 7 with a mason from a nearby village. When the Deputy Magistrate reached the spot, they found that arrangement of the marriage was complete and the bridegroom party was half-way. The parents complained about their poor economic condition and argued that the marriage was arranged with a relative demanding less dowry. They finally agreed to stop the marriage when the District Magistrate called them at his office and explained the implications of early marriage. Kanyashree Club members have also informed administration about 2 more early marriages of their classmates and the District Magistrate has promised to intervene in all these cases.
2	07-06-17, Anandabazar Patrika
	A meeting of nearly 200 stakeholders (Kanyashree members, Purohit, Moulobis, civic volunteers, Self Help Group (SHG) members, barbers, decorators) was organised by the Block administration at Purbasthali, Barddhaman to take pledge to prevent child marriage. The members agreed to look at the birth certificate before participating in any marriage.
3	23-06-17, Anandabazar Patrika
	A 'Child Marriage Prevention Committee' was formed of 28 girl students of Purbasthali Block studying in class 8 and 12 of Minapur Secondary School on 23 July. They organized a programme within the school premise and invited local Block Development Officer (BDO), Panchayat members and other officials to campaign against child marriage. With their help, the students decided to launch a policy called Sishusri to help newly born children monetarily. They have decided to collect funds from the villagers and keep it in a bank under the mother's name. The fund may be withdrawn only after the girl/boy reaches 18/21 years. The girls have decided to save a minimum ₹5,000 for each child.
	During the programme, the volunteers heard about early marriages of 3 girls and one boy of the locality. They immediately jumped into action with the help of the administration and stopped all these marriages. All those four students were later admitted to Dogachia High School. The poor inhabitants of the two villages (Minapur and Dogachiya) of Purbasthali marry their daughters early for economic reasons. They are mostly engaged either in agriculture or in jewellery making in other states.

TABLE 8.2 Newspaper Reports *(cont)*

Sl. No	Date, Source News Detail

4   01-07-17, Anandabazar Patrika

On the basis of confidential report of two Kanyashree Volunteers of Class 9 studying in Paligram D. S High School, the administration has prevented marriages of three minor girls. They also gave the telephone number (1098) of Childline to the girl student of class 10 of their school. When the Childline officials received the call, they went to her house the next day with the two Kanyashree Volunteers on 31 June. The family was then persuaded to sign the undertaking to the effect that they would not marry off their minor daughter. While on their way from the Majhikhara Village of Mongalkot, Katwa, the Kanyashree Volunteers requested the officials to go to another house where one of their classmates was getting married that day. These volunteers persuaded their friend to continue studies like them with financial help from the Kanyashree Scheme. On the whole, Childline officials have prevented 6 marriages of girl students of Class 9 and 10 in the locality. Interestingly, male students have also joined the officials along with Kanyashree beneficiaries to prevent those child marriages.

5   04-07-17, Ei Samay

Kanyashree Volunteers of Vita High School of Rayan-2 Village Panchayat under Barddhaman-1 have stopped the marriage of a girl student of Class 9 of the school living in Bhatar village. When one of the Kanyashree Volunteers received the marriage card, they collectively went to talk to the parents. But having failed to impress upon the parents, they reported the matter to their school teacher who in turn brought the matter to the notice of BDO. BDO then went to that house along with Deputy Panchayat Pradhan and members of Kanyashree club. Since the father of the girl was absent at that time, the BDO asked the family members to come to his office tomorrow. Next day the parents met the BDO and signed the undertaking. The BDO also asked the family of the bride groom of Bhatar to return the dowry failing which the administration will take legal action.

Interestingly, a Scheduled Tribe minor boy and a girl eloped from the same village a few days earlier. The parents of these families later brought them back and decided to wait until they attained legal age for the social marriage. But the tribal community leaders objected and said that they were already married and should stay together. The matter could not be resolved despite intervention of the BDO and local Panchayat.

TABLE 8.2 Newspaper Reports *(cont)*

Sl. No	Date, Source / News Detail
6	08-07-17, Anandabazar Patrika The district administration of Purbasthali-1 organized an innovative workshop at Nazrul Mancha on 7 July 2017 aiming to generate consciousness against early marriage of girls by involving ritual specialists and other stakeholders who come to know about such marriage early. Normally, the news of any early marriage reaches the administration at the last moment. Hence, the administration decided to take their help to take early action. At a late stage parents, relatives and neighbours strongly resist postponement of marriage because the expenses have been made. Nearly 200 participants attending the workshop took the pledge that they would take part in any marriage only after verifying the age certificate of the concerned girl. Some of the ritual specialists like priests and Imamsraised the issue of social pressure. Yet, they agreed to help the administration in future. The Officer-in-Charge of Nadanghat Thana claimed to have prevented 19 early marriages in the last two months though no case was filed. In the whole Kalna Block, the administration prevented 30 child marriages during the last two months. A village police constable was rewarded for his efforts. The workshop ended with the slogan: 'No Age Certificate of Girl, No Marriage'.
7	08-07-17, Ei Samay Members of Kanyashree Club of Purbasthali-1 came to know about the marriage of a Class 8 student of Golahat Junior High School. They informed their teachers who in turn confirmed the news by calling the would-be husband whose phone number was stated in the Kanyashree application form of the girl. Next morning, a team under BDO's leadership reached the house. When the BDO told them that child marriage is illegal, the parents promised to postpone the marriage and signed the undertaking. The BDO also stopped another marriage of a 17-year-old boy with another minor in Singhajuli of Kalna block after receiving the news from members of Kanyashree Club.
8	11-07-17, Ei Samay The district administration prevented a child marriage in Purbasthali-2 on the day of the marriage. The BDO came to know about such marriage from a confidential source. When the team went to stop it at a house at Mandirtala, invited guests were having lunch with a clarinet playing, making it public that a marriage ceremony is in full progress. The bride, who was just 14 and a student of Class 9, was performing some ritual acts. Incidentally, she was in a relationship with the boy, who is also a minor (20) and works in a different state.

TABLE 8.2 Newspaper Reports *(cont)*

Sl. No	Date, Source News Detail
8	11-07-17, Ei Samay *(cont)* The father, a daily labour, has four children and he was happy to receive a proposal from a groom from a nearby village. As the boy had started earning and would like to take his wife to his place of work, both the families had no objection to such a marriage. The marriage was formally stopped though no one knows what happened after such prevention.
9	15-07-17, Ei Samay A student of Class 9 of Hatgobindapur Mangobindachandra High School prevented her own marriage. She initially tried to argue against her marriage with her mother, grandmother and brother-in-law, who were arranging her marriage. Failing in her efforts, they, along with her school friends, met the Headmaster who called the local MLA. The girl also talked to the MLA over the phone. The Childline officials and police were then called to prevent the marriage. The father, who was not part of the plan, said that he was the only earner of his family and given their economic condition, his son-in-law had brought a good proposal. The parents signed the undertaking to allow their daughter to complete her studies.
10	17-07-17, Anandabazar Patrika Volunteers of Kanyashree Club of Vita High School of Mangalkot have prevented many child marriages in the area. They collect marriage invitation card as proof of marriage as parents very often deny the plan. When they fail to prevent a marriage on their own, they take help of BDO and other officials. In one such incidence, they went to a house with the BDO. When the parents denied the plan, they brought out the invitation card. These volunteers have prevented 4 marriages in Paligram. Interestingly, these volunteers take leadership in impressing the parents and block officials have to do nothing. The district administration has decided to felicitate these volunteers by giving them Kanyashree Badge and a mobile number, where they can send SMS or call. The school authority and the administration receive news of child marriage mostly through such volunteers. The formation of Kanyashree Club had empowered these girl students.

TABLE 8.2 Newspaper Reports *(cont)*

Sl. No	Date, Source / News Detail
11	20-07-17, Anandabazar Patrika
	Members of Kanyashree Club of Silut Basantpur High School of Ausgram noticed that a girl student of Class 9 was not attending classes for nearly a month. They then asked other students of Mallikpur village and came to know that her marriage was planned next Friday. They collectively went to the house and pleaded with the parents and others to stop the marriage. These girl students were threatened by the parents and relatives and told to go away immediately. The students then informed the matter to the BDO through their Head Master. The BDO immediately visited the house along with the Kanyashree volunteers and stopped the marriage. He also promised to take legal action if Kanyashree volunteers were targeted by anyone.
12	03-08-17, Anandabazar Patrika
	Just after Madhamik examination, poor parents of a girl student of Ichlabad High School at Barddhaman town forced their daughter to leave school and marry a man. The family of six, being dependent on the income of a carpenter, decided to marry off their minor daughter (15) as it was difficult for them to continue her education. As the daughter did not like the idea, she contacted Childline through her school teachers. But the family was adamant. Hence, she was shifted to a Home in Barddhaman from where she started studying in Class 11 and passed the examination with highest marks in Arts stream. She is now the leader of Kanyashree Club called Jagarani in the school and campaigns against child marriage within and outside the school. Her basic argument is that: 'girls are equally able to earn and stand by their parents like sons. So they should be allowed to.'
13	04-08-17, Anandabazar Patrika
	The girl students of Class 10 of Asansol Old Station High School noticed on Wednesday that one of their classmates was depressed. When asked, she started crying; her father was going to arrange her marriage next Sunday. She was then asked to write a formal complaint by the teachers. Next day, the father of the student was called to the school in the presence of two Deputy Magistrates. They told him that it is illegal to marry off girls before 18 and asked him to stop the marriage. The father, who is a barber and runs a small shop, finally signed the undertaking. The Headmaster also promised to meet the educational expenses of the student. The student was happy to continue her education.

TABLE 8.2 Newspaper Reports *(cont)*

Sl. No	Date, Source News Detail
14	04-08-17, Anandabazar Patrika
	The district administration of Purba Barddhaman organized a seminar on 13 July 2018 at Sanskriti Mancha in the Barddhaman town to campaign against early marriage of girls. The beneficiaries of Kanyashree were invited to attend the seminar and share their experience. A girl student of Ichlabad School told the story of how she gathered the courage to protest and stop her marriage with the help of school teachers and Childline officials. Another girl student of Madhavdihi School spoke of the insecurities of marriage. Others spoke about the capacity of girl children to lead their own life. The issue of dowry was also discussed.
15	06-08-17, Anandabazar Patrika
	The Block Administration of Purbasthali-I with help from local Panchayat had distributed sampling of valuable trees under the scheme *Sabujshree* to 170 families where a girl child was born in the last one year. Each family was given saplings of 11 trees to be planted close to their house. Later, the administration awarded 100 selected mothers who had nurtured the trees well in the last 6 months. The mothers were happy about the recognition and it created the awareness that women are not inferior.
16	11-8-17, Anandabazar Patrika
	Kanyashree volunteers of Galsi Saradapith School came to know about marriage of a Class 9 student of their school. They informed the Childline. When the officials reached Mirik Para along with the police one day before the marriage, they could not trace the girl. Later Kanyashree volunteers were able to trace her in a different location using their social network. The father, who is an agricultural labourer, then pleaded that they have arranged the marriage with a good bride-groom. The parents finally signed the undertaking. The Childline officials have also prevented marriage of a minor girl of Class 9 of Panuhat Rajmahisidevi High School. They have promised to check whether the student attended school regularly.
17	12-08-17, Ei Samay
	The BDO of Kalna-2 prevented a child marriage. The girl student was studying in Class 8 of Satgachi Girls School. After receiving the news that a girl of just 13 is getting married to a man of 29, the BDO went with local Panchayat members and police. They found that all arrangements for the marriage were complete. The parents pleaded that they have got a 'good bride-groom' even though he was 16 years older than the girl. The man works in the Gulf. The parents did not bother to find whether this is a case of trafficking.

TABLE 8.2 Newspaper Reports *(cont)*

Sl. No	Date, Source News Detail
18	12-08-17, Ei Samay
	Teachers of Jamalpur School noticed that a girl student of Class 9 (15) was absent in the school for more than a week. When they came to know of her marriage, they reported the matter to the Childline. When the officials along with the police reached the spot, the poor parents pleaded about getting a good bridegroom and making all the arrangements. They were not happy that the marriage was annulled at the last moment.
19	19-8-17, Anandabazar Patrika
	This is a unique case of police arresting the husband for marrying a minor girl of 12 from Benoy Pally of Memari. The girl hailing from Chinui village of Memari was studying in Class 6 of a local school. Her mother, a brick kiln worker, brought her up after the death of her husband. She forced her daughter to marry a 30-year-old man. Someone from this locality informed the Childline. When the team reached the spot they found the bride locked in a room as she did not want to stay with her husband. Police recovered the girl and sent her to a Home and filed a case under PCMA. The girl told the special judge that marriage was forced upon her by her mother. The nodal officer of Kanyashree Scheme from East Barddhaman promised to admit her to a school and link her with other Kanyashree volunteers to protect her.
20	22-01-18, Anandabazar Patrika
	Kanyashree members of Hutkirtinagar Balika Vidyalaya of Ausgram prevented four child marriages during the last one year. They have received letters of commendation from the Chief Minister for such activities. Interestingly, the girls whose marriage was prevented by the Kanyashree members are now their best friends.
21	26-01-18, Ei Samay
	Childline officials have stopped a child marriage in Bhatar with help from police and administration. They came to know that a girl child of Class 10 of Bamsore High School was getting married that very day. When they reached the house of the Muslim girl, all arrangements for the marriage were complete. The girl did not have a father and her mother was not at all willing to stop the marriage. The relatives and villagers also protested against cancellation of marriage at the last moment. The mother asked the officials: 'Who will take care of my daughter later?' 'Who will find a good bride groom for my daughter?' Amidst the chaos, the mother finally agreed to sign the undertaking. The mother, relatives and neighbours were not convinced, however, about the ills of child marriage.

TABLE 8.2 Newspaper Reports *(cont)*

Sl. No	Date, Source News Detai

22   01-02-18, Ei Samay

Kanyashree Club members of Bhandardihi P B Bidyamandir have prevented a marriage of their minor classmate after receiving secret information. They became suspicious when the student missed school for some days. On Wednesday, the Muslim girl of Class 10 was set for marriage. They informed the BDO, who sent a team to Nityanandapur village. But the villagers did not help them to locate the house. Next day when the team went with Kanyashree volunteers, the house could be traced. The marriage ceremony was then in full swing. By seeing the team, the mother of the girl started crying and argued that they are poor people and somehow found a bride groom. After much debate, the parents agreed to stop the marriage and signed the undertaking.

23   02-02-18, Ei Samay

In the Memari-2 block, the police arrested five persons for planning to traffic a girl child studying in Class 7 in a local school in the guise of marriage. The family of the girl fixed her marriage in Dakhalpur village under Memari Thana. When Childline officers came to know about it, they intervened with assistance from BDO and police. The girl complained to the BDO by writing that her father was selling her in the pretext of marriage. He had already taken money from the party. The mother of the girl also supported this view. Memari police then arrested five persons including the maternal aunt of the girl. Among those arrested, three came from Uttar Pradesh. The mother later changed her testimony and wrote to the police that they had taken ₹6,000 from the bride groom party to arrange the marriage.

24   02-02-18, Ei Samay

A father from Chandipur village of Goghat, Arambag arranged marriage of his daughter, a candidate for Madhyamik Examination that year. She was a good student. The Headmaster came to know about this marriage and informed the BDO. The BDO led a team to the girl's house. It was clear from the certificate that the girl was only 15. Yet, the parents expressed their inability to cancel the marriage, because they had already spent a lot of money including a huge dowry. BDO then explained the benefits of Kanyashree and Rupashree schemes and asked the groom's family to return the dowry. Finally, the father agreed to stop the marriage and sent his daughter to school from the next day.

TABLE 8.2 Newspaper Reports *(cont)*

Sl. No	Date, Source News Detai
25	13-02-18, Ei Samay

Marriage of a girl was delayed by 10 days following the intervention of district administration of Bhatar under Barddhaman East District. The Kanyashree Officer of Bhatar along with local police did not consider the appeal of the parents and villagers though the girl would become 18 after 10 days only. The villagers were very angry with the administration as they could have come earlier and argued that the administration should consider the problems of parents.

26	21-02-18, Ei Samay

The Headmaster of A. A. P. G. High School of Kalna came to know that a Muslim student has not come to the school to receive her cycle under *Sabooj Sathi.* He immediately went to her house along with Kanyashree members and Panchayat Pradhan. Members of a local NGO also joined them. The father of the girl works in Maharashtra as a contract labourer. He had arranged the marriage in April. The parents agreed to delay the marriage as the process was yet to start. They also came to know about the marriage of a tribal girl student of Class 10. The teacher talked to her parents and stopped that marriage also. The Kalna administration also prevented marriage of another Hindu girl near Purbasthali new market.

27	23-02-18, Anandabazar Patrika

The District administration of Barddhaman had organised several rallies, meetings, street plays, and posters to campaign against child marriage. A large number of school and college students participated in these programmes. This is done because the practice of child marriage is very high in certain areas of the district. One such awareness camp was held in Ausgram on 22 February 2018. During the proceedings, Kanyashree volunteers came to know about a child marriage. With the help of police and administration, the volunteers reached the spot and found that the girl herself, a student of Class 9 of Ausgram High School, wanted to get married. Incidentally, this family had been prevented from arranging the marriage earlier. But when the girl eloped, the parents decided to socially arrange their marriage. This time too the marriage was prevented and no one knows what happened later.

28	23-02-18, Ei Samay

Katwa District Administration took several steps (as above) to create awareness as despite many efforts, they are unable to impress upon the villagers to stop child marriages. Bhatar Block Administration also organized similar programmes.

TABLE 8.2 Newspaper Reports *(cont)*

Sl. No	Date, Source News Detai
29	23-02-18, Ei Samay A student of Class 7 told the Kanyashree leader of her school that she did not want to get married. Her parents were forcing marriage on her. The brother of the student also told them that he was earlier beaten up for opposing the marriage of his other sister. The Kanyashree leader immediately reported the matter to the Kanyashree nodal teacher. The team led by the BDO reached the house on the day of the marriage. After much persuasion, the parents agreed to delay it and signed the undertaking.
30	27-02-18, Ei Samay The block administration of Purbasthali-2 prevented two cases of child marriage. The news came through Childline.
31	03-03-18, Ei Samay Kanyashree Club members of Kaligram High School have prevented another marriage in Dewan Dighi at Barddhaman. This story is similar to others.
32	04-03-18, Ei Samay Students of Class 11 of Borobainan Krishi Samit Siksha Niketan organized a drama to campaign against child marriage in the annual programme of the school. The drama named 'Jagaran' was written by a school teacher. The storyline resolves around the ill fate of a minor girl child after the marriage. They invited district officials, teachers, guardians, villagers and all students of the school to attend it. The district administration has prevented 25 child marriages in Raina-2 block during the last few months. In all such efforts, Kanyashree volunteers have played a major role.
33	05-03-18, Ei Samay A student of Class 10 of Amarun Station Shiksa Niketan, Bhatar, objected to her marriage and prevented all efforts by her father to fix the marriage. Her father is a daily labourer and has three daughters. Earlier, family members did not allow her to fill up the Madhyamik examination form. This time the school Headmaster helped her to do so.
34	11-05-18, Ei Samay The district administration of Durgapur faced public fury when they tried to postpone a child marriage. When the team reached the spot, the marriage ceremony was in full swing. Although marriage was stopped temporarily, the parents did not sign the undertaking. There was no reporting about what happened later.

TABLE 8.2 Newspaper Reports *(cont)*

Sl. No	Date, Source News Detai

35   05-06-18, Ei Samay

A father from Mandardihi village of Bhatar sought financial assistance under the Rupashree Scheme. He is a daily labourer. On inspection of the documents submitted, it was found that his daughter is yet to reach 18. The marriage, scheduled on 18 May 2018, was therefore postponed till 18 December and the father was asked to submit an undertaking. But the parents were unhappy as they had made arrangements by taking out a loan.

36   29-06-18, Ei Samay

A father from Bamunara Panchayat of Bhatar complained to the BDO against his son eloping with another minor girl student of the same school. The boy and the girl, studying in Classes 10 and 7 respectively at Amarun Station Shiksa Niketan were in a relationship. When the father of the boy asked him to withdraw from it, the couple eloped and took shelter in girl's house. The father of the son then complained to the BDO and the administration then brought the girl to a Home. But it was difficult to keep her at Home for long as she was found to be pregnant. The case shocked the whole administration. No police case was filed against the boy.

37   30-06-18, Ei Samay

The Kalna administration intervened in the marriage of a girl who was 17. The parents agreed to stop the marriage until the girl attained legal age; but no further information was available.

38   13-07-18, Anandabazar Patrika

A student of Class 9 continued to attend school against her parent's wishes. Citing reasons like poverty, security of the girl child and social pressure, they wanted to get her married. The parents were finally persuaded by stakeholders to postpone the marriage and sign the undertaking. The school teachers and Kanyashree volunteers also promised to keep an eye.

39   09-08-18, Ei Samay

The block authority of Ausgram was surprised to find a false claim of grant under the Rupashree Scheme. The girl got married three years earlier and had a child. Thus, false claims for Rupashree and Kanyashree cannot be ruled out.

TABLE 8.2 Newspaper Reports *(cont)*

Sl. No	Date, Source News Detail
40	25-11-18, Anandabazar Patrika A Kanyashree Club member came to know about the marriage of a minor girl. When the BDO along with Panchayat members and Childline officials went to the house, they did not find any one there. The villagers told them that the girl had been taken to a relative's house at another village for a secret marriage. The officials chased the case and the father finally admitted his attempts to get his daughter of 16 married with a 25-year-old man. The way several relatives were involved in keeping the marriage secret puzzled the team. The case was shared with Kanyashree volunteers as they need to be more vigilant now to prevent early marriage.
41	19-01-19, Anandabazar Patrika The Vice President of Katwa Panchayat Samiti went on his own to prevent a marriage of 13-year-old girl. When he reached, the family was busy receiving engagement gifts (called *tatta* in Bengali). He asked the father, a daily labourer, to stop the marriage. He also called the groom's family on the phone and explained why the marriage should be delayed. The bridegroom agreed and the Vice President took personal responsibility to meet the expenses of her education and marriage when she attains 18.
42	20-01-19, Ei Samay Khandaghosh Block Administration took responsibility to meet all expenses of education of the minor girl student of 16 years, whose marriage was cancelled by them. The girl was very happy as she wanted to continue her education. The parents signed the undertaking and acknowledged their mistake.
43	24-02-19, Anandabazar Patrika In Sridharpur area of Memari-2, the stakeholders arguing for late marriage had a tough time preventing an early marriage. At first, the parents agreed to delay the marriage and signed the undertaking. Yet, the officials came to know that later at night the marriage was being performed secretly. They called the bridegroom who was on his way and explained the illegality of the marriage. The marriage was cancelled for that day. This story reveals how villagers try to bypass the pressure to prevent early marriage.

TABLE 8.2 Newspaper Reports *(cont)*

Sl. No	Date, Source News Detail

44   14-03-19, Ei Samay

An elected Municipal councillor of CPI(M) Party was found marrying a 16-year-old girl on 12 April 2019. Childline officials received a phone call and they immediately reached the house of the girl along with Block administration and local police. But, by the time they reached the spot, the marriage was complete and the bridegroom had taken his wife to his house. The team could not trace the councillor, but brought the newly wed wife. Her mother was also arrested but later released on bail. A police case has been filed against the husband. It is not clear from the report what happened to the girl, who was in a relationship with the man and did not object to her marriage.

45   27-04-19, Anandabazar Patrika

A minor student of Palita High School of Ketugram-1 Block used her father's mobile phone to call the Headmaster of her school and requested him to stop her marriage scheduled next day. She gave her Madhyamik Examination that year and her family had arranged her marriage with a daily labourer of nearby village. The matter was kept secret and the girl was not told about such an arrangement. She was asked to get ready for the marriage ceremony just three days before the event. Confused, she contacted her school teachers. Next day, the usual team reached the spot and cancelled the marriage by asking the parents to sign the undertaking.

46   14-05-19, Ei Samay

Two daughters complained to the District Magistrate of Katwa against their father. The father, who works in Delhi, forced one of his minor daughters to marry a person aged 39 having taken them to Tarapith in the pretext of a tour. The problem started when the married daughter fled from the in-laws' house complaining of violence. The father was forcing her to return to the marital home. The matter was under inquiry.

47   17-05-19, Anandabazar Patrika

The Superintendent of a Madrasa Md. Zakiuruddin Seikh from Katwa was given the prestigious Shiksharatna award in 2015 for preventing many early marriages and drop out of Muslim girl students. A girl student of his Madrasa, whose marriage he prevented when she was in Class 9, has scored 87 percent in board examination (Fazil) for Class 12. Her father is a tailor and is now proud of her daughter. Though she got married after attaining 18 years, she continued her education and wants to become a teacher.

TABLE 8.2 Newspaper Reports *(cont)*

Sl. No	Date, Source News Detai
47	17-05-19, Anandabazar Patrika l *(cont)*
	Another student has also scored good marks. Kanyashree Club has helped in generating positive consciousness about education for girl children and delaying marriage. They have also formed a group called Mina Mancha to carry out door to door campaigns against child marriage. As a result of such campaign, rate of dropout has reduced.
48	22-06-19, Ei Samay
	Two non-official Marriage (Hindu) Registrars of Barddhaman West District were suspended by the state government for illegally validating child marriages. They were first issued show cause notices, towhich they did not reply. It was alleged that they forged documents to marry off minor children. The report indicated that such acts were common in some other parts of the state.
49	13-07-19, Ei Samay
	A police team was attacked by villagers when they went to stop early marriage of a Muslim girl. Two policemen were physically assaulted by a person. The perpetrator was later arrested and the marriage was finally stopped.
50	04-08-2019, Anandabazar Patrika
	A tribal woman, Rashmoni Kisku of Saheb Danga village, Galsi-2, applied for financial help under the Rupashree scheme though she had got married five years earlier and had a 3-year-old child.
51	16-08-19, Anandabazar Patrika
	On 14 August, which is celebrated in the state as a Kanyashree Day, the parents of a minor girl tried to arrange a marriage with a boy of 21 at a relative's house to evade social pressure. Her father is a daily labourer. The Block administration came to know about the plan and prevented it.
52	170-08-19, Anandabazar Patrika
	A case of torture was lodged with the police by parents of a 17-year-old boy who eloped with a local girl of 15 years. The matter was referred to the Child Welfare Committee who asked the couple to stay separately until they attain the legal age of marriage.

TABLE 8.2 Newspaper Reports *(cont)*

Sl. No	Date, Source News Detai
53	17-08-19, Anandabazar Patrika
	This report is of a case of solemnizing a child marriage after parents had given assurance to the administration that they will defer it. The parents went to a local temple the same night and solemnized the marriage. The administration is yet to take any action against the persons involved.
54	17-08-18, Ei Samay
	On 15 August, parents of a 13-year-old girl from Manteswar arranged her marriage. The girl stopped going to school after taking admission in class seven. But on the day of marriage, the Block officials along with local police stopped the marriage at the last moment and asked the parents to sign the undertaking. The administration also stopped the marriage of another 13-year-old girl from the same block.

in 2017, there were 19 cases of reporting on the issue in the two newspapers, the figures slightly went up to 21 in the whole of 2018 and came down to just 14 within 229 days in 2019. It is worth noting here that in 2015, not a single news item on such prevention in the district was published in these newspapers and in 2016, only 2 news items were published.

In order to compensate for my failure to take note of non-reported or other cases (reported in other newspapers) of prevention of child marriage, I did look at data uploaded at the Kanyashree portal. And my search revealed that I did miss nearly 86 cases of prevention in both the districts of Barddhaman, mostly from Purba Barddhaman in between 2017 and 2019. Though these stories are not given in detail like those in the two newspapers, yet on the whole, we may presume that there were more than 200 cases of prevention of child marriage in the two districts of Barddhaman during the last three years. This is no mean achievement given the large-scale prevalence of early marriage in Barddhaman. We, however, have little knowledge about any follow up action carried out by the administration after a marriage is prevented at the very last moment. On the contrary, a few cases of parents arranging the marriage even after signing undertakings are reported. Besides, some cases of false claim for grants under both Rupashree and Kanyashree as well as falsification of marriage documents by registered Marriage Registrars are also reported. These violations confirm that societal impulse for early marriage is still very strong.

Nevertheless, it appears from my listing that there is a gradual decline in the number of cases reported from Barddhaman, Purba and Paschim districts since its peak in the middle of 2017 and 2018. Going by the tenor of the reports published, the major reason for the decline is secret solemnization of marriage by parents and relatives. Initially, news about occurrence of child marriage could be easily traced by Kanyashree volunteers from their respective schools and it was they who took initiative to stop those marriages with help from others including teachers. Later, other stakeholders have also started receiving such news from anonymous callers. The large-scale campaign among students, Panchayat and Self Help Group members, ritual specialists and rural people at large is proving to be beneficial. This also proves that the agenda of preventing early marriage has spread to a large group of villagers and not only to Kanyashree members. Most remarkably, this includes adolescent male students. Use of Sabujshree scheme to distribute saplings of trees to the mothers of newborn daughters and sons is also encouraging. Due to such activities, there might be a sharp decline in the percentage of child marriage in the state in years to come.

Yet, with more and more cases of forceful prevention of child marriage, on the day of the wedding, parents are seen developing counter strategies: *(a)* denying any plan of marriage by not printing cards or inviting fewer guests; *(b)* secret arrangement of marriage despite signing the undertaking; *(c)* arranging the marriage in a relative's home; and *(d)* often attacking the prevention team with local support. Newspaper reports also clearly demonstrate that the prevention team is reaching the spot at the last moment. This is mostly because news of marriage of minor girls is kept secret by parents and relatives till the final day. As a corollary, there is a decline in the number of prevention cases reported by the media. Incidentally, news published in local media during Covid 19 pandemic reveal increasing instances of early marriage from all parts of the state. Parents are finding it easy now to arrange such marriages secretly as schools are closed, teachers, neighbours and Kanyashree volunteers are confined to the homes, local administration and police are busy tackling the pandemic and parents are also asked to keep the number of guests at a minimum at social functions. Concurrently, networks of traffickers have also revived in areas facing natural calamity[5] and acute unemployment. The traffickers are turning the situation into an opportunity to lure girls with good proposals, including that of marriage.

Another trend noticed in such reporting is that parents consider cases of elopement by minor girls and boys as a threat to their prestige and status. Such 'love marriage' very often acts against the arguments for late marriage. Parents prefer to fix a marriage early if there is any hint of a possibility that children — boys and girls — may choose their own partners. After a marriage is solemnized, it is not considered 'proper' for administrative or legal intervention. It has been seen (case no 12) that if the family remains adamant in fixing the marriage even against the wishes of the girl child, she has to be provided shelter in a Home, which is often not possible for the administration. In other words, once a marriage is solemnized, there is little protest or action against it unless the matter is reported to the police for reasons like violence/torture committed after the marriage. As a result, I could could trace only three instances of police arrest amongst the 54 marriages listed. In two of them, the case was filed against the husband (no. 19 and 44), and in another, police arrested some persons coming from Uttar Pradesh for trafficking a minor girl under the guise of marriage (no. 23). The issue of early marriage of boys is also reported by the media. As I have have noted earlier, these boys have migrated to different places for work and are considered 'good bride-grooms' in a rural society where the prospect of employment looks remote.

Interestingly, in most cases, the age of girls being married is found to be in between 14–17 though a few cases of marriage of 12- or 13-year-old girl child have been reported. The news-paper reporting also confirms one of our earlier findings. Early marriage is practised mostly by marginalized people living in less developed blocks of Purba Barddhaman like Katwa, Kalna, Purbasthali, Ausgram, Mangalkot, and Bhatar. There are only two instances of such marriage from the more developed blocks such as Durgapur and Asansol of Paschim Barddhaman.

CONCLUSION

It appears that the task of preventing child marriage is tough, continuous and long drawn and any abnormal situation like Covid-19 or Cyclone Amphan makes it more challenging. Looking into the way Kanyashree Yodhyas have become role models in rural Bengal to stand against the wishes of their parents, to campaign for late marriage and prevent early marriages by collecting information from different sources, we may argue that KP has served its purpose. It is true that the financial assistance under K1 is too little even though the combined monetary benefit under both K2 and Rupashree is ₹50,000 for a girl of 19. But as most marriages are arranged before a girl reaches 17, the more effective aspect of K1 is not the money, the money is just a peg to draw in parents and hang the scheme on; its real efficacy is in awareness and the social action around the scheme. So, publicity of the scheme by the state government has increased its impact. A great deal of awareness of child marriage is occurring around the scheme, especially in rural West Bengal.

Yet, there is little change in the notion that marriage is essential for a girl child among marginalized communities of rural Bengal. Also, issues like unemployment, poverty, natural and health calamity, early marriage of boys, lack of employment options for girls, cases of elopement and concern for security of girl child, and police approach to the crime,[6] allow the practice to continue. From the newspaper reporting, it is pretty clear that after solemnization of marriage even police or administration do not consider it appropriate to separate the child couple or take legal action against the parties arranging marriage. Once the task gets restricted only to 'prevention before marriage', it becomes easy for parents to look for ways of accomplishing the marriage; sometimes arranging it secretly. Notwithstanding certain positive developments, therefore, the process of 'institution building' through popular participation appears to be a long-drawn task. Much, therefore, needs to be done in years to come, which would call for all round synergy in action on the part of stakeholders. Going by the limits of financial schemes in restricting child marriage, strong legal actions against the offenders also need to be taken to develop a counter-culture of late marriage.

NOTES

1   In 13 of the 30 villages surveyed in Malda, the rate of early marriage was found to be above 80 percent.
2   Along with my Department, Department of Economics of both Calcutta and North Bengal Universities were involved in this survey.
3   The administrative boundary of the erstwhile Barddhaman district was bifurcated into Purba (East) and Paschim (West) Barddhaman from 7 April 2017.
4   Government of West Bengal. 2011. *District Human Development Report— Barddhaman*. Kolkata: Development and Planning Department.
5   Cyclone Amphan has in May 2020 caused severe damage in districts like East Midnapur, North 24-Parganas and South 24-Parganas.
6   Only 348 police cases were registered in the state in between 2011 and 2018 and 68 percent of those were filed in last five years.

REFERENCES

Das, U., and A. Pal. 2019. 'Kanyashree Safal, Abar Cheleder Shisker Janyao Prakalpya Chai Ki?' (Kanyashree Is Successful, Do We Now Also Need Scheme for Boys?), 16 March, *Anandabazar Patrika*, Barddhaman edition.

Ghosh, Biswajit. 2010. 'Delaying the Age of Marriage in Malda: A Document to Design Interventions for Changing Norms'. Kolkata: UNICEF.

Ghosh, Biswajit, and Ananda Mohan Kar. 2010. 'Child Marriage in Rural West Bengal: Status and Challenges', *Indian Journal of Development Research and Social Action* 7, 1 & 2: 49–62.

Ghosh, Biswajit. 2011a. 'Child Marriage and Its Prevention: Role of Adolescent Girls', *Indian Journal of Development Research and Social Action* 6, 1 & 2: 1–23.

———. 2011b. 'Early Marriage of Girls in Contemporary Bengal: A Field View', *Social Change* 41, 1: 41–61.

———. 2011c. 'Child Marriage, Society and the Law: A Study in a Rural Context in West Bengal, India', *International Journal of Law, Policy and the Family* 25, 2: 199–219.

———. 2011d. 'Child Marriage, Community, and Adolescent Girls: The Salience of Tradition and Modernity in the Malda District of West Bengal', *Sociological Bulletin* 60, 2: 307–326.

———. 2019. 'Social Structure in Barddhaman', *Burdwan District Gazetteer*, Chapter XV. Unpublished.

International Institute for Population Sciences. 2007. *National Family Health Survey 2005–06 (NFHS-3)*. Government of India. New Delhi: Ministry of Health and Family Welfare.

———. 2008. *District Level Household and Facility Survey under Reproductive and Child Health Project 2007–08* (DLHS-3), Government of India. New Delhi: Ministry of Health and Family Welfare.

———. 2017. *National Family Health Survey 2015–16 (NFHS-4)*. Government of India. New Delhi: Ministry of Health and Family Welfare.

Khanna, Akshay, and Akhil Khan. 2018. 'Searching for the Boys: A Review of Literature, Analyses and Practices Relating to Early and Child Marriages, with a Focus on Boys, Men and Masculinity', *American Jewish World Service* (AJWS), https://ajws.org/our-impact/research-early-child-marriage/, accessed on 8 September 2019.

Mukherjee, Aparna, and T. V. Sekher. 2017. 'Do Only Girls Suffer? We Too!' Early Marriage Repercussions on Boys in Rural India', *EPW* 52, 1: 75–82.

Pratham. 2019. *Annual Status of Education Report* (ASER, January). https://www.asercentre.org, accessed on 8 September 2019.

Sen, Anindita, and Arijita Dutta. 2018. 'West Bengal's Successful Kanyashree Prakalpa Programme Needs More Push From State and Beneficiaries', *engage*, *EPW* 53, 17, https://www.epw.in › engage › article › West-Bengal-Successful-Kanya..., accessed on 7 September 2018.

Times of India. 2019. 'Kanyashree Scheme Has Helped 60 Lakh Girl Children: Mamata', 14 August, https://timesofindia.indiatimes.com › Education, accessed on 9 September 2019.

UNICEF. 2009. 'State Consultation on Child Marriage in West Bengal – Background Notes'. Kolkata: UNICEF.

A Select Bibliography

Elvira Graner and Samita Sen

W E HAVE MENTIONED in the introduction and in several essays in this book that the research literature on child marriage reflects a wide range of approaches to this topic. From the mid-twentieth century, child marriage has been seen more as a policy issue than a social problem. Overall, a demographic approach to the study of child marriage has been predominant. In contrast, there have been fewer attempts at understanding the subjective reasoning of those personally involved, at whatever level of agency. In order to strengthen the latter perspective, this project has been part of an international effort to formulate new research questions and chart fresh directions for discussions on child marriage. With this larger aim in view, we are appending this bibliography, which is a combination of our own individual lists put together for our various projects on child marriage. We hope that this will be useful for future researchers.

Agarwala, S.N. 1961. *Age at Marriage in India*. Allahabad: Kitab-Mahal Publishers.
Agnes, Flavia. 2001. *Law and Gender Inequality: The Politics of Women's Rrights in India*. New Delhi: Oxford University Press.
Anagol, Padma. 2005. *The Emergence of Feminism in India, 1850–1920*. Aldershot: Ashgate.

Asian Forum of Parliamentarians on Population and Development. ca. 2013. 'Review of National Legislations and Policies on Child Marriage in South Asia'. Bangkok: AFPPD.

Bannerji, Himani. 2001. *Inventing Subjects: Studies in Hegemony, Patriarchy and Colonialism*. New Delhi: Tulika, 2001.

Bhagat, R. B. 2002. 'Child Marriage Restraint Act'. In *Child Marriages and the Law in India*. New Delhi: HRLN: 139–41.

Boyden, Jo, and S. Dercon. 2012. *Child Development and Economic Development. Lessons and Future Challenges*. Oxford: Young Lives; http:// www.younglives.org.uk/publications/PP/child-development-and-economic-development/boyden-and-dercon-child-development-and-economic-development

Caldwell, J. C, P. H. Reddy, and P. Caldwell. 1983. 'The Causes of Marriage Change in South India', *Population Studies* 37: 343–61. http://gsdl. ewubd.edu/greenstone/collect/admin-mprhgdco/index/assoc/ HASH014b.dir/P0008.pdf

Center for Reproductive Rights. ca. 2014. 'Child Marriage in South Asia: Stop the Impunity'. New York: CFRR. www.reproductive rights; org/sites/crr.civicactions.net/files/documents/ChildMarriage_ BriefingPaper_Web.pdf

Centre for Social Research. 2013. 'A Study on Child Marriage in India. Situational Analysis in Three States'. New Delhi: CSR India. www. csrindia.org/images/download/case-studies/Child-Marriage-Report.pdf

Chakrabarty, R. 2012. 'India Emerges World's Child Marriage Capital. *The Times of India*. 12 Oct. http://timesofindia.indiatimes.com/india/ India-emerges-worlds-child-marriage-capital/articleshow/16774 381.cms

Chandra, Aparna. 2017. 'Privacy and Women's Rights', *Economic and Political Weekly* (henceforth *EPW*) 52, 51.

Chatterjee, P. 2011. 'India Grapples with Its Child Marriage Challenge'. *Lancet* 378: 1987–88.

Chidambaram, S. 2013. Marriage Is No Child's Play: *The Hindu*. Virudhunagar, 4 Oct. http://www.thehindu.com/news/cities/ Madurai/marriage-is-no-childs-play/article5199852.ece

Das, N. P. and D. Dey. 1998. 'Female Age at Marriage in India. Trends and Determinants'. *Demography India* 27: 91–115. http://www.women studies.in/elib/fertility/fr_female_age.pdf

DeSouza, Peter Ronald, Sanjay Kumar and Sandeep Shastri, eds. 2009. *Indian Youth in a Transforming World: Attitudes and Perceptions.* New Delhi: CSDS, KAS and Sage.

DFID. 2006. *Why Governance Matters.* London: DFID.

Dhillon, A. 2015. 'Child Marriage in India Finally Meets Its Match as Young Brides Turn to Courts', *The Guardian.* May 27. http://www.theguardian.com/global-development/2015/may/27/india-child-marriage-annulment-brides-go-to-court

The Economist. 2011. 'Child Brides. For Poorer, Most of the Time'. *Economist* (28 Feb). http/:www.economist.com/blogs/dailychart/2011/02/child_brides (henceforth *EPW*) 94, 15: 7.

EPW Editorials. 2013. 'Will Child Marriages Ever End? '*EPW* 48, 44: 9.

———. 2014. 'Not Made in Heaven'. *EPW* 49, 51: 8.

———. Letters 2013. 'Child Marriage', *EPW* 48, 52: 4–6.

Fukuyama, Francis. 2013. 'What Is Governance?' *Governance* 26, 3: 347–68.

Forbes, Geraldine. 1999. *Women in Modern India,* Cambridge: Cambridge University Press.

Ghosh, Biswajit, and Ananda Mohan Kar. 2010. 'Child Marriage in Rural West Bengal: Status and Challenges', *Indian Journal of Development Research and Social Action* 6, 1–2 (Jan.–Dec.): 1–23.

Ghosh. Biswajit. 2010. 'Delaying the Age of Marriage in Malda: A Document to Design Interventions for Changing Norms', UNICEF, Kolkata.

———. 2011a. 'Early Marriage of Girls in Contemporary Bengal: A Field View', *Social Change,* New Delhi: Sage, CSD, 41, 1:, 41–61.

———, 2011b. 'Child Marriage, Society and the Law: A Study in a Rural Context in West Bengal, India', *International Journal of Law, Policy and Family* 25, 2: 199–219.

———. 2011c. 'Child Marriage, Community, and Adolescent Girls: The Salience of Tradition and Modernity in the Malda District of West Bengal', *Sociological Bulletin, Indian Sociological Society* 60, 2 (May-Aug): 307–26.

———. 2011d. 'Child Marriage and Its Prevention: Role of Adolescent Girls', *Indian Journal of Development Research and Social Action: An International Journal* 7, 1–2: 49–62.

GOI and IIPS. 2017. *National Family Health Survey 4.* New Delhi/Mumbai: GOI and IIPS.

GOI. 2011. *India Human Development Report.* New Delhi: OUP and GOI/Planning Commission. http://www.iamrindia.gov.in/ihdr_book.*pdf*

GOI/Law Commission of India. 2008. 'Proposal to Amend the Prohibition of Child Marriage Act 2006 and Other Allied Laws'. New Delhi: LCI (ReportNo.205).http://lawcommissionofindia.nic.in/reports/report 205.pdf

GOI/MHA/Registrar General. 2014. *Vital Statistics of India. Based on the Civil Registration System 2011.* New Delhi: GOI.

GOI/MHFW and IIPS. 2009. *Profile of Youth in India. NFHS-3 from 2005/06.* New Delhi: GOI. www.dhsprogram.com/pubs/pdf/OD59/OD59. pdf

GOI/MHFW, IIPS and Population Council. 2010a. *Youth in India. Situation and Needs.* New Delhi and Mumbai: GOI/IIPS/Population Council. http://www.popcouncil.org/uploads/pdfs/2010PGY_YouthIn IndiaBrief33.pdf

———. 2010b. *Youth in India. Situation and Needs. Bihar.* New Delhi and Mumbai: GOI/IIPS/Population Council.

GOI/Ministry of Human Resource Development, Department of Women and Child Development. 2001. 'Convention on the Rights of the Child. First Periodic Report'. New Delhi: GOI.

GOI/Ministry of Law and Justice. 2006. 'Right to Education Act 2006'. New Delhi: Bharat ka Rajpatra/India Gazette.

———. 2007. 'Prevention of Child Marriage Act 2006'. New Delhi: Bharat ka Rajpatra/India Gazette (18Jan.).

———. 2013. 'Registration of Births and Death Act. Amendment for Registration of Marriages'. New Delhi: Bharat ka Rajpatra; http://www. prsindia.org/uploads media/Registration%20of%20births%20and %20deaths/REegistration%20of%20Births%20and%20Deaths%20 (Amendment)%20bill,%202012.pdf

———. 1949. 'Amendment to the Child Marriage Restraint Act'. Bharat ka Rajpatra/India Gazette.

———. 1955. *Hindu Marriage Act 1955.* New Delhi: Bharat ka Rajpatra/ India Gazette.

———. 1969. *Registration of Births and Death Act.* New Delhi: Bharat ka Rajpatra/India Gazette.

———. 1978. *Amendment to the Child Marriage Restraint Act.* New Delhi: GOI/Bharat ka Rajpatra.

———. 2004. *The Prevention of Child Marriage Bill.* New Delhi: Bharat ka Rajpatra/India Gazette.

GOI/MSPI. 2014. *Millennium Development Goals India Country Report.* New Delhi: GOI/Ministry of Statistics and Programme Implementation.

GOI/MWCD. 2011. *Report on CEDAW (Convention on the Elimination of All Forms of Discrimination against Women)*. New Delhi: GOI; www.wcd. nic.in/cedawdraft20nov2011.pdf

———. 2012. *National Strategy Document on Prevention of Child Marriage*. New Delhi: GOI. http://www.khubmarriage18.org/sites/default/files/207.pdf

———. 2013. *National Policy for Child*. New Delhi: GOI/MWCD. http://wcd.nic.in/childwelfare/ npc2013dtd29042013.pdf

GOI/ORG and UNPFA. 2014. *A Profile of Adolescents and Youth in India*. New Delhi: GOI and UNFPA.

Governance and Social Development Resource Centre. 2010. *Helpdesk Research Report. Early Marriage and Sexual and Reproductive Health*. London: GSD.

Government of India. 2014. Population Census 2011. New Delhi: GOI. http://censusindia.gov.in/

Graner, Elvira, Fatema Samina Yasmin and Syeda Salina Aziz. 2012. *Giving Youth a Voice. Bangladesh Youth Survey 2011*. Dhaka: UNDP/SDC/ Institute of Governance Studies; www.igs-bracu.ac.bd/ research/ bangladesh-youth-survey.

Graner, Elvira. 2015. 'Unkept Promises. The (Mal)Governance of Universal Education for Youth in South Asia'. Oxford: paper presented at the Conference on "Grounded. Youth in South Asia (22–23 May).

———. 2019. 'Governing Childhood in India. The Up-Hill Battle to Abolish Child Marriage', *Studies on Sociology of Childhood and Youth* 35, 35–57.

Green, Margaret E.2014. *Ending Child Marriage in a Generation*. New York: Ford Foundation. http://www.fordfoundation.org/pdfs/library/ EndingChildMarriage.pdf

Greening, Justine. 2014. *Girl Marriage Is Not Only a Tragedy for Girls*. London: DFID. www.girlsnotbrides.org child-marriage-just-tragedy-girls-disaster-development-says-uk-secretary-state-development/

Guttmacher Institute. 1987. 'Age of Indian Brides Rising, but Many Still Marry at Younger Ages than the Minimum Set by Law'. *International Family Planning Perspective* 13, 4: 148–50.

HAQ. ca. 2010. *Child Marriage in India. Achievements, Gaps and Challenges. Response to Questions for OHCHR Report on Preventing Child, Early and Forced Marriages for Twenty-Sixth Session of the Human Rights Council*. New Delhi: HAQ Centre for Child Rights. www.ohchr.

org/Documents/ Issues/ Women/WRGS/ForcedMarriage/NGO/ HAQCentreForChildRights1.pdf

Haug, Werner. 2012. Editorial. Too Young to Wed. Child Marriage in Eastern Europe and Central Asia. *Entre Nous* (76): 1. www.euro.who. int/data/assets/pdf_file/0007/178531/Entre-Nous-76-Eng-v2.pdf

The Hindu. 2008. 'Fix Marriageable Age for Boys and Girls at 18, says Law Commission'. (7 Feb). http://www.thehindu.com/todays-paper/ fix-marriageable-age-for-boys-and-girls-at-18-says-law-commission/ article1194481.ece

———. 2013. 'Concern over India's Refusal to Sign Child Marriage Resolution', (27 Oct.). http://www.thehindu.com/todays-paper/ tp-national/tp-newdelhi/concern-over-indias-refusal-to-sign-child-marriage-resolution/article5276990.ece

———. 2014. 'White Bindi' Project Campaigns against Child Marriage', (29 March). http://www.thehindu.com/todays-paper/tp-in-school/ white-bindi-project-campaigns-against-child-marriage/article 5845636.ece

———. 2014. 'Keeping Girls in School Cuts Child Maternal Mortality', (10 July). http://www.thehindu.com/todays-paper/tp-features/ tp-sci-tech-and-agri/keeping-girls-in-school-cuts-child-maternal-mortality/article6194938.ece

———. 2014. 'The Highest Rate of Child Marriage is in Bangladesh', (12 Sept.).

Hindustan Times. 2014. 'Child Marriage "Worst Form of Domestic Violence" Against Child'. Delhi court PTI, New Delhi (7 Sept.) http://www.hindustantimes.com/india-news/delhi-court-abhors-the-custom-of-child-marriage/article1-1261160.aspx

———. 2015. 'Child Marriage: A Scourge That Needs To Be Weeded Out'. (13 May). http://www.hindustantimes.com/comment/child-marriage-a-scourge-that-needs-to-be-weeded-out/article1-1346915. aspx

Human Rights Law Network. 2006. *Child Marriages and the Law in India*. New Delhi: HRLN: 139–41.

ICRW. 2010. *New Insights on Preventing Child Marriage. A Global Analysis of Factors and Programmes*. Washington, DC: ICRW. https://www. icrw.org/files/publications/New-Insights-on-Preventing-Child-Marriage.pdf

IIPS and GOI/MHFW. 2007. *India. National Family Health Survey-3*. Mumbai: IIPS and GOI. www.dhsprogram.com/pubs/pdf/FRIND3/ FRIND3-vosl.1, 2.pdf.

Indian Express. 2007. 'SC to Govt: Clearly Define Law against Child Marriage'. *Express News Service* (18 Sept.). www.archive.indianexpress. com/news/sc-to-govt-clearly-define-law-against-child-marriage/ 218075/

Indian Legislature. 1929. *Child Marriage Restraint Act 1929*. Indian Gazette Act NO. XIX (1 Oct.).

International Center for the Rights of Women. 2014. *Too Young to Wed. Education and Action towards Ending Child Marriage. Policy Solutions.* Washington, DC: ICRW; www.icrw.org/files/ publications/ Too-Young-to-Wed-Education-and-Action-Toward-Ending-Child-Marriage.pdf

IPPF. 2007. *Ending Child Marriage: A Guide for Gobal Policy Action.* London: International Planned Parenthood Federation and Forum on Marriage and the Rights of Women and Girls. Downloads/ending_ child_marriage.pdf

Jayal, Niraja Gopal. 2003. 'Locating Gender in the Governance Discourse'. In *Essays on Gender and Governance*. Niraja Gopal Jayal et.al. New Delhi: UNDP: 96–120. http://www.undp.org/content/dam/ india/ docs/essays_on_gender_and_governance.pdf

Jejeebhoy, Shireen, K. G. Santhya and Rajib J. Acharya. 2010. *Health and Social Consequences of Marital Violence. A Synthesis of Evidence from India*. New Delhi: Population Council and UNPFA. http://www. popcouncil.org/uploads/pdfs/2010PGY_IndiaMaritalViolence.pdf

John, M.E. 2011. 'Census 2011. Governing Populations and the Girl Child', *EPW* 46, 16: 10–12. https://www.unfpa.org/sites/default/ files/resource-pdf/ UNFPA _Publication-39866.pdf

Kakkar, A. K. 2009. *Child Marriage in India: Issues and Challenges*. New Delhi: Cyber Tech.

Kamal, S. M. M., and Hassan, C.H. 2015. 'Child Marriage and Its Association with Adverse Reproductive Outcomes for Women in Bangladesh', *Asia-Pacific Journal of Public Health* 27, 2: 1492–1506.

Kaur, R. 2004. 'Across-Region Marriages: Poverty, Female Migration and the Sex Ratio', *EPW* 39: 2595–603.

Kaur, R., and R. Palriwala, eds. 2014. *Marrying in South Asia. Shifting Concepts: Changing Practices in a Globalising World*. New Delhi: Orient Blackswan.

Kazi, Seema. 2011. '*Gender, Governance and Women's Rights in South Asia*'. New Delhi: Centre for Women's Development Studies. http://www. cwds.ac.in/OCPaper/occasional-paper-September-57-seema-2011. pdf.

Kulkarni, M.N. 1994. 'Child Marriages and State', *EPW* 29: 1884.

Lal, Ruby. 2013. *Coming of Age in Nineteenth-Century India: The Girl Child and the Art of Playfulness*, Cambridge: Cambridge University Press.

Lal, B. Suresh. 2013. 'Child Marriage in India. Factors and Problems', *International Journal of Science and Research* 4, 4: 2292–97; www.ijsr.net/archive/v4i4/SUB1536991.pdf

Malhotra, A., A. Warner, A. McGonagle and S. Lee–Rife. 2011. *Solutions to End Child Marriage: What the Evidence Shows*. Washington DC: ICRW. http://www.icrw.org/files/publications/Solutions-to-End-Child Marriage.pdf

MAMTA. 2006. 'Early Marriage and Early Pregnancy in India'. In *Child Marriages and the Law in India*. New Delhi: Human Rights Law Network, 143–60.

Masoodi, Ashwaq. 2014. 'Child Marriages in India. Untying the Knot'. New Delhi: Round Table India. www.roundtableindia.co.in/ index.php?option=com_content&view=article&id=7249:child-marriages-untying-the-knot&catid=61:opinion&Itemid=56

Mathur, M., S. Green and A. Malhotra. 2003. *Too Young to Wed: The Lives, Rights and Health of Young Married Girls*. Washington, DC.: ICRW; https://www.icrw.org/files/publications/Too-Young-to-Wed-the-Lives-Rights-and-Health-of-Young-Married-Girls.pdf

Menon, Pratibha P. 2006. 'State Responses to the Petition'. In *Child Marriages and the Law in India*. New Delhi: Human Rights Law Network, 139–41.

Moore, A. M., et al. 2009. *Adolescent Marriage and Childbearing in India: Current Situation and Recent Trends*. NY and Washington, DC: Guttmacher Institute. http://www.guttmacher.org/pubs/2009/ 06/04/ AdolescentMarriageIndia.pdf

Mukerjee, Arpana. 2015. 'Boys Also Suffer Early Marriage in India. Case Studies from Uttar Pradesh'. Kuala Lumpur: Asia Population Association Bi-Annual Conference (July 27–29, unpublished paper).

Mukherjee S., S. Singh, S. Das Gupta, R. Pande, and S. Basu. 2008. *Knot Ready: Lessons from India on Delaying Marriage for Girls*. Washington, DC: ICRW; http://www.atria-kennisinstituut.nl/ epublications/2008/ Knot_ready.pdf

Nadendla, Veda. 2014. 'How An Indian Tradition Is Destroying the Lives of Young Girls in the Name of Marriage'. New Delhi: Breakthrough – Youth Ki Awaaz (19 Sept.). www.youthkiawaaz.com/ 2014/09/ indian-tradition-destroying-lives-young-girls-name-marriage

A Select Bibliography

259

Nagi, B. S. 1993. Child Marriage in India: A Study of Differential Patterns in Rajasthan. New Delhi: Mittal. www.sappdf.org/1j5om4_pdf-book-child-marriage-in-india.pdf

National Commission for Protection of Child Rights (NCPCR) and Young Lives. 2017. 'A Statistical Analysis of Child Marriage in India based on Census 2011'.

Navarro, Sonia Chager. 2012. 'Educational Expansion and Early Marriage in India: Time and Regional Trends'. Paper presented at Population Conf. Stockholm. www.epc2012.princeton.edu/papers/120729

NBC staff. 2012. 'Indian Baby Bride Wins Annulment'. NBC (25 April). www.worldnews.nbcnews.com/ _news/ 2012/04/25/11394397-indian-baby-bride-laxmi-sargara-wins-annulment-in-landmark-case?lite

Newbigin, Eleanor. 2013. The Hindu Family and the Emergence of Modern India. Cambridge: Cambridge University Press.

Nguyen, Minh Cong, and Quentin Wodon. 2012. Global Trends in Child Marriage. Washington, DC.: World Bank. http://www.ungei.org/files/Child_Marriage_Trends3.pdf

Nihlén, Åsa, and Isabel Yordi Aguirre. 2012. 'Early Marriage. Cause and Consequence of Gender Inequality and a Violation of Human Rights'. Entre Nous 76: 2–4; www.euro.who.int/data/assets/pdf_file/ 0007/178531/Entre-Nous-76-Eng-v2.pdf

Nirantar Trust. 2015. Early and Child Marriage in India: A Landscape Analysis. Nirantar Trust, Supported by American Jewish World Service.

North, D.C. 1990. Institutions, Institutional Change and Economic Performance. Cambridge: Cambridge University Press.

———. 1995. 'The New Institutional Economics and Third World Development'. In: The New Institutional Economics and Third World Development, J. Harriss et al., eds. London/New York, 17–26.

Pande, Ishita. 2012. Medicine, Race and Liberalism in British Bengal: Symptoms of Empire. New Delhi: Routledge.

Parashar, Archana. 1992. Women and Family Law Reform in India: Uniform Civil Code and Gender Equality, Delhi: Sage.

Plan Asia Regional Office and ICRW. 2013. Asia Child Marriage Initiative: Summary of Research in Bangladesh, India and Nepal. Bangkok. PARO. www.planinternational.org/files/Asia/publications/asia-child-marriageinitiative-summary-of-research-in-bangladesh-india-and-nepal.pdf

Plan International. 2011. Breaking Vows: Early and Forced Marriage and Girls' Education. London: Plan International. http://www.plan-uk.

org/resources/documents/Breaking-Vows-Early-and-Forced-Marriage-and-Girls-Education/

PRAXIS. 2012. *Marriage Can Wait, Our Rights Not. A Study Exploring Causes, Impacts and Resistance in the Context of Early Marriages in Bihar and Jharkhand.* New Delhi. PRAXIS. http://www.praxisindia; org/user_praxis/file/Marriage%20Can%20Wait,%20Our%20Rights%20Can't%20-%20A%20 Study.pdf

Raj, A. 2010. 'When the Mother Is a Child. The Impact of Child Marriage on the Health and Human Rights of Girls'. *Archives of Disease in Childhood* 95: 931–935. http://adc.bmj.com/content/early/ 2010/10/07/ ad3c.2009.178707.full.pdf

Raj, A. et al. 2014. 'Brief Report: Parents–Adolescent Child Concordance in Social Norms Related to Gender Equity in Marriage: Findings from Rural India', *Journal of Adolescence* 37: 1181–84.

The Red Elephant Foundation. 2013. *Child Marriages in India: An Insight into Law and Policy.* New Delhi: TREF, submitted to OHCHR. http:// www.ohchr.org/Documents/Issues/Women/WRGS/ Forced Marriage/NGO/TheRedElephantFoundation.pdf

Roberts, Helen. 2015. 'Baby Bride Who Wed at One and Divorced at 18 Marries Again', *Daily Mail* (21 Oct.). http://www.dailymail.co.uk/news/article-2274350/Baby-bride-Laxmi-Sargara-marries-second-time.html#ixzz3i7r5cuSc

Rohatgi, M. 2014. '30% Girls in Maharashtra Are Child Brides: Study'. *The Times of India* (6 July); http://timesofindia.indiatimes.com/city/pune/30-girls-in-Maharashtra-are-child-brides-Study/articleshow/37870524.cms

Roy, Raj Coomar. 1888. 'Child Marriage in India'. *The North American Review* 147, 383: 415–4–23. www.jstor.org/stable/25101631

Rukmini S. 2014. 'Consent Does Not Matter, Says Study', *The Hindu,* (14 Sept.). www.thehindu.com/news/national/child-marriages-still-rampant/article6668638.ece

Sagade, Jaya. 2005. *Child Marriage in India: Socio-Legal and Human Rights Dimensions.* New Delhi: Oxford University Press.

Salvi, Vinita. 2009. 'Child Marriage in India: A Tradition with Alarming Implications', *The Lancet* 373, 9678: 1826–27.

Santhya, K. G., and J. Jejeebhoy. 2007. 'Young People's Sexual and Reproductive Health in India: Policies, Programmes and Realities'. New Delhi: Population Council (Rep. No. 19).

Santhya, K.G. et al. 2010. 'Associations between Early Marriage and Young Women's Marital and Reproductive Health Outcomes: Evidence from India', *International Perspectives on Sexual and Reproductive Health* 36, 3: 132–39.

Sarkar, Tanika. 2001. *Hindu Wife, Hindu Nation: Community, Religion and Cultural Nationalism,* New Delhi: Permanent Black.

Save the Children. 2004. *The State of the World's Mothers: Adolescent Mothers.* Westport, CT.: Save the Children. www.savethechildren.org/atf/cf/ {9def2ebe-10ae-432c-9bd0-df91d2eba74a}/ SOWM_2004_final.pdf

———. 2014. *WINGS 2014. The World of India's Girls.* New Delhi: Save the Children. http://resourcecentre.savethechildren.se/sites/default/ files/documents/wingsreportpdf.pdf

———. 2015. *The State of the World's Mothers. Urban Disadvantage.* Westport, CT.: Save the Children.

Sekher, T.V. 2010. 'Special Financial Incentive Schemes for Girl Child in India. A Review. New Delhi: GOI and UNFPA. https://www.unfpa. org/sites/default/files/resource-pdf/UNFPA_Publication-39772. pdf

Sen, Samita. 2009. 'Religious Conversion, Infant Marriage and Polygamy: Regulating Marriage in India in the Late Nineteenth Century', *Journal of History* 26: 99–145.

———. 2012. 'Crossing Communities: Religious Conversion, Rights in Marriage, and Personal . In *Negotiating Spaces: Legal Domains, Gender Concerns and Community Constructs,* Flavia Agnes and Shoba Venkatesh Ghosh, eds. New Delhi: Oxford University Press.

Sethuraman, K., et al. 2007. 'Delaying the First Pregnancy: A Survey in Maharashtra, Rajasthan and Bangladesh'. *EPW* 44 (3 Nov.): 79–89.

Seymour, S. C. 1999. *Women, Family, and Child Care in India: A World in Ttransition.* Cambridge: Cambridge University Press.

Shobhan, R., ed. 2008. *A Ship Adrift: Governance and Development in Bangladesh.* Dhaka: CPD.

Sieczkowski, Cavan. 2012. 'Indian Child Bride, Laxmi Sargara, Has Marriage Annulled After Marrying at One-Year-Old'. *International Business Times* (26 April 26). www.ibtimes.com/indian-child-bride-laxmi-sargara-has-marriage-annulled-after-marrying-one-year-old-693198.

Singh, Renu, and Uma Vennam. 2016. 'Factors Shaping Trajectories to Child and Early Marriage; Evidence from Young Lives in India', Working Paper 149, Young Lives (May 2016).

Singh, Renu. 2017. *A Statistical Analysis of Child Marriage in India.* Oxford: Young Lives.

Singh, S., and R. Sharma. 1996. 'Early Marriage among Women in Developing Countries', *International Family Planning Perspectives* 22, 4: 148–57.

Singh, S., Dey, N. and A. Roy. 1994. 'Child Marriage, Government and NGOs', *EPW* 29: 1377–79.

Singh, Susheela, et al. 2014. *Adding It Up: The Costs and Benefits of Investing in Sexual and Reproductive Health 2014*. New York: Guttmacher Institute and UNFPA.

Sivanandan, T.V. 2015. 'Minor Girl Rescued from 'Marriage', *The Hindu* (7 August).

Srinivasan, K., and James, K.S. 2015. 'The Golden Cage: Stability of the Institution of Marriage in India'. *EPW* 50, 13: 38–45.

Sureender, S. 1993. 'Importance of Increasing the Female Age at Marriage', *New Times*. Bombay: IIPS, 5.

Svanemyr, J., et al. 2012. 'Preventing Child Marriages: First International Day of the Girl Child: My Life, My Right, End Child Marriage', *Reproductive Health* 9, 31: 3.

Tambe, Ashwini. 2009. *Codes of Misconduct: Regulating Prostitution in Late Colonial Bombay*, Minneapolis, MN: University of Minnesota Press.

———. 2019. *Defining Girlhood in India: A Transnational History of Sexual Maturity Laws*, Urbana, IL: University of Illinois Press.

Tembhekar, Chittaranjan . 2015. 'Government Is Under-Reporting Child Marriages in Maharashtra', *Times of India* (14 April). www.timesofindia. indiatimes.com/city/mumbai/Govt-is-under-reporting-child-marriages-in-Maharashtra/articleshow/46914503.cms

Tewari, S. 2014. 'At 240 million, India Has a Third of Child Marriages in the World', *Hindustan Times* (12 Aug.). http://www.hindustantimes. com/india-news/at-240-million-india-has-a-third-of-child-marriages -in-the-world/article1-1251139.aspx

Thapar, Sumitra. 2007. 'Save the Girl Child', *The Hindu* (19 March). http://www.countercurrents.org/gen-thapar190307.htm

Uberoi, Patricia. 1993. *Family, Kinship and Marriage in India*. New Delhi: Oxford University Press.

UN Women. 2011. *Progress of the World's Women: In Pursuit of Justice*. New York: UN Women. http://www.unwomen.org/~/media/ headquarters/attachments/sections/library/publications/2011/ progressoftheworldswomen-2011-en.pdf

———. 2015. *Progress of the World's Women: Transforming Economies, Realizing Rights*. New York: UN Women. http://progress.unwomen. org/en/2015/pdf/UNW_progressreport.pdf

———. ca. 2010. *Definition of Forced and Child Marriage*. New York: UN Women. www.endvawnow. org/en/articles/614-definition-of-forced-and-child-marriage.html

UNDP. 2012. *Maharashtra Human Development Report: Towards Inclusive Human Development*. New Delhi: Sage. http://www.in.undp.org/content/dam/india/docs/human-development/MHDR%20English-2012.pdf

———. 2014. *Human Development Report. Sustainable Development*. New York: UNDP. www.hdr.undp. org/sites/default/files/hdr14-report-en-1.pdf.

UNESCO. 2009. *EFA Global Monitoring Report. Overcoming Inequality. Why Governance Matters*. Paris: UNESCO. www.download.ei-ie.org/docs/IRISDocuments/Education/Education for All/Global Monitoring Report 2009/2009-00090-01-E.pdf

———. 2010. *EFA Global Monitoring Report Reaching the Marginalized*. Paris: UNESCO. www.unesdoc.unesco.org/images/0018/001865/186525e.pdf

———. 2015. *EFA Annual Report: Achievements and Challenges*. Paris: UNESCO.www.unesdoc.unesco.org/images/0023/002322/232205e.pdf

UNFPA. 2003. *A Profile of Adolescents in India*. New Delhi: UNFPA. www.apollospectra.com/files/resources_pdf/ UNFPA India Report-Adolescent Health and Development.pdf

———. 2005. *State of World Population: The Promise of Equality*. New York: UNFPA. www.unfpa.org/ sites/ default/files/pub-pdf/swp05_eng.pdf

———. 2012a. *State of World Population: By Choice, Not by Chance*. New York: UNFPA. https://www.unfpa.org/sites/default/files/pub-pdf/EN_SWOP2012_Report.pdf

———. 2012b. *Marrying Too Young*. New York: UNFPA. http://www.unfpa.org/sites/default/files/pub-pdf/MarryingTooYoung.pdf

———. 2013. *Motherhood in Childhood: Facing the Challenge of Adolescent Pregnancy*. New York: UNFPA. www.unfpa.org/sites/default/files/pub-pdf/EN-SWOP2013-final.pdf

———. 2014. *State of World Population 2014: The Power of 1.8 billion, Adolescents, Youth, and the Transformation of the Future*. New York: UNFPA. www.unfpa.org/sites/default/files/pub-pdf/EN-SWOP14-Report_FINAL-web.pdf

———. 2018. *State of World Population 2018*. New York: UNFPA. www.unfpa.org/sites/default/files/pub-pdf/EN-SWOP18-Report_FINAL-web.pdf

UNFPA/ICRW/AusAID and AFPPD. 2010. *Child Marriage in Southern Asia. Policy Options for Action.* Bangkok: UNFPA www.icrw.org/publications/child-marriagesouthern- asia.

Unicef. 2001. 'Early Marriage: Child Spouses', *Innocenti Digest* (7); http://www.unicef-icdc.org/ publications/pdf/digest7e.pdf

———. 2005. *Early Marriage: A Harmful Traditional Practice. A Statistical Exploration.* New York: Unicef. http://www.unicef.org/publications/files/Early_Marriage_12.lo.pdf

———. 2010. *Progress for Children: Achieving the MDGs with Equity Number 9.* New York: Unicef. www.unicef.org/publications/fi les/Progress_for_Children-No.9_EN_081710.pdf

———. 2011. *The State of World's Children: Adolescence: An Age of Opportunity.* New York: Unicef. www.unicef.org/adolescence/files/SOWC_2011_Main_Report_EN_02092011.pdf

———. 2012. *Child Marriage in India.* New Delhi: unicef. http://www.unicef.in/Itstartswithme/ childmarriage.pdf

———. 2013a. *The State of the World's Children 2014: Revealing Disparities, Advancing Children's Rights.* New York: unicef. www.unicef.org/gambia/SOWC_report_2014.pdf

———. 2013b.'Deepshikha: Educating and Empowering Adolescent Girls in Remote Communities'. New Delhi: Unicef (unpublished document).

———. 2014a. *The State of the World's Children 2015 Reimagine the Future. Innovation for Every Child.* New York: Unicef. http://www.unicef.org/publications/files/ SOWC_2015_Summary_and_Tables.pdf

———. 2014c. *Ending Child Marriage Progress and Prospects.* New York. Unicef. www.unicef.org/ media iles/Child_Marriage_Report_7_17_LR.pdf

———. 2017. *Ending Child Marriage in India.* New Delhi: Unicef India.

USAID. 2005. *Ending Child Marriage and Meeting the Needs of Married Children. The USAID Vision for Action.* Washington, DC: USAID. www.pdf.usaid.gov/ pdf_docs/pdacu300.pdf

Wadlof, Rene. 2007. Child Marriage in India. Socio-Legal and Human Rights Dimensions. Book Review. In *Theological Obs. Service* (x).

Warner, Anne et al. 2014. *More Power to Her. How Empowering Girls Can Help End Child Marriage.* New York: ICRW. http://www.icrw.org/sites/default/files/publications/More%20Power%20pages%20Web.pdf

WHO. 1993. *The Health of Young people. A Challenge and a Promise.* Geneva: WHO.

———. 2006. *Married Adolescents. No Place for Safety.* Geneva: WHO.

————. 2011. *The Sexual and Reproductive Health of Younger Adolescents: Research Issues in Developing Countries. Background paper for a consultation.* Geneva: World Health Organization. http://www.who.int/reproductivehealth/publications/adolescence/rhr_11_15/en/index.html

————. 2012. *Adolescent Sexual and Reproductive Health. Global Research Priorities.* Geneva: WHO.

World Bank. 2004. *Attaining the Millennium Development Goals in India. How Likely and What Will It Take to Reduce Infant Mortality, Child Malnutrition, Gender Disparities and Hunger- Poverty to Increase School Enrollment and Completion?* Washington, DC: World Bank/ Human Development Unit. https://openknowledge.worldbank.org/bitstream/handle/10986/8627/318460rev.pdf?sequence=1

————. 2007. *World Development Report. The Next Generation.* Washington, DC: World Bank. http://www-wds.worldbank.org/external/default/WDSContentServer/IW3P/IB/2006/09/13/000112742_20060913111024/Rendered/PDF/359990WDR0complete.pdf

————. 2014. *Understanding the Economic Costs of Child Marriage.* Washington, DC: World Bank. www.worldbank.org/en/topic/education/brief/understanding-the-economic-impacts-of-child-marriage

————. 2017. *World Development Report 2017. Governance and Development.* Washington, D.C.: World Bank.

World Health Organization. 2012. *Early Marriages, Adolescent and Young Pregnancies.* Geneva; WHO. http://apps.who.int/gb/ebwha/pdf_files/WHA65/A65_13-en.pdf

Yadav, K. P. 2006. *Child Marriage in India.* New Delhi: Adhyayan Publ.

Yadava, S.S. and J.G. Chadney. 1994. 'Female Education, Modernity, and Fertility in India', *Journal of Asian and African Studies* (29/1): 110–119.

Young Lives. 2013. *Delivering the MDGs in India. Targeting Children's Nutrition and Education.* India Policy Brief No. 3 New Delhi: Young Lives. http://www.younglives-india.org/files/policy-papers/mdgs-targeting-children-nutrition-and-education

————. 2017. *Incidence of Child Marriage. New Findings Form the 2011 Census of India.* Policy Brief 32. Oxford: Young Lives.

About the Editors and Contributors

Samita Sen is Vere Harmsworth Professor in Imperial and Naval History at the University of Cambridge. She was the first Vice Chancellor, Diamond Harbour Women's University, West Bengal. She has taught at the universities of Calcutta and Jadavpur. Among her publications are *Women and Labour in Late Colonial India* (Cambridge University Press 1999) that won the Trevor Reese Prize in Commonwealth History; with Nilanjana Sengupta, *Domestic Days: Women, Work, and Politics in Contemporary Kolkata* (Oxford University Press 2016) and *Passage to Bondage: Labour in the Assam Tea Plantations* (Stree 2016). Presently working on women's migration and history of marriage, she has published papers on education, the women's movement, religious conversion, informal labour and domestic violence. She has participated in action research on gender budgeting, women in governance and women's land rights.

Anindita Ghosh received her Ph.D from Jadavpur University and worked with research projects of the School of Women's Studies, Jadavpur University. She is a member of Sachetana, Kolkata, a voluntary women's organization. Currently, she is a consultant for Headword, a national publishing house.

LIST OF CONTRIBUTORS

Deepita Chakravarty received her Ph.D from JNU and is Professor in the School of Development Studies, Ambedkar University, Delhi. She received the Sir Ratan Tata Post-Doctoral Fellowship at London School of Economics and Political Science in London in 2010–11. She has taught at CESS, Hyderabad, IIM Kozhikode, and SOAS, University of London.

She has written jointly with Ishita Chakravarty, *Women, Labour and the Economy: From Migrant Men Servants to Uprooted Girl Children Maids* (Routledge, 2016).She has primarily published on labour market behaviours of women and men in India in *EPW*, *Indian Journal of Gender Studies*, *Modern Asian Studies*, *Journal of South Asian Development* and *Journal of Economic Asymmetries*, and *Indian Journal of Labour Economics* among others.

Bhaswati Chatterjee is Associate Professor in History, Vidyasagar College, Kolkata. She received her Ph.D from the University of Calcutta, 2017. She has published on women's autobiography, gender, politics and social reform in the colonial and postcolonial periods and is presently co-editing *Her Story*, a festschrift on Professor Geraldine Forbes.

Ishita Chowdhury is Assistant Professor, Department of Sociology, Mount Carmel College, Bengaluru. She has a Masters in Sociology from Presidency University, Kolkata, and was previously research assistant, School of Women's Studies, Jadavpur University. She has undertaken several qualitative research projects as a research officer in an R &D organization in Bengaluru. She is passionate about Gender Studies and the sociology of everyday life.

Biswajit Ghosh is Professor of Sociology, University of Burdwan, West Bengal. He received his Ph.D from Jawaharlal Nehru University, New Delhi. He has been Visiting Faculty at JNU, Shivaji University, Tripura University, and Vidyasagar University. He has written five books, 92 articles, and three major policy documents for UNICEF, Government of West Bengal and Save the Children Fund. He was a Module Coordinator of UGC E–Pathshala e–content on research methodology and social movement courses in Sociology. He is on the editorial board of many peer–reviewed journals.

Elvira Graner joined the South Asia Institute of Heidelberg University in 1995, where she obtained her Habilitation

(Privatdozentin), after completing her Ph.D at Freiburg University. Her assignments in South Asia include heading Heidelberg University´s Heidelberg Centre South Asia (HCSA) and being the Deputy Director of the International Centre for Advanced Studies 'Metamorphoses of the Political' (ICAS: MP), both in New Delhi. Her interest in governance and social policies began during her fellowship at BRAC University's Institute of Governance Studies (Dhaka). Currently, she is based at the Institute of Labour Science and Social Affairs (ILSSA) at Hanoi.

Mary E John is Professor, Centre for Women's Development Studies, New Delhi, where she was Director, 2006–2012. She was Deputy Director of the Women's Studies Programme at JNU, 2001–2006. She writes and speaks widely on issues related to Women's Studies and feminism. Major recent publications include *The Political and Social Economy of Sex Selection: Forging Family-Development Linkages* (UNFA, 2018), *Child Marriage in an International Frame: A Feminist Review from India* (in press), and co-edited with Meena Gopal, *Women in the Worlds of Labour: Interdisciplinary and Intersectional Perspectives* (in press). She was the co-chair of the UGC appointed Task Force for the Saksham Report guidelines for Sexual Harassment and Gender Sensitization in Indian Universities (2013).

Juanita Kakoty has an M.Phil. in Sociology from Jawaharlal Nehru University, New Delhi. Her academic articles have appeared in books published by Routledge and Anwesha and in international journals. She edited the Sage journal, *Antyajaa: Indian Journal of Women and Social Change,* 2015–2019. She has also written many feature stories for the *Deccan Herald*, *The Assam Tribune*, *Thomson Reuters News Foundation*, *The Book Review* and *The Thumbprint*. Her short stories have been published by *Himal South Asia, The Assam Tribune, Kitaab, Earthen Lamp Journal, Eastlit*, and *Kaani*. She was one of the founding faculty members of Sociology in Gauhati University. She has taught Sociology at Jamia Milia Islamia, New Delhi.

She has been working on prevention of abuse and violence, particularly sexual abuse.

Tinku Khanna, currently serving as the Director, Apne Aap Women Worldwide India Trust, has been working for last 18 years to end sex-trafficking among caste-communities trapped in inter-generational prostitution. She has played a significant role in the landmark anti-trafficking judgement passed by Patna High Court to a Writ filed by Apne Aap Women Worldwide. She has also contributed to several publications and research reports by Apne Aap Women Worldwide, and co-authored the article: 'Sexual Slavery without Borders: Trafficking for Commercial Sexual Exploitation in India', *International Journal for Equity in Health* (25 September 2008). She is keenly interested in understanding feminist politics, especially the feminist interpretation of law.

Utsarjana Mutsuddi has completed her M.Phil in Women's Studies from Jadavpur University. Her research interests include family, kinship, marriage, exotic dance, Denotified Tribes and travelling communities of India. She has an M.A. in English Literature where she specialized in History of Theatre, and has designed lights for national-level and Kolkata-based plays, including *Otho Hidimba Kotha*. She is interested in feminist representation/memory of women and marginal communities.

Lightning Source UK Ltd.
Milton Keynes UK
UKHW012112050422
401139UK00001B/139